The Origin of Sin

A VOLUME IN THE SERIES

Cornell Studies in Classical Philology

Edited by Frederick M. Ahl, Theodore R. Brennan, Charles F. Brittain, Kevin M. Clinton, Gail J. Fine, David P. Mankin, Sturt W. Manning, Alan J. Nussbaum, Hayden N. Pelliccia, Pietro Pucci, Hunter R. Rawlings, III, Éric Rebillard, Jeffrey S. Rusten, Barry S. Strauss

VOLUME LXI

THE ORIGIN OF SIN

An English Translation of the *Hamartigenia*

Prudentius

Translated and with an Interpretive Essay by Martha A. Malamud

A list of titles in this series is available at www.cornellpress.cornell.edu.

The Origin of Sin

An English Translation of the *Hamartigenia*

PRUDENTIUS

Translated and with an Interpretive Essay by
MARTHA A. MALAMUD

CORNELL UNIVERSITY PRESS   ITHACA AND LONDON

Copyright © 2011 by Cornell University

All rights reserved. Except for brief quotations in a review, this book, or parts thereof, must not be reproduced in any form without permission in writing from the publisher. For information, address Cornell University Press, Sage House, 512 East State Street, Ithaca, New York 14850.

First published 2011 by Cornell University Press
First printing, Cornell Paperbacks, 2011

Printed in the United States of America

Library of Congress Cataloging-in-Publication Data

Prudentius, b. 348.
 [Hamartigenia. English]
 The origin of sin : an English translation of the Hamartigenia / Prudentius ; translated and with an interpretive essay by Martha A. Malamud.
     p. cm. — (Cornell studies in classical philology ; v. 61)
 Includes bibliographical references and index.
 ISBN 978-0-8014-4222-3 (cloth : alk. paper)
 ISBN 978-0-8014-8872-6 (pbk. : alk. paper)
   1. Christian poetry, Latin—Translations into English.   I. Malamud, Martha A., 1957–   II. Title.   III. Series : Cornell studies in classical philology ; v. 61.
 PA6648.P6 H3313
 871'.01—dc23
                                                              2011021222

Cornell University Press strives to use environmentally responsible suppliers and materials to the fullest extent possible in the publishing of its books. Such materials include vegetable-based, low-VOC inks and acid-free papers that are recycled, totally chlorine-free, or partly composed of nonwood fibers. For further information, visit our website at www.cornellpress.cornell.edu.

Cloth printing   10 9 8 7 6 5 4 3 2 1
Paperback printing   10 9 8 7 6 5 4 3 2 1

In memory of my beloved aunt,
GISELA WEHRHAN CHRISTIAN

> ...though fall'n on evil dayes,
> On evil days though fall'n, and evil tongues;
> In darkness, and with dangers compast round,
> And solitude; yet not alone...
>
> MILTON, *Paradise Lost*

CONTENTS

Acknowledgments   ix

Note on Translations and Editions   xi

THE ORIGIN OF SIN: AN ENGLISH TRANSLATION

Preface   3

The Origin of Sin   7

AN INTERPRETIVE ESSAY

Introduction   51

1. Writing in Chains   56
2. Figuring It Out   76
3. Seeking Hidden Truth   85
4. Falling into Language   96
5. Under Assault   112
6. Generation of Vipers   129
7. Signs of Woe   140
8. *In Aenigmate*   170

Notes   197

References   213

Index   223

ACKNOWLEDGMENTS

THIS BOOK HAS BENEFITED GREATLY from the hard work of others—especially Christopher Francese and Marc Mastrangelo, who had no reason, other than collegiality at the highest level, and love of scholarship, for expending so much effort on a project not their own. Chris Francese sent me detailed, cogent comments on almost every page of the translation, and Marc Mastrangelo provided equally detailed and challenging comments on the essay. I gratefully acknowledge their expertise and generosity.

Emily Albu read and commented on both the text and the translation in several versions and helped clarify the structure of the argument and the placement of notes in the translation. Rebecca Krawiec made me aware of significant bibliography that would have otherwise escaped me. Margaret Malamud and Don McGuire put up with reading and hearing about innumerable versions of the evolving manuscript; I thank them for their patience and encouragement. Neil Coffee deserves thanks for taking up the slack in the department when I was on leave and distracted by administrative duties. Brad Ault and Renee Bush provided crucial support in the late stages of the project. John Dugan, coeditor of *Arethusa*, shouldered an extra editorial burden and provided advice, encouragement, and friendship throughout the writing of this book. And I thank Frederick Ahl, who has been an inspiration for many years; my approach to Latin poetry bears his indelible stamp.

The anonymous readers for Cornell University Press set high standards and offered incisive comments that have substantially improved the translation. I also benefited from the comments of the lively students and faculty of the University of Toronto Department of Classics, and the participants in the Pacific Rim Roman Literature Seminar in Christchurch, New Zealand. Portions of this essay (Malamud 2002) first appeared in the *Journal of Early Christian Studies*, whose anonymous readers were extremely helpful. I thank Bruce McCombe, dean of the College of Arts and Sciences at the University at Buffalo, and the Department of Classics there for granting me a semester of research leave that enabled me to complete this project.

NOTE ON TRANSLATIONS AND EDITIONS

PRUDENTIUS is a pivotal poet: his poetry is steeped in the work of his classical predecessors, especially Vergil, Lucretius, Horace, Ovid, Statius, and Juvenal, but it also anticipates the Christian worldview and the sophisticated allegorical and linguistic experiments of his successors Dante, Chaucer, Spenser, and Milton. Like the Roman god Janus, Prudentius looks forward and back at the same time. His radically experimental verse earns him a place in the European epic tradition, though he has been largely underappreciated because those radical qualities have been for the most part ignored. The goal of this translation, and of the essay that accompanies it, is to make his fascinating and complicated verse accessible to a wider audience.

But Prudentius is a difficult poet on every level: syntax, style, diction, and content. The *Hamartigenia* consists of a preface, composed of sixty-three lines in iambic senarii, and the poem proper, 966 lines of dactylic hexameter, the meter of classical epic and didactic poetry. Prudentius used his prefaces to provide an interpretive framework for the poems they introduce, and the words are chosen and arranged with great care. Though the preface to the *Hamartigenia* is brief, it is densely packed with meaning. I have chosen to translate it line for line, in prose that reflects as closely as possible the literal meaning of the Latin, and provide notes to explain subtleties I was unable to render in the translation. The poem itself I have translated into loosely iambic pentameter verse, a meter that evokes the long tradition of epic poetry in English, much as Prudentius's hexameters would have evoked the tradition of the great Latin hexameter writers—especially Lucretius, Vergil, and Ovid. Consequently, although the line numbering in my English translation of the preface is the same as the Latin, the line numbering of the English translation of the poem is not. For easy reference, the lines of the translation are numbered in the margins of every page, and at the top of every other page the reader will find the line numbers corresponding to Prudentius's Latin text. In the essay, when both the text and translation are quoted, the line numbers of the Latin appear below the Latin text; the line numbers of the translation appear below the English text. When only the English translation is quoted, the English line numbers appear first, followed by reference to the Latin line numbers, e.g., (*H.* 173–280; Lat. 124–205).

Translations of biblical passages are from the New King James Version. Translations of *Aeneid* passages are by Frederick Ahl. Except when otherwise noted, all other translations are my own. I have used Thomson's edition of the *Hamartigenia*, which is the most easily accessible for readers who wish to consult the Latin, with frequent recourse, especially in the notes to the translation, to Palla's 1981 edition and commentary. Both Thomson's and Palla's texts are based on Bergman's 1926 CSEL edition. Quotations from *Paradise Lost* are from the second edition (1674).

The Origin of Sin

An English Translation

PREFACE

Adolescent brothers,[1] a digger and a shepherd,[2] the two
born first to the first of women,
set on the altar firstfruits of their labors,
offered up as holy gifts to God.[3]
One offers earth's crops, the other living things.[4] 5
In conflict, they make rival pledges:
one the young of a sheep, the other the yield of his trench.[5]

---

1. The first word of the poem is *fratres*, "brothers." The brothers, as we learn in line 11, are Cain and Abel; Prudentius is referring to the story told in Genesis 4. Abel's murder was commonly believed by early Christian writers to be a prefiguration of the suffering and death of Christ, but Prudentius sees Cain as prefiguring dualist heretics who, in his view, split the one true God into warring gods, one good, one evil. Enmity between brothers is also a significant motif in Roman myth and literature: Prudentius's readers would likely have been reminded of Rome's foundational fratricide, the slaying of Remus by Romulus, as well as of Eteocles and Polyneices, the fratricidal sons of Oedipus. Prudentius's use of the Greek word *ephebus* ("adolescent," the Greek term for a youth between sixteen and twenty years old) suggests that he may have had the Greek sons of Oedipus especially in mind. The strife between the brothers is the subject of the *Thebaid*, written by Prudentius's great epic predecessor Statius.

2. "Digger": The Latin is *fossor*, a word used for various kinds of manual laborers, including miners, ditchdiggers, and gravediggers. All of these menial professions were held in contempt. *Fossor* was also used colloquially to mean "fornicator."

3. The text places great emphasis on the word *primus*, "first" (*prima primos procreat*, H. praef. 2, and *primordia*, H. praef. 4), drawing attention to the importance of this story as a paradigm for later sins.

4. The opposition *terrulentis* (earthly) . . . *vivis* (living) reflects the association of the earth with death throughout the *Hamartigenia*. It also reflects the brothers' parentage: Eve's name means "life" in Hebrew; the name Adam was associated with *ha-adamah*, the earth or ground.

5. The two brothers offer the produce (*fetum*) of their respective professions. The word Prudentius uses for Abel's sheep is *bidens*, a word commonly used to denote sacrificial animals, that literally means "with two teeth." There is an untranslatable pun here: *bidens* also means a two-pronged hoe, which would more appropriately belong to Cain. Cain will use a hoe (*sarculus*) to kill Abel in line 16. Cain offers the produce of his "trench," *scrobis*, a word that has negative associations in

God approved the victim of the younger brother
and rejected what the older had acquired.[6]
Look! A voice resounds from the throne on high: 10
"Cain, be still! If you rightly make your offering
and yet do not divide it up correctly,
your perverted gifts will bring black guilt."
Then the brother arms his murderous hand,
jealous of the holiness God had approved;   15
with his curved hoe he breaks his brother's neck,[7]
his wicked carnage staining the new-made earth,
which would be redeemed later, in its old age,
by the holy blood of Christ that kills its killer.
Death[8] first came to be through the wounds of an innocent,   20
then passed away through the wounds of a guiltless one;
Death, who arose through crime, is dissolved by crime;
before, she struck down Abel, and then Christ;
she met her end attacking one who has no end.[9]
So the ancient story began with things yet to be,   25
and the last things were marked out by that first deed,
when the crude farmer who invented death
brought his bungled, unsalted[10] offerings of earth,

Latin. At Ovid *Met.* 7.243, it is used for the trenches dug by Medea to collect victims' blood for a magic ritual; another common meaning is "grave."

6. Why God refused Cain's sacrifice is never made clear in Genesis and was the subject of much exegetical discussion. Among the reasons proposed by patristic interpreters are that God prefers the pastoral to the agricultural way of life; that what grows spontaneously is better than what is cultivated; that Cain offered not the firstfruits, but just the fruits of his labor; and that Cain offered an inferior product. Prudentius associates the earth with death in this passage, so Cain's offering is tainted by its association with the earth. Prudentius's specification that God rejected the things Cain had *acquired* (*paratis*) may be a play on Cain's name, which biblical commentators thought was derived from the Hebrew word *kinyan*, meaning to possess, get, or acquire, or *kin'ah*, "jealousy" (a meaning Prudentius brings out with the words *aemulus, H. praef.* 15; *aemulator, H. praef.* 31; and *invidus, H. praef.* 33). Cf. Genesis 4:1: Eve bore Cain and said, "I have gotten a man from the Lord." Hayward 2009 discusses Jewish and Christian exegetical approaches to answering the question of what was wrong with Cain's sacrifice.

7. Prudentius reinforces the connection between agriculture, the earth, death, and sin by having Cain slay his brother with a hoe. Genesis 4 does not specify the weapon used. Again, there is a parallel in the Roman story of Romulus and Remus. According to Ovid (*Fasti* 4.843), Romulus killed Remus with a digging tool (*rutro*).

8. *Mors*, "Death," is feminine in Latin. Prudentius frequently uses personified nouns as actors in his poems; the Virtues and Vices in his *Psychomachia* are all personified feminine abstract nouns.

9. Death came into the world with the death of Abel, the first human to die; after the voluntary death of Christ, Death's power over humanity was broken.

10. I have translated *insulsa* as "bungled, unsalted" to bring out two aspects of its meaning. *Insulsus* literally means "unsalted," "tasteless," and figuratively, "stupid"; it is the opposite of *salsus*,

and thinking[11] God a god of lifeless things,
believed the yield of his hoe worth offering   30
in his dark bravery of the living victim.[12]
    I recognize, of course, whom this figure implies,[13]
the killer of his brother, the jealous slayer,
who perversely divides holy doctrine
and reckons his own offerings more just—   35
he's Marcion.[14] Shaped from utterly corrupted earth,[15]
he teaches dualists to differ from the Spirit,
offering up his gifts of tainted flesh
and worshipping the everlasting power in separate shapes.[16]
If he could heed the warning and be still,[17]   40
then quiet brotherhood could cultivate peace
and acknowledge that the one God of the living lives.
But this man, an initiate of a transitory cult,[18]

---

which literally means "salted," and figuratively, "witty." In addition to casting Cain as a rustic boor, as the juxtaposition of *rusticus* and *insulsa* would suggest, Prudentius may be using the word here to reinforce the inappropriate nature of Cain's offering by making an analogy with pagan Roman ritual. *Mola salsa*, "salted grain," was an important component in many Roman sacrificial rites; its use was believed to have been instituted by Numa, the king who established religious ritual for Rome. Prepared by the Vestal Virgins, it was sprinkled on the forehead of sacrificial victims. A sacrifice performed without this necessary component would be not only bungled but ill-omened.

11. *Deputans*, "thinking," carries on the agricultural metaphor that associates Cain with the earth. The primary meaning of *deputo* is "to prune"; in ante- and postclassical Latin it is used to mean "consider, allot, count as." It is a compound of *puto*, whose meanings include "to cleanse, to prune, to set in order, to think."

12. Although God prefers Abel's offering of an animal, Prudentius is not providing an argument in favor of animal sacrifice, of which he and other orthodox Christians did not approve. Rather, the offering of crops produced from the earth stresses Cain's association with earth and mortality. The sacrificial lamb also foreshadows the sacrifice of Christ, the Lamb of God.

13. A key line: Prudentius here reads the story of Cain and Abel as a typological allegory (*figura*) that needs to be interpreted.

14. Marcion was known for his dualist teaching that there was a punitive God who created man, the world, and the law, and a good God revealed by Christ, who saved man. He also created a drastically reduced New Testament consisting only of parts of the Gospel of Luke and ten Epistles of Paul. He lived during the second century, and Marcionism as a sect died out in the fourth century. Gnilka (2000, 291–357) argues, but does not conclusively prove, that *H. praef.* 36–47 are an interpolation.

15. Marcion's creation from corrupt earth is a distorted version of God's creation of Adam from earth, and taints him by association with Cain, who is linked consistently with earth and flesh.

16. Although Marcion is singled out here, the philosophy ascribed to him (belief in two divine forces, one good and one evil) is more characteristic of Manichaeism, a dualistic belief popular in Prudentius's day. Saint Augustine was deeply attracted by its teachings before his conversion.

17. "Be still," *quiescat*, is the same verb used in line 11, when God commands Cain to be still, *quiesce*.

18. *Caduco ... mysterio*, "transitory cult": *Caducus* literally means "that falls, has fallen, falling," and is derived from the verb *cado*, "to fall." By extension it comes to mean "transitory, frail, fleeting, doomed." It was used technically in law to refer to property "that is not, or cannot be, taken up by the heir or legatee and consequently falls to the treasury, escheatable, caducary" (*OLD* s.v. 10).

profanely divides the highest being,
separating good and bad, as if two Gods could rule, 45
and sets up two opposing powers, and believes
the one that he himself admits is evil is a God.
He is a cruel, bloody Cain, a tenant farmer[19]
of this world, jealous of unity, a baleful sacrificer
whose filthy offering smacks of earth, 50
the earth of the fallen body, foul flesh,
lumped together from thick fluid and dust.
Its nature flourishes with fertile fraud,
pouring from her womb the teeming sins of guilty men,
and kills the life of the soul through the fall of flesh.[20] 55
Flesh turns her shafts against her sister, Mind;
Mind fans the flames within the drunken brain,
where she gathers potent passions,
drunk with Flesh's maddening poisons.
Eternal God she splits into two; she dares 60
divide the Godhead indivisible.
Murdered, she falls, denying God is one:
Cain triumphs in his brother Spirit's death.[21]

Prudentius was a lawyer, and legal language permeates the poem. A *mysterium* is a mystery cult whose initiates are sworn to silence about its rituals.

19. *Colonus* can mean simply "farmer" or "tiller of the soil," but it frequently means a farmer who cultivates another's land. It can also mean "colonist." Prudentius uses language (*caducus, colonus*) that suggests that Marcion/Cain is dispossessed, neither a true heir nor a true owner of his land.

20. Prudentius opposes the body, made of earth, to the intellectual part of man—*mens*, "mind"—and personifies them. He uses both *terra* (earth) and *caro* (flesh) to describe the earthly, tainted element in man. The struggle between Earth/Flesh and Mind takes place within the individual's disordered brain (*cerebrum*). The preface ends with the triumph of Cain/Earth/Flesh over Abel/Mind.

21. Palla ad loc. recapitulates the arguments in favor of the reading *halitus*, "breath" or "spirit," instead of *allitus*, which Thomson adopts in his Loeb translation ("Cain in his triumph bears the marks of his brother's death"). To corroborate Palla, if his reading is correct, the last word of the preface contains a significant etymological wordplay on the name Abel, which commentators believed was derived from the Hebrew *hebel*, "breath" or "spirit" (also associated with "vanity" or "ephemerality").

THE ORIGIN OF SIN

Where does your madness hurl you, treacherous Cain,[22]
blasphemer, you who split our God in two?
Isn't the one creator clear to you?
Is your divided vision darkened by mist?[23]
Your keen gaze, spoiled, pursues two different paths,[24] 5
its sight deceived by double phantom figures.
The twofold shape of earthly things makes sport
of you and makes you stupidly believe
a God divided reigns above the heavens.
But though this sordid world confuses two 10
opposing elements of good and evil,
Heaven itself submits to a single God.
Because there are two different sorts of works
that stir anxieties in human hearts,
it does not therefore follow that the heavens 15
retain two rulers. It is the outer man

---

22. Cain, whom we have seen in the preface making an improper division of his sacrifice, is identified with Marcion and by extension with other heretical thinkers who fail to comprehend the unity of God. The divisiveness that characterizes heretical thought is compounded by the social effect of heresy, which destroys the unity of the church.

23. The first appearance of one of the key thematic elements in the poem, vision. Man's imperfect vision leads him to incorrect perception of the true nature of the universe.

24. "Two paths": The Latin is *divortia*, from *divortium*, "a separation, a place where the road divides, a fork." The word is part of a network of imagery of being lost, or going astray, related to the poem's central concept, sin. The Greek word *hamartia*, from which the title of the poem is formed, means "error, failure, sin," and is derived from the verb *hamartano*, "to miss the mark, go astray, err." Rather than following the single true path, Cain/Marcion's gaze is tricked into following two paths. The image of the fork in the road is developed more fully at *H*. 1051–67 (Lat. 789–801) in a parable illustrating Adam's dilemma at the moment of choosing to sin.

born of the earth, who, when he apprehends
that things are so, is led to the conclusion
that two powers exist for different realms.
Because he thinks there is a God who once 20
created evil and likewise one who shaped
all good things and brought them into being,
he then concludes a pair of Gods exists,
both supreme but having different natures.
What twofold nature can maintain itself 25
or rule for long if a divided source
separates it from the throne and checks it
by constant change of ruler? Either God
is one and holds the highest power, or
the two that now exist are both diminished: 30
both cannot have supremacy. It's clear
that nothing is supreme if it's not one,
omnipotent, since separate things claim power
each for itself, rejecting the other's rule,
and so are not supreme and not almighty. 35
Dispersed authority is not complete:
one cannot have a thing another has.
If you divide the pile, it grows smaller.
We testify that God is whole and One
and indivisible; in Him is Christ 40
who, like Him, is whole and One, who lives
now, has lived before all things, and will
live, and brook no partner, as agreed.
The Father is the summit of all powers,
the ruler who holds sway over everything, 45
the source sublime of virtue, nature's crown,
the universal single fountainhead,
the author of beginning and of birth,
from whom all things, light and time and years
and number flow; who willed that after One 50
another thing will follow: numbers start
with One and One alone cannot be counted.
    And since there is no other God and Father,
and Christ cannot be second to the Father,
the One who has a single Son exists 55
before all number, God, and rightly God,
for He is first and one: first in power
and first in whom He sired. But how does pure

generation make a difference?²⁵ Both
begetter and the One begot from One 60
before the darkness of primeval chaos,
free of number and time, will always be
One. What man has dared to say the power
that governs in one majesty, belongs
to itself alone, and was eternal 65
before the world began, is two? Who dares
to rip apart a single nature's strength?
Did the Father adopt a second son
of foreign origin, to make the number
two—a separate being to introduce 70
a second godly power? God's true Son
is in the form of his true Father and keeps
the same form, duly proving He is One.
No adoptive bond allies the two,
no pledge of faith unites them; rather, true 75
love and a single substance, which is God,
make them One.²⁶

                 This path displeases you,
Marcion; your sect condemns our faith
after dividing heaven for different lords.
What fogs bewilder you? What nightmare plagues 80
your sleeping mind, wherein a double form
appears in visions and stands divided in
a twofold heaven? If torpor saps your mental
strength, at least observe the elements²⁷
our earthly eyes encounter, signs through which 85
the mystery of God is manifested.
The Lord's prophetic majesty foresaw
long ago the heresy that would
divide the ruler of this world, the Lord

---

25. *Generatio simplex*, "pure generation," implies generation from a single source or through a single channel, and is attributed only to God. It is a key concept for Prudentius, who fills the *Hamartigenia* with examples of the problems that arise from *generatio* that is not *simplex*, which produces offspring that are not identical in nature with their parent. The problem of evil is closely related to the issue of reproduction, for if God created man in his own image, how can we account for the presence of evil? Dualists solve the problem by positing two gods who are unlike. Prudentius here attempts to prove the unity of God.

26. In the next section (77-133; Lat. 56-94) Prudentius argues that God has provided a visible symbol of divine unity, the sun, to give man a way to comprehend the divine unity.

27. The Latin *elementa* means both elements and the letters of the alphabet. Studying nature is analogous to reading a book or interpreting signs.

of light, in two, to make a twofold God 90
divided for a separated realm.
He placed this symbol right before our eyes,
a visible proof that shows that we should not
place our faith in two divine powers:
a single fire furnishes the days 95
that roll along through heaven's enormous vault:
one sun alone weaves the year together
from the days, and yet it is threefold,
reliant on three qualities without
distinction: light and speed and heat. Its speed 100
propels it; heat provides its warmth, and light
its radiance. These three exist at once:
light and heat and speed, but nonetheless
the selfsame starry orb puts forth all three
without distinction: in its single orbit 105
it performs these disparate duties: a single
substance underlies three different things.

I wouldn't venture to compare any
thing to God as if it were His equal,
nor think a sign,[28] His servant, to be His peer. 110
But the Father Himself has willed that we
deduce that He is great from smaller things,
since we are not allowed to see or visit
higher things.[29] But looking in a mirror,
we see in smaller things the images 115
of what our minds can't comprehend, and He
has granted us to search for hidden truth
in the closest things. No man has ever seen
two suns, unless he sees them through a cataract
that veils his eyes, or a dusky mantle spreads 120
across the clear heaven and makes it blush,
when clouds block shafts of light, reflect their fire,

28. 'Sign': The Latin *signum* means "sign," but also "constellation" or "star." God, the *logos*, is pure meaning; no sign can represent Him adequately; similarly, a good Christian would not worship the sun, a created being, as a god, even though it can by analogy hint at the nature of God.

29. Here Prudentius claims that he can provide proper interpretation through strategies of figural reading taught by God (for a good discussion of interpretive strategies in the *Hamartigenia*, see Conybeare 2007, esp. 232 for this particular passage). He returns at important moments in the poem to the question of how to interpret signs and figures, e.g., the interpretation of the tale of Lot's wife at H. 1023-26 (Lat. 723-24) and of the contest between David and Absalom ("his standard, / set against his father" (*signis contraria signa paternis*, H. 742-43; Lat. 567).

and scatter them into counterfeited orbs.[30]
Each mind is shrouded over with its own
opaque atmosphere: a cataract
with watery veil dulls our keen gaze, blocks
the flow of our freed contemplation's thrust
up into heaven's softness, and obstructs
our rapid senses' comprehension that
our God is One. And our malfunctioning sight
fractures the image, strives to follow two
sources of light, and builds a pair of altars
to twin creators.
     —If there are two, why not
a thousand gods? Why should Deity
content itself with being two in number?
Would it not be better to flood the nations
with far-flung troops of gods and fill up every
part of earth without discrimination
with monstrous demigods to whom the wild
savage offers up his sacrifice
that counts for nothing?[31] If contesting gods
retain their hold over a divided heaven,
then it makes sense to assign to clouds, to springs,
to bellowing ocean and to woods and hills
and caves and streams, to winds, to forges, and to mines:
to each a god with his own authority.
Or, if worshipping the Gentiles' spirits
seems vulgar, yet you're happy with the thought
of two gods, equal, sharing power, then come
and tell me, which one holds the lands by lot,
and which one rules the ocean storms with ever-
lasting law? Explain to me how power
co-inherited can be divided.
"One sits on high," you say,[32] "inside a grim

---

30. Marcion's disordered mental state is reflected in his double vision. In a vivid description of Dido's love-inspired madness, Vergil compares her nightmares to the visions of two famous figures from the tragic stage (Ahl's translation): "She was like Pentheus, stripped of his mind, seeing armies of Furies, / Seeing the sole sun double, and Thebes in a duplicate presence; / Like Agamemnon's child, driven mad in a drama: Orestes, / Fleeing his mother who's armoured with flames and with dark hissing serpents, / While, at the door of the palace, avenging Furies sit waiting" (*Aen.* 4.469–73).

31. "A sacrifice that will count for nothing": *perituros honores*. See Thomson 1946, 116, and Henry 1940, 154.

32. "You" is Marcion, who is given a speech laying out the dualistic view that there is one stern Old Testament God who is responsible for evil in the world, and a gentle, loving God responsible for

citadel: the author of wickedness, 155
the god of vices, harsh, unjust, who sowed
whatever ills ferment in this corrupted
globe. Imbuing his new spawn with snaky
poison, he struck the spark of our beginning
from death's combustible matter.[33] He himself, 160
the maker of the world, created stars
and earth and sea; and he himself shaped
limbs from clay, creating man, a thing
for illness to devour, to be debased
by many sins, a thing the grave could make 165
dissolve with hideous decay. The other
is marked by love of piety and gentle
healing arts, restoring man and saving
creatures bound by death. Two Testaments
were issued, one from either power: the New 170
Testament was given by the better
God, the Old by the savage one." This voice,
—oppressive, dialectical—is yours,
Marcion; it's proof of the psychosis
of your stricken brain. We know a father 175
of sin exists; we also know that he
is not a god at all.[34] No, he is damned
to servitude in hell, condemned to live
in Stygian Avernus—Marcion's God,
severe and grim, a treacherous betrayer, 180
his head erect, his snaky brow surrounded
by somber clouds, dense-wrapped in smoky flame.
Envy, who cannot stand to see the joys
of just men, fills his bruised and spiteful eyes
with burning gall.[35] The roving snakes that crowd 185

---

the New Testament. This is an example of the device prosopopoeia, ascribing particular words or acts to a character.

33. Stam translates "derived the beginning of the world from the sting of death" (*de fomite mortis*); Henry (1940, 155) suggests instead that *de fomite mortis* means "a deadly substance"; Thomson translates "that which derives from death."

34. Prudentius asserts that what Marcion takes to be the Old Testament god is actually the devil, an angel who was good when God created him, but who voluntarily turned away from God. The description of Satan, with his flame and smoke, snares and snakes, is one of the most striking examples of *enargeia* (vividly visual language: see pp. 60–61 below).

35. Envy, *Invidia* (another personified abstract feminine noun), is etymologically linked to the Latin *invideo*, "to look askance at, regard with envy." It is significant that she attacks the devil's eyes and spoils the clear vision that characterized the angel before his fall. Envy is thus associated with

his mane cover up his bristling shoulders,
while crested bright-green serpents lick his face.
With his hand he coaxes coils of twisted
cord in snares, and weaving tangled fetters
in easy knots, he stretches nets for traps. 190
It is his art to capture wild creatures,
to lie in wait for beasts, to set his snares
for wandering animals in hidden places,
undetected. This one, this is Nimrod[36]
the savage hunter, one who never rests 195
from punishing the careless souls of men
with ceaseless slaughter. Cunningly, he circles
the earth with its craggy peaks and tufted forests
and winding labyrinthine paths, to trap
some by fraud and hidden tricks, to wrestle 200
others to the ground with his giant arms,
and spread his deadly triumphs far and wide.
Bold Death! How you drive the hearts of men![37]
Man—how shameful—worships his own doom,
scorns the source of life, adores that bloody 205
butcher, bowing to him even when the
sword-edge reaches for his throat! How sweet
is death to poor compulsive souls, addicted
to sin's intoxicating nectar, how
much pleasure those in darkness take from bane! 210
That one who first gave birth to evil, who
perverted good with sin and light with darkness,
is thought to be a God? This madness equals

---

the misdirected gaze, which for Prudentius is emblematic of failure to align one's will with God's will. Cain, who kills his brother out of envy, is characterized by the adjective *invidus* in *H. praef.* 33.

36. Here Prudentius equates Satan with Nimrod (Prudentius uses the form Nebroth), who appears at Genesis 10:8–12 as a mighty hunter "before the Lord" and ruler of several important southern Mesopotamian cities, including Uruk, Akkad, and Babel. He is not characterized as evil in Genesis, and some later Christian writers characterize him as a just ruler. The Jewish historian Josephus (*Antiquitates* 1.113–14) relates that he was the grandson of Noah who wanted revenge for the Flood and built the Tower of Babel to be high enough to serve as a refuge if God chose to flood the world once more, and he appears in rabbinical and Christian commentators as a highly negative figure, often associated with Zoroaster. See van der Toorn and van der Horst (1990), which discusses the ancient sources for the figure of Nimrod in detail. Like Cain, Nimrod was associated with the corrupting arts of civilization, including hunting, warfare, and the more arcane art of astronomy, hence the emphasis in line 191 (Lat. 139), *ars olli*, on his arts. See Fyler 2007, 35–42 on Nimrod's association with Cain, the building of cities, and the Tower of Babel.

37. Here Prudentius punningly echoes *Aeneid* 4.412, "Improbe Amor, quid non mortalia pectora cogis!" substituting *mors* (death) for Vergil's *amor* (love).

that of those who, so the story goes,
consecrated shrines to Rust and Fever, 215
as if they were divinities.³⁸
                But Sin
was not invented by a god: a fallen
angel conceived and birthed it in his sordid
mind.³⁹ Once he was a brilliant star,
majestic, bright in the firmament, a blaze 220
of glory nourished out of nothingness.⁴⁰
For everything existing comes from nothing,⁴¹
all things before they were created came
from nothing: and yet God is not from nothing,
nor is Wisdom, nor the Holy Ghost, 225
a substance everlasting, unbegun,
the one who shaped the angels of the air.
    Of this troop one, most beautiful of face,
majestic, fierce, and grown too great in strength,
became puffed up, tumescent, carrying 230
himself too proudly, and displayed his fires⁴²
with too much arrogance. Persuasively⁴³
he taught that he was generated from
his own powers, and from himself he drew
the substance for himself, from which he first 235
came into being, and was conceived without
a maker. Hence his followers design
a secret cult that teaches that a tyrant

    38. Prudentius names *Scabies*, Itch, or the skin disease scabies, and *Febris*, Fever. A typical Christian attack on Roman religion was that they worshipped evils as divinities. Lactantius (*Inst.* 1.20.17) contemptuously cites the worship of *Febris* and *Robigo* (Rust or Mildew). Since there are no other sources for the worship of *Scabies*, Thomson (ad loc.) conjectures that Prudentius here uses *Scabies* as a synonym for *Robigo*. The Romans celebrated a festival, the Robigalia, in honor of Robigus (or the feminine Robigo), a deity who protected crops against rust or mildew (Pliny, *HN* 18.29). Pliny also mentions shrines to Fever (*Febris*), Orbona (a goddess of stillbirths and dead babies), and Ill Fortune (*Mala Fortuna*) (*HN* 2.5.16).
    39. Milton brilliantly elaborates the claim that Sin was born from Satan's mind. He describes the birth of Sin from the head of Satan, and their subsequent incestuous coupling, which resulted in the birth of their offspring, Death, at *PL* 2.746ff.
    40. Prudentius here follows other early Christian writers in identifying Satan, the fallen angel, with Lucifer, the "Day Star" or "Morning Star." See Isaiah 14.3–20, with [Tertullian], *Contra Marcionem* 5.11, 17.
    41. Prudentius counters a prime tenet of Epicureanism, argued at length by Lucretius in his poem *On the Nature of the Universe*, that nothing comes from nothing.
    42. Again Prudentius identifies Satan the angel with Lucifer the star.
    43. Prudentius uses the verb *persuasit*, and will go on to emphasize Satan's persuasive powers and command of rhetoric.

from the shadows suddenly leaped forth,
who'd lived concealed in a kind of endless night 240
for ages past and always ruled since time
began.[44] In sudden jealousy, they say,
he thrust his head up from the gloomy darkness,
keen to ruin the works of God. But this
our reasoning[45] denies: for we are not 245
permitted to invalidate the one
faith that scripture teaches: "Without God,"
it says, "no thing is made; but rather, all
are made through Him, and no one else is made
unless by Him."[46]

                    And even he[47] was good 250
at first, and meant for goodness, clear and bright
from the first beginning of his being.
Soon, though, of his own free will he sank
into evil, when Envy, that discolored
creature, infected him and spurred him on 255
with bitter pricks and goads. For a spark of hate
struck by Envy, caught and blazed, and sudden
anguish ignited his impatient mind.
He had seen a simulacrum fashioned
of clay[48] and warmed to life by God's own breath 260
and given dominion over earth; he saw
all of nature—earth and sky and ocean—
had learned to pour forth harvests, and to give
her riches liberally for the use of man,
the earthly ruler. The savage beast swelled up, 265
his heart disturbed by sour anger, and drew
upon the strength within his acid marrow.
Once he was a stainless creature: upright
wisdom kept his tall young body free
of knots. But look! In sinuous curves he coils 270

   44. Satan's followers are adherents of Marcionism (and by extension other dualistic religions such as Manichaeism); the tyrant they teach about is the punitive Creator God they believed coexisted with the merciful god of the New Testament.
   45. Prudentius uses the Latin *ratio*. Reason is not allowed to weaken the faith (*fides*) handed down by scripture.
   46. A paraphrase of John 1:3, "Through him all things were made; without him nothing was made that has been made." Augustine cites this verse in his attack on Manichaeism, a contemporary dualist theology, in *Sermo* 1 (discussed by Conybeare 2007, 230).
   47. The corrupted angel.
   48. Adam, whom God creates from clay.

himself in new complexities, and bends
his shining belly in sliding spirals. His tongue,
once single, now is treacherously split,
and flickers with the art of varied speaking,
its fissured words reechoing.[49] And hence 275
the origin, the source, the fountainhead
of sin! The origin of evil flowed
from that prince first:[50] not needing any teacher
he first discovered how to ruin himself,
and soon he ruined man. The world—with all 280
the earth's resources undermined, and man,
its guardian, corrupted—met its doom.
No different from a thief who chances on
a careless traveler, to rob him: first
unmindful of the spoils, he stabs the master 285
(the struggle is slow and difficult), and then,
victorious, he strips the spoils from
the unresisting corpse that's made him rich.[51]
Just so the mansion under man's dominion,
the rich and fruitful earth, fell easily to ruin 290
when its master sinned and, prone to sin
already, drained to the dregs its master's evil.
Then it was that the malignant land
from its infertile soil bore hybrid crops
and flimsy burrs and weeds, and spoiled the grain 295
with useless straw. Now savage lions learned
to kill the shepherd and drain the guiltless cattle
of blood, and rip apart with savage jaws
young bulls already broken to the yoke.
The wolf too, irked by plaintive bleating, burst 300
boldly into crowded pens at midnight. Skill,
experienced in cruel stratagems,
stained every beast, and craft honed twisted senses
keen: although a wall surrounds a blooming

---

49. Prudentius explicitly identifies the origin of sin with the splitting of Satan's tongue, the last step in his transformation from angel to devil. In Latin, *lingua* means both the tongue, the physical instrument of language, and language itself.

50. "From that prince first": Augustus was the first to use the title *princeps*, "first citizen." As the the actual power of the emperor increased over time, the title *princeps* took on the meaning of "ruler," hence the English "prince."

51. Prudentius has used various rhetorical devices thus far—ekphrastic description, biblical typology, allusion to both scripture and classical literature, apostrophe, prosopopoeia, and analogy; this is the first sustained epic simile in the poem.

garden, or thick hedges guard the vineyard, 305
the devastating locust will devour
the budding plants, and wild birds attack
and scatter clustered grapes. Why should I speak
of stems of plants, imbued with poisoned drugs,
whose deadly sap drips with danger? Look: 310
envenomed juices bubble in tender shrubs,
though nature once gave birth to harmless hemlock;
the dewy flower that clothes the oleander's
branches once safely pastured frisky goats.

But when the established bond was overthrown, 315
the elements themselves transgress the bounds
laid down for them, and plunder and destroy
all things, and shake the world with lawless might.
The battling winds shatter shady groves;
uprooted by the savage blasts, the woods 320
come crashing down, while over here the raging
river's swollen waters leap across
the banks placed opposite to check their path,
and wandering far and wide, the river rules
the devastated fields. But the Creator 325
did not plant such rage in newborn things:
instead, the unchecked license of the world,
without restraint, disturbed the peaceful laws.
And is it any wonder if the world's
parts are shaken and spun about, or if 330
the engine of the universe, harassed
by its own faults, is struggling, or if plague
exhausts the lands? It's human life that gives
the pattern for the world's sin—human life![52]
Madness and Error stimulate our actions,[53] 335
causing wars to rage, and Pleasure to flood
the world, and Lust to burn with filthy fire,
and hungry Greed to suck down heaps of coins
with gaping jaws. No limit of possessing
slows Greed from adding hope for more and more 340

---

52. Contrast this passage, in which the exemplum of man's sin corrupts the universe, with the analogy of the sun earlier, in which the universe provides an exemplum to help man understand God.

53. In another example of enargeia, or writing that brings a visual image to mind, Prudentius introduces a host of personified Vices, several of which appear later in the *Psychomachia*, the poem that is the first sustained personification allegory in Latin literature.

to money she's amassed. The thirst for gold
grows when gold's acquired. Hence a harvest
of woes, sole root of evil, while Ornament,
a pimp for dissipated Honor,[54] pans
for gold in rushing streams and digs for hidden   345
ores, and foolish Ambition scratches in
the veins of dirty earth, clawing up
the hidden secrets of nature, as if she might
find sparkling stones by rooting in the ditches.[55]
For Woman, not content with natural beauty,   350
puts on borrowed glamour; she even binds
the pearly stones from seashells in her gleaming
hair, or plaits her braids with golden chains,
as if the hand of God, the master craftsman,
had left her face unfinished, so she had   355
to decorate her brow with woven sapphires,
wind blazing gems around her flawless neck,
or weight her ears with dangling emerald stones.
It would be dull to run in detail through
the sacrilegious efforts made by married   360
women, who stain with dye the gifts with which
God endowed their forms. Makeup now
destroys the former beauty of their skin,
unrecognizable beneath its coat
of false color—but that's the weaker sex.   365
Within the narrow confines of her breast
a tide of sins batters her fragile mind.
And what about the fact that Man—the head
of a woman's body, the king who rules the small
and fragile creature carved from his own flesh,   370
he who rules the tender vessel with
his governance—is also dissipated
in hedonism? Look at the aging athletes,
softened by good living, men to whom
the Maker gave hard bodies and strong limbs   375
scaffolded by bones. Yet they're ashamed
of being men and chase whatever vanities

---

54. "Honor": The Latin is *Pudor*, here in the sense of sexual restraint, modesty (*OLD* s.v. 2b).

55. After the troop of personified Vices, Prudentius turns to a stock theme from moral diatribes and satire: the vices of women and homosexuals. Women are attacked for their love of artifice, exemplified by makeup and ornament; effeminate men are accused of improperly abandoning their masculine qualities (self-control, strength) in their lust for luxury goods and feminine display.

will make them beautiful, and foolishly
dissolve their native strength. Flowing robes
delight them—robes not made of wool from sheep, 380
but culled from the spoil of Oriental trees,[56]
and diamond shapes and checkered patterns ripple
when they flex their muscles. They invented
the art of steeping threads in dye to make
figures in different-colored fibers. Fleeces 385
from exotic fauna, soft to touch,
are spun for yarn. This man, a mighty hunter,
chases after sexy tunics, weaving
feather boas (a novel fabric made
from multicolored birds), while another 390
minces about in clouds of scent and lotions
and imported powder. The Creator
placed our vital powers in our senses:
self-indulgence now controls all five![57]
The use we make of ears and eyes, of nose 395
and palate, is ruined by vice: even touch,
which rules all of our body, now solicits
the sensuous caress of heated lotions.
Oh, what anguish! Nature's laws lie low,
her captured dowry dragged behind the tyrant 400
Lust. Perverted justice prospers; every
thing that God Almighty gave to men
they twist to different ends. I ask you,
was the watchful pupil set below
the delicate lid in order to pollute 405
its sight with gross delight, or watch the foul
bodies of transvestites swept away
by floods of stage emotion? Does our breath
make its way through tunnels branching down
from the center of the brain's high fortress 410
to our twin nostrils just so Pleasure, basely
bought, can revel in the sweet enticement
of a harlot letting down her scented hair?

56. I.e., silk, which the Romans imported from China and valued highly. The fabric was woven from the threads produced by silkworms that fed on the leaves of mulberry trees.
57. It was thought that the senses were gateways through which the soul could be attacked (cf. John Chrysostom, *On Vainglory and the Education of the Young* 27); Prudentius here enumerates the assaults to which each sense is vulnerable. Sight is by far the most dangerous of the senses, as it leaves the strongest impression on the mind.

Did God open our ears and make a way
for sound to enter their intricate canals 415
so we could hear the lute girls' pointless strumming,
the sound of strings, and wild drinking songs?
Inside the mouth's damp cave, does taste exist
so spicy foreign entrées can ensnare
the gourmand's jaded palate and greedy maw, 420
enabling him to spend entire nights
eating meals composed of many courses
and every kind of flavor, until his belly,
stuffed with food and wine, can take no more?
God wanted us to learn what's hard or soft, 425
what's smooth, and what is rough, what's hot or cold
through an interpreter: our sense of touch.
But we cocoon ourselves with downy pillows
and linen cloths that soothe and smooth our skin
whenever we recline upon our couches. 430

The man who is able to find the golden mean
is happy—the man who can with moderation
enjoy the gifts he has been given, and use
them sparingly. The rich appearance of this
world, its lovely charm, the overflowing 435
abundance of its glittering toys cannot
trick or capture him as if he were
a child, cannot enslave him to a love
unsuitable, if once he has discovered
beneath the sweet appearance of a seeming 440
good the deadly poison that lurks inside.
Once it was holy and good for us, when God,
in the beginning, created the universe.
God saw that it was good indeed, as Moses,
our historian, bore witness[58]—Moses, 445
who wrote the story of the infant world
and said, "The Lord saw that everything
He made was good."[59] And I will follow this,

---

58. Moses is described in two very different Latin phrases: *historicus* and *sanctus vaticinator*, "historian" and "holy seer." *Historicus*, an unpoetic word, appears only here in Prudentius's works. Conybeare (2007, 231) argues that Moses bridges the gap between literary culture (*historicus*) and feigned orality (*vaticinator* combines the concepts of *vates*, "bard" or "seer," and song (-*cinator*, from *cano*, "to sing"), and mediates between the Old and New Testaments.

59. Genesis 1:31.

and steadily hold within my mind the concept
uttered by the holy seer, inspired 450
by God, as he went over in his mind
the origins of ancient light: "Whatever
God and Wisdom have created is good."
The Father, then, created what is good,
and with the Father, Christ, for he is God, 455
and God the Father and the Son are one.
For nature makes them one: one nature
of will, of law, of strength, of love exists
in both. It doesn't mean, therefore, that there
are *two* divinities or *two* creators 460
of things, since there is no discrepancy
in kind, no separation of powers, none
of intellect: everything that's good
was born from one creator. From this spring
no mud can flow, no murky waters rise; 465
its source, still pure, remains intact. But as
its crystal waters, uncorrupted, lap
against the dirty sands, the sad decay
surrounding it infects its purity.
Now, did a horse, did iron or bull or lion, 470
rope or olive tree have any evil
power within them when they first were shaped?
It isn't iron blades that commit murder:
it takes a human hand. The horse does not
create the frenzied madness of the circus, 475
or its folly, or its wild applause:
it's mob mentality, completely brainless,
that runs amok—don't blame the racing horses.
So vile passion ruins a useful gift.
In just this way, we know, the gyms in Sparta 480
were drenched with olive oil: that soothing extract
was used for crime; in just this way a tumbler
sure-footedly ascends the lofty stage
suspended in midair upon a rope,
and daring bodies somersault across 485
the backs of wild beasts and flirt with death.
By popular demand we put on shows
that feature human blood! Our laws demand
that humans suffer punishment from beasts,
and human limbs are torn by cruel jaws 490

to entertain the happy crowd with slaughter!
It's tedious to go through the thousand other
frenzied pleasures of this stupid world,
forgetful of the one true Thunderer,
that shroud our human life in clouds of wretched   495
error.[60] Is there anyone now who can
recall his heavenly Father, or attempt
to make his mind ascend the heights? Any
one who breathes a sigh to heaven and turns
his thoughts to his ancestral throne on high   500
and turns his gaze back to his Creator,
or sends his hope toward heaven on balanced wing?

    Instead, Man sells his soul to a lord unworthy,
content to grunt beneath a load of heavy
cares. With downcast eyes and senses bent,   505
he chases the fleeting, earthly things he loves.
What does he find sweet? What earth produces,
what slippery reputation brings, what fatal
pleasure recommends, what passes like
a breath of wind that stirs the dust, or like   510
the flitting of an insubstantial shadow.
The highwayman[61] attacks our weakened souls
with these diseases and plagues; with hidden force
he penetrates the thirsty hearts of men.
He sows the seeds of every wickedness   515
deep within, and scatters his agents through
all the body's parts. And there, enslaved
to such a prince, a vast array of forces
takes the field, attacks our sickened souls
with dreadful weapons:[62] Anger, Superstition,   520

---

    60. Two words close together in the Latin suggest that in this passage about human enslavement to the pleasures of the world, Prudentius wants us to recall worship of the pagan gods: *bacchantia* (Lat. 375), lit. "raving like a bacchante," which I have translated as "frenzied," and *Tonantis* (Lat. 376), "the Thunderer." The bacchantes were the wild female cult worshippers of Bacchus. *Tonans* was a common epithet of Jupiter, the king of the gods, whose attribute was the thunderbolt. Prudentius frequently uses the epithet as a synonym for *Deus*, God, perhaps for the sake of meter, or perhaps to bring the pagan pantheon to the reader's mind.

    61. "Highwayman": Latin *praedo*. The image of the devil as a highwayman or robber was very common in early Christian writings. See Bartelink 1967 and Fontaine 1964. In this section of the poem (through line 720; Lat. 552) Prudentius portrays the soul under attack by Satan and his agents.

    62. Prudentius included a short list of personified Vices who threaten the soul through the senses at 250ff. This more elaborate allegorical set piece presents twenty-one personified abstractions.

Grief, Despair, Discord, and Thirst for Blood,
Thirst for Wine and Thirst for Gold, and Spite,
and Cunning, Slander, Theft, Adultery,
and Malice. Hideous, with deformed faces,
their every gesture threatens. Swelled Ambition 525
swaggers, Learning boasts, and Oratory
thunders, while Deceit, in hiding, weaves her snares.
On this side, bitchy Eloquence fills the forum
with barking,[63] and on that, cut-rate Philosophy,
her staff the size of Hercules' club, 530
draws a crowd with her troupe of naked sages.
Idolatrous Religion prays before
the smoky statues, and pale with fear, she bows
down low before unhearing altars. Ah!
How the evil enemy oppresses man 535
with his multitudes of troops, and wages
iron war with countless mercenaries!
How powerfully he triumphs over the conquered![64]
The Canaanite, his ally, helmed in dread,
attacks with all his ranks of troops; his beard 540
bristles on his jutting chin; he shakes
a heavy spear in his right hand. And over
there, the Amorite's raging army blazes
and Girgashites in thousands skim the field
in strict array, some striking from afar, 545
some fighting hand to hand. And look! A troop
on fire for battle—the Jebusites. Their golden
weapons, dipped in dragon's blood, gleam
and kill with deadly splendor. Hittite, you
enjoy equipping fearsome squads with lances; 550
the tribe of Perizzites attacks with arrows,
just as brave, with different arms; and last,
the Hivite king, clad in a scaly breastplate

---

63. *Caninus*, literally "doglike," is an adjective that characterizes an aggressive, offensive kind of speech, particularly associatied with oratory, satire, and the Cynic philosophers. See Palla 1981, 218 for examples. "Philosophy" translates the Latin *Sapientia*, "Wisdom." This is a rather striking use of the word, which Prudentius usually uses to refer to divine wisdom. Cut-rate Philosophy with her Herculean club is a likely reference to Cynic philosophers, famous for their aggressive attacks on conventional morality, extreme ascetic lifestyle, and rejection of religion (Augustine, *Civ. Dei* 14.20, mentions Cynic philosophers in their cheap cloaks carrying clubs, and the Cynics were said to regard Heracles as a role model: Palla 1981, 219; Goossens 1947).

64. Now biblical figures, the seven tribes who were expelled from Palestine to make way for the Israelites, join the personified Vices in their attack on the soul (Exodus 23:24; Joshua 24).

of serpent skin. Relying on these heroes,
the vile ruler of sins subdues weak souls, 555
and they, guileless in their simplicity,
unused to war and trusting in a false
pledge of peace, believe at first those troops
are allies, and out of love for peace, pursue
a truce with Mammon. Off they go in chains, 560
without a fight, willing to bow their necks
beneath the harsh yoke—they *choose* to follow
the harsh commands of worthless spirits! A man
adds to his property with fields he doesn't
need, eyeing his neighbor's yard, ignoring 565
boundary lines. In shackles he's paraded
before the victor's chariot, little knowing
that he's condemned already to the cruel
lash. The lawyer reaches lofty heights,
his empty fame inflating him with pride.[65] 570
He thinks the highest and the soundest good
is constituted by career success—
by scaring prisoners (who tremble when
the bailiffs shout at them), by breaking rods
on the backs of wretched clients, and swinging 575
the dreaded legal ax against them ... Now
the rope's around his neck, his ankles chained,
his feet will wear the iron fetters smooth.
O, you captive mortals, who are now
confined in prison by your enemy, 580
the virtue that you couldn't comprehend
condemns you to this servitude.[66] Believe me,
this is Babylon, our Captivity,
this the fearful triumph of the Assyrian
king that tearful Jeremiah mourned 585
in *Lamentations*: a city deprived of all
her people.[67] Is it secret? Who could doubt

---

65. Prudentius himself was a highly successful lawyer, as he states in the preface to his collected works, and had personal experience with the long speeches, dramatic rhetoric, and public punishment that characterized legal proceedings in late antiquity.

66. Prudentius now compares the soul's captivity to scriptural episodes describing the bondage and deliverance of the Israelites.

67. This refers to the Babylonian Captivity or Exile. The Babylonian king Nebuchadnezzar laid siege to Jerusalem and captured much of the Jewish population in 599 BCE. After the Persian victory over the Babylonian Empire in 538 BCE, Cyrus the Great gave permission for Jews to return to the land of Judah.

that souls descended from the seed of Jacob
live in exile among the Gentiles, captured
by the Mede and forced into alliance? 590
In Babylon they've lost the habit of living
as their fathers did: degenerate,
they shuffle off ancestral ways and turn
to foreign laws, they take up foreign clothes
and speech: they learn to wallow in profane 595
rituals and banish Mother Zion
from their wicked hearts. It pains them to
recall their native country; now they break
their harps and cymbals and praise the sacred rites
of a kingdom not their own. Should their fathers 600
have chosen to tolerate the savage rule
of Memphis, squatting down at Pharaoh's feet
by the cruel hearth of the palace, ready to slave
away at making bricks from clay and straw
as long as their guts are stuffed with food, while they 605
belch up meat they can't digest? Is that
what should have happened? Why did the Lord pour out
so much help by means of marvelous omens—
aid His rebel people don't deserve?
Why did He loosen the fetters from their necks, 610
and curb the might of Egypt with a rod
of snakes? What good is it to have the seas
retreat, to tread a dusty path across
the waters, for rocks that once knew only Ocean's
depths to be exposed to unknown heaven, 615
for thirsty mud to dry up in the waves?
Where's the good, if the once-victorious army
that cut through darkness with a pillar of light
has lost the fertile valley where the grapes
grew in clusters;[68] if they have forgotten 620
how to till the land where snowy streams

68. Numbers 13:17–20, 23–25: "Then Moses sent them to spy out the land of Canaan, and said to them, 'Go up this way into the South, and go up to the mountains, and see what the land is like: whether the people who dwell in it are strong or weak, few or many; whether the land they dwell in is good or bad; whether the cities they inhabit are like camps or strongholds; whether the land is rich or poor; and whether there are forests there or not. Be of good courage. And bring some of the fruit of the land.' Now the time was the season of the first ripe grapes. . . . Then they came to the Valley of Eshcol, and there cut down a branch with one cluster of grapes; they carried it between two of them on a pole."

of milk forever mix with flowing honey?
if they allow the walls of Jericho,
toppled long ago by the trumpet's blast,
to rise again to their former height; if, forced   625
back from the banks of backward-flowing Jordan,
they leave the land of their inheritance[69]
and can't defend the City built with toil
and sweat, whose towers rise above the thunder-
clouds, if they don't know which stone it is   630
that stands against the foe, a tower of strength
that can't be conquered even by the bronzed
beak of a battering ram or shaken by iron
missiles? This is the keystone in the arch,
that locks the other stones in their positions,   635
securing the foundation.[70] One who knows
the Stone is properly centered in his ramparts,
and takes his stand atop the citadel
reliant on his love of the Stone,[71]
is ever vigilant, and keeps his weapons   640
pure, and guards himself and his defensive
walls with a triple row of palisades—
such a man the Queen of Tyre will not
defeat, nor the Parthian who lives
by great Euphrates, nor the dusky Hindu   645
sporting feathered arrows on his black
brow.[72] Why, even if a foreign tyrant[73]

---

69. Numbers 34:13: "Moses commanded the Israelites: 'Assign this land by lot as an inheritance.'"

70. As Taddei notes, the image of the cornerstone is centrally located—close to the perfect center of the poem in terms of lines—and is meant to recall Christ, who is called the capstone or cornerstone (1 Peter 2:7, Ephesians 2:20, Romans 9:33).

71. Prudentius uses the Greek loanword *petra*, alluding to the famous passage (Matthew 16:18) where Christ said, "Thou art Peter (*Petros*) and on this rock (*petra*) I will found my church." *Amore petrae*, which I have translated as "his love of the Stone," could also mean "the Stone's love for him."

72. Possibly the Phoenician Jezebel, but more likely, given the context and parallels with the Parthians and Indians, the Queen of Tyre refers to Dido, a princess of Tyre who founded the city of Carthage. According to the influential version of her story in the *Aeneid*, after being deserted by the Trojan prince Aeneas, who was called by destiny to leave her and found Rome, Dido cursed the Trojans and their descendants, with the result that Carthage became Rome's great enemy in the Punic Wars. The Parthians and the Indians were also traditional enemies of Rome, mentioned, e.g., by Horace at *Carm.* 1.12.93–96. Prudentius thus associates the enemies of Israel with the traditional enemies of Rome.

73. "Foreign tyrant": The Latin word for "foreign," borrowed from Greek, is *allophilus*, a term that in ecclesiastical writings is used to refer to the Philistines (Palla ad loc., citing *ThLL* 1:1692). The devil here is identified as the tyrant of the Philistines, one of the seven hostile tribes the Israelites

should wake the giants who hurl the thunderbolt
to blast your camps, *you*'ll be safe.[74] The god
of Marcion, that Charon[75] of our world
who ushers souls to hell, will never move you
from your well-defended post, although
he rules the empty shadows that extend
beneath this transitory sun.[76]
                       For every-
thing the sun looks down upon is empty:
all things consist of ever-changing elements
and all can be dissolved. Am I lying?
No, the apostle Paul, our teacher, said
the whole created world, against its will,
is subject to toil in vain;[77] in pity
he wept that all creation is in bondage
to this treacherous robber. "He who thinks,"
he says,[78] "that our combat is with blood
and flesh, with burning heart and poisonous bile,[79]
that heat in our very marrow drives the soul
to sin, is wrong! The body doesn't oppress
the mind; no earthly power besieges
our clear understanding and provokes it

---

fought against in their quest to gain the promised land. "The giants who hurl the thunderbolt": In classical mythology, the giants, born of the earth goddess Gaea, led a rebellion against the rule of Zeus; the successful suppression of the revolt by the Olympian gods that led to the restoration of order to the cosmos was a frequent subject of visual arts and literature. Prudentius associates the Philistines with the giants who threaten cosmic order, an association perhaps inspired by the figure of Goliath, the gigantic Philistine slain by David. Similarly, the devil in the guise of Nimrod is associated with the giants in line 201 (Lat. 147), where he is said to have "giant arms," *giganteis . . . lacertis*.

74. Prudentius uses the rhetorical device of apostrophe as he moves from describing the ideal Christian in the abstract, *ille* ("that one" or "he who"), to addressing the reader in particular (presumably also a Christian), using the second person.

75. In classical literature, Charon is the boatman who ferries the souls of the dead across the river Styx.

76. Prudentius now sets out the argument that man struggles not against the material body but against the spirits of darkness, demons who dwell in the atmosphere (the space between earth and heaven). This argument does not directly contradict but is significantly different from the one set out the preface, which envisions inevitable combat between flesh and spirit.

77. Romans 8:20–22: "For the creation was subjected to frustration, not by its own choice, but by the will of the one who subjected it, in hope that the creation itself will be liberated from its bondage to decay and brought into the glorious freedom of the children of God. We know that the whole creation has been groaning as in the pains of childbirth right up to the present time."

78. Prudentius presents this paraphrase of Paul as a direct quotation.

79. "Heart": The Latin is *venis*, lit. "veins"; it can also mean "innermost quality, inner feeling." *Fel*, "bile," was used for both the gallbladder and bile in the sense of animosity, bitterness.

to war. We fight by night and day with dark
powers who rule the numbing mists and heavy
clouded air."⁸⁰
                      THIS MIDDLE region, as you
know, that lies between the heavens and
the earth below, whose sheer abyss contains
the floating clouds, endures the rule of many
different powers, and under the command
of Belial, its wicked rulers strike
the heart with dread.⁸¹ *These* are the robbers we
must fight: the holy words of the apostle
testify to that. No sinner should
accuse his body's impulses, or blame
sin on innate nature. It is easy
to curb rebellious passions of the body,
to restrain the eager drives of frail
matter, to conquer and subdue the flesh.
It's clear the mind, descended from the heights
of heaven, is a higher thing by far:
if it should wish to tame its subject limbs
with harsh authority and turn them over
to strict command, no power could resist
the master's rule.
                      Man has, however, a greater
force within, attacking with a breath
of venom, striking at his subtle mind
with subtle mist. It comes more quickly than
an arrow from a Parthian bow, whose path
it is impossible to see:⁸² a feathered
thing that flies across the rapid breezes
of the atmosphere, it takes us by
surprise—no hiss announces death's approach,

---

80. Ephesians 6:12: "For our struggle is not against flesh and blood, but against the rulers, against the authorities, against the powers of this dark world and against the spiritual forces of evil in the heavenly realms."

81. Heaven (*aether*), home of the angels, is separated from the earth by *aer*, the region of the atmosphere, the realm of Satan, the fallen angel. Cf. Ephesians 2:1–2: "As for you, you were dead in your transgressions and sins, in which you used to live when you followed the ways of this world and of the ruler of the kingdom of the air, the spirit who is now at work in those who are disobedient."

82. The Parthians were famous for perfecting a battle tactic called the Parthian shot, in which they feigned retreat and galloped off, then turned backward in their saddles as their horses continued to retreat, and shot at the enemy.

but silently it bursts the heart's interior
and pierces the secure abode of life   700
with poisoned wound. On swifter wings
than that, its point imbued with drug more fatal,
flies the arrow hurled by the slippery power
that rules our darkened world: in flight, the arrow
baffles sight, its feathered shaft hurtling   705
through the air to pierce the inmost heart.
The soul is not by nature lazy, or slow
to guard against such wounds, since God endowed
her with a fiery nature,[83] pure and wise,
subtle, tranquil, flighty, restless, rapid,   710
mobile, and sharp: let her but remain
pure and worship her creator, fighting
by His side, and unintoxicated,
let her overcome this world and trample
it underfoot. Better she should never   715
taste the fool's delight of fatal wealth
and deceptive spoils of many lands
than that, lying prone beneath this burden
and subject to a foreign power, she
should find she can't evade her foe's sharp arrows.   720

    But why do I distort things, blaming all
the evil of the world and of humanity
on our spiteful foe, when our own faults
are nurtured in our souls, and take their birth,
their source, their strength, their being, their potential   725
from the heart that fathered them?[84] Indeed,
he gives us spark and kindling for our sins,
but he can only trick and trouble us
as much as we allow. For we provide
weapons for the toothless lion; the lazy   730
beast would gnash his jaws in vain if we
did not applaud and give the favor he feeds
upon. For we give birth to all our sins
from our own bodies, just as David did,
who was the best of fathers otherwise,   735
though he produced as offspring Absalom,

---

83. "Fiery nature," *ignitum . . . ingenium*: A wordplay that associates the soul's innate character (*ingenium*) with fire (*ignis*), the element closest to the divine.

84. Prudentius now turns to the soul's own responsibility for sin.

his only crime. The father of many righteous
children, David also fathered one
parricide, an evil son who dared
to draw his sword against the author of 740
his being, who came to battle with his standard
set against his father and opposed
his army, fighting his own flesh and blood.
Alas for loyalty! In just the same
way our hearts give birth to dreadful children, 745
a painful generation, whose habit is
to turn their teeth against us from the start
and live by the pain of those that gave them life,
for they destroy their parents' all-too-fertile
flesh and feed on the family's dying stock. 750
But that royal David, king of kings,
God's prophet, and a forefather of Mary,
the virgin mother, had begot a mixed
breed of children, the good and loyal with
the bad. And so it was that Absalom, 755
the good king's brother, sowed his crimes among
the upright children and brought bitter woe
to that sweet home, so that no Solomon
exists in us; we're Absalom—corrupt,
we turn our knives against our family's flesh.[85] 760

      Let us, if we may, take a fable from
the pagan natural historians.[86]
It goes like this: the viper issues offspring
from her womb: they bite her, and she dies,
becoming mother in the throes of death. 765
It isn't her genitals that make her fertile,
it isn't intercourse that swells her womb.
No, when she's in heat, inflamed by female
lust, the obscene creature opens wide
her gaping jaws, thirsting for her mate 770
who's soon to die. Into his spouse's jaws

---

    85. Palla draws attention to the series of antitheses in these lines: *tristibus-piis, crimina-iustis, dulcem-amaris*, culminating in the antithetical brothers Solomon and Absalom.

    86. Palla 254–56 lists numerous sources for ancient beliefs about the generative habits of the viper, esp. Hdt. 3.109, Pliny *NH* 10.62.169–70, and *Physiologus* 10. Salvatore (1958: 20–23) has shown that this passage is also influenced by Lucretius's description of sex in *DRN* 4 (cf. *H.* 589 and *DRN* 4.1030–31; *H.* 590–91 and *DRN* 4.1048 and 4.1084–85).

he thrusts his three-tongued head; aflame with passion,
he enters her mouth, injecting poisoned semen
through oral sex. Amid the sweet accords
and covenants of love, the bride, wounded 775
by such violent delight, draws down
her lover's head into her mouth and snaps
his neck between her teeth, drinking in
the last ejaculation from her dying
lover's lips. These pleasures kill the father; 780
the offspring in the womb destroy their mother:
for when the seed matures, the little tiny
bodies begin to crawl in their warm den,
and lashing about they strike her shaken womb.
This internal treachery enflames 785
the mother, conscious of her guilty sex,
and she bemoans her children, now become
her executioners, as they break down
the barriers to birth. For since no birth canal
provides an easy path, the young, struggling 790
toward the light, attack her laboring womb
and open up a way through her torn loins.
At last, as their nurturing mother dies, the brood
of sorrows emerges, barely forcing their way
out into life, carving out their birth 795
by crime. The puppies[87] creep about and lick
the corpse that bore them—a generation orphaned
at birth, bereft of their poor mother before
they ever saw the light of day. The way
our soul conceives is not dissimilar:[88] in just 800
this way, with Belial as mate, the soul
guzzles venom gushing from the viper's
mouth and sucks his kisses down and draws
them deep inside; in just this way, aflame
with venomous lust, she joins her spouse, so soon 805
to die, and fills her womb with sins. Pregnant, then,
she carries a deadly race: fruits of an evil
nature, sprung from her coupling with the snake,

---

87. "Puppies": *Catuli*, which can mean the whelp of any animal (usually of mammals, but Vergil uses it of snakes in *G.* 3.438), but was most commonly used to mean "puppy." Varro (*L.L.* 9.74) takes it as a diminutive of *canis* (dog).

88. Prudentius moves from an example drawn from nature (the mating habits of vipers) to an allegory: the personified soul mates with Satan (Belial) in his familiar snaky form.

the snake, who must pay first for what he's done:
the soul corrupted and the earth in ruins! 810
And she, in turn, will struggle in childbirth,
torn by a thousand wounds, until she bears
unnatural offspring, a litter of sins, children
gorged and fattened on their mother's corpse.
Hence[89] that just rebuke of Christ when He 815
accused, "Is your father not a demon, sinners?
Were you not begotten when he joined
with flesh that thirsted for his evil seed?"
Reader,[90] go through the holy book: you'll see
that as I said, the Lord brought true indictments 820
against iniquitous men: "Holiness
itself, or works of holiness, would prove
that you were truly offspring of my Father."

How blind is lust! The soul, though good, though knowing
she's legally betrothed and that the ever- 825
youthful king himself, whose ageless face
forever keeps its godlike beauty, the king
will call her to the marriage bed—what can
it mean when she instead decides to choose
adultery, and prostitutes herself 830
for cheap sex with a Hindu, black as night,[91]
rejecting the son of God, the Virgin-born,
and calls the children born in a brothel sweet?[92]
I know how well seductive rhetoric

---

89. Prudentius turns from the example of the vipers to a biblical passage, John 8:44, where Christ says, "You belong to your father the devil, and you want to carry out your father's desire." Conybeare (2007, 234) argues persuasively that the next statement ascribed to Christ (H. 821-23; Lat. 626-28)—"Holiness / itself, or works of holiness, would prove / that you were truly offspring of my Father"—is also an allusion, to John 8:31-32: "If you hold to my teaching, you are really my disciples. Then you will know the truth, and the truth will set you free."

90. As Conybeare (2007, 233) notes, this is a startling apostrophe. In the Latin text, which would have had no quotation marks, it appears at first to be Christ himself who addresses the reader—it is not clear that it is Prudentius speaking until we reach the word "Lord" (*dominum*). Since the pronoun "you" and second person verbs have so far in the poem referred to Marcion (with the exception of H. 501, where "you" seems to refer to the just soul), the reader has reason to be surprised at being addressed so suddenly and forcefully. Conybeare (2007, 34) argues that Prudentius is here conflating his own voice with that of God: in her words, "There is a remarkable displacement of authority going on here."

91. Jerome seems to see Indians, or Hindus, as especially promiscuous: *Ad Iovinianum* 1.44 col. 286: *Indi, ut omnes paene barbari, uxores plurimas habent*; 2.7, col. 309: *Persae, Medi, Indi, et Aethiopes, regna non modica, et Romano regno paria, cum matribus et aviis, cum filiabus et nepotibus copulantur.*

92. The sinful soul rejects her proper bridegroom, Christ, in favor of Satan.

can argue on the other side and make 835
its case, and how malicious fraud fights
with sharpened teeth and shreds the truth, inciting
us to fight, and says, "If God does not
want evil to exist, why does He not
forbid it? It doesn't matter whether He's 840
the author who created evil, or
just allows His lovely works to be
turned to sinful use when he could stop it.
If *He,* omnipotent, should will that all
humanity live out life innocent, 845
our pure and pious will would never weaken
nor would our hand be stained by any act.
The Lord, then, must have put in place the evil
deeds He watches from on high, allows
to happen, and approves of, just as if 850
He had created it himself. For He
himself, indeed, created that which, though
He could exclude it, He does not destroy:
instead, by long-established precedent
He lets it roam unchecked."
                             Condemn my ears, 855
kind Father, and close off the channels of
my brutish head! Don't let their paths receive
such sounds! It's well worth losing vital function
in part of the brain if the fortunate soul
with deafened ear stays safe and hears no evil.[93] 860
What man, who recollects that he excels
in rank all other creatures by God's grace,
would stand to hear such insults hurled at God?
There's much I will not mention. This alone
proves God is good: that from their graves He raises 865
all who died from love of what's forbidden
and bids them share forever in His kingdom.
But if He were the author and preserver
of evil, after the harm done to salvation
and death of the unrighteous, He would not 870

---

93. As in 392–430 (Lat. 298–329), the soul is portrayed as vulnerable to attack through the senses: in this case, Prudentius would prefer to lose his sense of hearing than to fall victim to dangerous rhetoric (the dangerous rhetoric here is the argument that if God created all things, He must logically have created evil as well).

have come with loving kindness to bring aid
and restore the lost. To fall is human,
to save, divine. Man deserves to die,
but God wipes out the actions of the dying
man and frees him from them: this is proof 875
overwhelming that the Lord, who offers
us so much, does not will evil, nor
approve it first, then wash it afterward
away.
    "Does anyone have the power to sin
against the Thunderer's will? For Him, it's easy 880
to put inside man's heart whatever feelings
suit Him, to instill his every fiber
with chaste desires, to flood his veins with pure
integrity."
        You fool, don't you know
the strength of your own freedom, given by 885
the one who shaped you? Don't you know how great
a power you've always had over this world,
your servant, and over your own character
and will, free of all constraints, the will
to make decisions and follow what you want, 890
your mind not forced to suffer servitude?
When He made you lord of all creation
and bade the subject world to follow your
commands, when He bestowed on you the fertile
fields and skies and sea, the flowing streams 895
and winds, would He begrudge to trust you with
free will and thus deny you freedom as if
you were unworthy? What would it mean if you
were chosen to be king of this great world
but not be king of your own self, your honor 900
spoiled by being thus curtailed? Or what
distinction is there for a lord who has
no mental freedom, whose only thought must serve
the law imposed upon it? What praise or credit
does a man deserve for living justly 905
without a real decision between two paths?
The man who does not have authority
to choose a different course, to bend and change
the inclinations of his mind: that man
will never of his own free will be good. 910

The man who's good involuntarily
is neither praiseworthy nor even good,
because no glory comes to him from forced
integrity, and virtue without glory
is sordid—it is only virtue if, 915
rejecting what is bad, it flashes out
on its own and by its better nature
seeks the proper path.[94]
                         "Go forth," says Adam's
Father, the Maker and Creator, "Go forth,
O man,[95] ennobled by my mouth's own breath, 920
slave to no one, powerful, the ruler
of the world and judge of your own mind.
Subject yourself to me of your own will
so that obedience itself will come about
through your own free judgment. I don't force you 925
or constrain you with my might; I do
remind you that you must avoid injustice
and follow after justice. Light befriends
the just, but shivering death awaits the sinner.
Choose a way of life: for virtue could 930
advance you to eternal life, or else
your sin condemn you for eternity.
With the freedom you've been granted, make
your choice between the fates."
                         Such kindness
leaves him free to roam down any road;[96] 935
rejoicing in the richness of his gift,

---

94. At this point Prudentius turns to the pivotal moment of original sin: God gives Adam free will, and he is faced with the decision of whether to heed the words of his wife or to obey God.

95. There is a complex etymological wordplay in the Latin (696–97): "'Vade,' ait ipse parens opifexque et conditor Adae, / 'Vade, homo.'" *Vade*, "go forth," is a near anagram of *Adae*, "Adam"; it is significant here because Adam's choice will result in his having to go forth permanently from Eden. *Homo* is a bilingual pun; it translates the Hebrew *Adam*, which means "man" or "mankind," and was thought to be related to the word *ha-adamah*, "ground" or "dirt." Similarly, in Latin *homo* was thought to be related to *humus*.

96. "Down any road": This is not in the Latin; I added it to convey the idea in English that *vagus*, "free to roam," is part of a complex of imagery of the traveler on the road, often lost and prey to robbers, that is a feature of the *Hamartigenia* and of other poems of Prudentius as well (Bartelink 1967, 197), e.g., the simile of the devil as a highwayman attacking a traveler (208–15); the brothers who come to a fork in the road and have to determine which is the right path (789–801); and Prudentius's prayer that his own soul not be confronted with the devil as highwayman after his death. Similarly, the thematic preface to *Apotheosis* opens with an extended metaphor that equates heretical beliefs with being lost amid a confusion of twisting paths (*praef. Apoth.* 1–16).

he goes against the law laid down for him,
and with knowledge[97] and free will he chooses
the things of death, believing all the while
that what the clever serpent urged, against   940
the will of God, would be more useful to him.[98]
He, indeed, persuaded by rhetoric
and not by harsh command. The woman, when
indicted for the crime, made this reply
to the charges of the Lord: herself seduced   945
by crafty arguments, she had persuaded
her husband; freely then did man himself
consent.[99] Given the freedom of his upright soul,
could he not have spurned her arguments?
He could! For God had urged him earlier   950
to follow what is better willingly,
but he, rejecting wisdom, trusted more
in that cruel enemy. And now he stands
between the Lord of life and Master of death:
God summons him from one side, from the other   955
calls the tyrant: impulse drives him one way,
then the other.[100]
                    LISTEN and remember
these famous monuments of deeds long past,
a prelude staged by History, a sign
well worth looking at. While fleeing from   960
the ruins of burning Sodom, Lot abandoned
his house in haste, taking with him all

---

97. The Latin is *prudens*, an important word. God alone has true foresight, *providentia*. The adjective characterizing Adam at the moment of his fateful choice is also a pun on the poet's own name, *Prudentius*, and thus associates Prudentius with the sinful Adam.

98. Note that here it seems to be the snake, not Eve, who convinces Adam. Contrast Genesis 3:6, and below, lines 946–47 (Lat. 715, *suasisse viro*) and 982 (Lat. 741, *traxerat Eva virum*).

99. The first appearance of Eve in the poem since the preface (*feminarum prima*, line 2). Here too she is unnamed, referred to only as "woman" (*mulier*). In the *Hamartigenia*, Eve's actions are almost entirely superseded by Adam's, and her actions and the serpent's are elided—both persuade Adam. The language in this passage is laden with legal imagery, which would have come naturally to Prudentius, who had a distinguished legal career: *rea* (defendant, one who is indicted), *crimen* (crime or charge), *exprobanti* (making a legal charge); Adam is referred to as *arbiter* (699) and *iudex* (700).

100. This is the end of the tale of Adam and Eve. Instead of recounting Adam's sin and its consequences, Prudentius leaves Adam frozen in the moment of decision, and turns to a series of elaborate figures to represent his dilemma (and our dilemma, for it is shared by each human soul): two biblical tales (the fate of Lot and his wife; the story of Ruth and Orpah); the tale of two brothers at a crossroads who take different paths, one to virtue and one to ruin; and the simile of the wise and foolish doves.

of his dear family,[101] to escape the storm
that rained devouring fire on the town.
The air already was alight; it veiled 965
the sky with clouds of sulfur; rattling hail
kindled the blazing day. An angel guest
sent in double form by the power of God
had written in advance the Lord's command:
that all the house should exit from the gates 970
and, never straying, keep their eyes ahead,
facing open country, never turning
back their gaze to see the fires lording
it over the city's walls.[102] "Whoever recalls
Sodom, the model that says the universe 975
will end in fire, must never turn his gaze
back to look upon the death of everything."
Wise Lot obeyed this warning, but his fickle
wife, her heart as light as any woman's,
bent her mind and will behind her, toward 980
her city's lamentation. And there she stuck.
Eve had drawn her husband to be partner
to her dreadful crime, but *she* destroyed
only herself by sinning.[103] Growing stiff
and petrified, she turns to fragile ore; 985
transformed to solvent stone, the woman stands
just as she had stood before, but now
she's formed into a lofty pillar stamped
into the salt, preserving all her features:
her loveliness, her graceful dress, her brow 990
and eyes and hair, her face turned back
to look behind her, with her chin just barely

---

101. "Family": The Latin is *pignora*, "pledges," commonly used to mean children. Lot had two daughters who left Sodom with him and his wife. After Sodom was destroyed and Lot's wife was transformed into a pillar of salt, Lot had no male heirs. His daughters got him drunk and became pregnant by him in order to preserve the family line (Genesis 19:31–33).

102. According to ancient optical theory, the viewer is physically connected to the object he views, hence the vital importance of directing one's gaze toward the proper object. Miles (1983, 128) summarizes Augustine's understanding of the visual process: "The soul of the viewer both initially projects the visual ray, and it also 'absorbs into itself' the form or image of the object, which is then permanently retained by the memory." Lot's wife's emblematic sin is to direct her gaze, and hence her will and attention, to an unsuitable object (the sinful cities of the plain), despite the angels' warning.

103. 'Eve . . . *she*': The only mention of Eve's name in the poem occurs here, embedded within the typological tale of Lot's wife. Eve is contrasted with Lot's wife—whereas Eve had destroyed both Adam and herself, Lot's wife ("*she*") destroyed only herself.

lifted over her shoulder—now a stiffening
monument of ancient sin.[104] Although
she's wet, dissolving into salty sweats, 995
she feels no loss to her full shape resulting
from that dripping flow. No matter how
much the cattle wear away the tasty
stone, the same amount of fluid remains
and forms again the skin their tongues had worn 1000
away. She stands as a reminder, warning
passersby. The sinful woman got
what she deserved for heeding slippery counsel,
her weak and fluid intellect dissolving,
too fragile to uphold the will of heaven.[105] 1005
But Lot, once he has started on his way,
keeps his purpose firm, unhesitating.
He doesn't turn around to look upon
the ruined walls collapsing into ash,
or at the people and their customs, all 1010
now burnt: their public archives, laws, and markets,
vendors, baths, and brothels, temples, theaters,
the circus and its crowd, the drunken bars.
Sodom's fires engulf in righteous flames
the everyday activities of men, 1015
condemning them to hell with Christ as judge.[106]
    It is enough to have escaped them once:
our good man Lot does not look back. His fragile,
fickle wife, however, did look back,
turning her eyes to see what she had fled, 1020
and, hardened into stone amid her native
city's ashes, she stands there to this day.

LOOK! this allegory offers proof
of freedom for you: through it God desired
us to know the choice of path to follow 1025
remains our own; which road to take is always

---

104. In addition to drawing on the brief Genesis account (Genesis 19:26) of the transformation of Lot's wife into a pillar of salt, Prudentius draws extensively from Ovid's description of the transformation of Niobe into a statue in *Met.* 6.

105. This imagery of fluidity and mobility aligns Lot's wife with the qualities of the made-up woman and the effeminate males at *H.* 264–99.

106. Gnilka (2000, 68–90) argues that the next lines, *H.* 917–22 (Lat. 765–68) are an interpolation, based on the fact that they repeat what was just narrated.

up to us. Two were given orders
to leave from Sodom: one departs in haste,
the other hesitates; *he* flees with ever-
increasing speed, while *she* refuses to go. 1030
Both are free to decide; the will of each
is different. Every man is split in two:
desire pulls in opposite directions.
   The cycle of tales in holy scripture
offers many such examples. Look 1035
at Ruth the Moabite and Orpah.[107] Ruth
lovingly attends her mother-in-law,
Naomi; Orpah leaves her. Both had been
released from marriage and the law of wedlock,
bound no longer by the Hebrew rites, 1040
and both enjoyed the liberty of their own
free will. Her old religion's rites and shrines
persuaded Orpah to prefer the foreskins
of savages and bear[108] and raise a monstrous
hybrid son, Goliath.[109] Ruth, meanwhile, 1045
sweltered through the stubble in the heat
of summer and earned the marriage bed of Boaz;
admitted to his chaste embrace, she soon
conceived and bore the family of Christ,
the royal line of David, and mingled 1050
human offspring with divine.
                              Often
I remind myself of how, in a time

---

107. Told in 1 Ruth. Ruth and Orpah are both Moabites, and thus descendants of Lot and his wife's daughters. Naomi's family had moved to Moab during a time of famine in Israel. Her sons married the Moab women Ruth and Orpah, and then died, leaving the two young women widows. Naomi decides to return to Israel, and urges her daughters-in-law to return to their families and remarry. Orpah reluctantly does so; Ruth insists on accompanying Naomi back to Bethlehem.

108. Ruth and Orpah each bear hybrid children: Orpah gives birth to the monstrous Goliath (Prudentius calls him *semiferus*, literally "half-beast," 784), while Ruth's descendant through David is Christ, who mingles human and divine (*Deo mortales miscuit ortus*, 788).

109. Orpah receives considerable negative attention in the exegetical literature, despite her positive portrayal in 1 Ruth. Her name was believed to be derived from the root *'orep*, meaning "nape of the neck," since she turned her back on Naomi (she thus typologically recalls the sin of her ancestress, Lot's wife). Prudentius's assertion that she was persuaded by the (plural) "foreskins of barbarians" may indicate his knowledge of the tradition that Goliath was conceived by polyspermy and had a hundred Philistine fathers (Jerusalem Talmud Yebamoth 24b. See Bronner 1993). David, the descendant of Ruth and slayer of Goliath, is told by Saul that he can have Saul's daughter Michal in marriage in exchange for the foreskins of one hundred Philistines; David brings him two hundred (1 Samuel 24–26).

of indecision, a pair of youthful brothers
arrived together at a crossroads; long
they hesitated by the branching fork   1055
and wondered which would prove the better path.[110]
On the right, the road is choked by thorns
and brambles and a rocky path ascends
steeply up a narrow ridge, while on
the left, through pleasant lawns adorned with shady   1060
orchards bearing golden fruit, the broad
and gently sloping road descends. Content
with thorns, one brother creeps along the jagged
ridge; the other, self-indulgent, takes
the level left-hand path. One raises up   1065
his head nearly to the stars; the other
slipped and fell into a muddy swamp.
Although all men share in a single nature,
the outcome of their lives is not the same:
each man's decision takes a different shape.   1070
Just as sometimes doves in a milk-white cloud,
descending through the bright and lucid sky,
settle in a wheat field, where a clever
fowler set his snares and smeared the twigs
with sticky lime, baiting his traps with peas   1075
and poisoned grain,[111] and some are tempted by
the treacherous grain and caught by nets of woven
cord that choke their greedy throats, or else
soft glue traps and binds their wings: but others,
not seduced by love of eating, stroll   1080
at ease, unharmed, about the barren grass
and take good care not to turn their eyes
toward the suspect food. Soon, when it comes
time to fly back toward the sky, some freely
seek the starry heaven and clap their wings   1085
above the clouds, while others, taken captive,

---

110. The topos of the crossroads symbolizing an ethical choice has a long history, usefully summarized with bibliography by Palla (285–86). See Hesiod, *WD* 286–91; Xenophon, *Mem.* 2.1.20ff.; Cicero, *Tusc.* 1.30.72; Servius, *ad Aen.* 6.136; Philo, *Spec. leg.* 4.108 and 1.12; Lactantius, *Inst.* 6.3–4; Jerome, *Contra Ruf.* 3.39 (*PL* 23, 508x); Ausonius, *Prof.* 11.5. A scriptural parallel appears at Matthew 7:13–14.

111. The final figure describing the dilemma of Adam and the soul: the fate of doves confronted by tempting food, which will prove to be the undoing of those who go after it. This is the last sustained simile in the poem.

lie wounded, struggling on the ground, their feathers
torn, looking up in vain at the passing
breezes. In just this way, nature showers
spotless souls from heaven onto earth, 1090
but there they are retained, entrapped by sweet
delights, and very few ascend again
to heaven; the sticky food entices many
and keeps them from advancing to the upper
regions.[112]

        And so the Father, knowing all 1095
in advance, set livid Tartarus[113] on fire
with molten lead and under grim Avernus
dug channels filled with pitch and hellish water
and ordered greedy worms to dwell beneath
the fiery waves of Phlegethon, eternal 1100
punishment for sinners. For He knew
the soul, the living force of His own breath
shaped by His own mouth, can never die,
but neither, stained by sin, can she again
return to heaven but must be plunged 1105
into the boiling abyss. To worms and flames
and tortures he gave eternal life, to keep
her punishment from perishing with age,
since the soul's immortal; torments foster
and gnaw on matter given without end,[114] 1110
and Death herself retreats from the endless groaning
and forces sobbing souls to keep on living.
But far away in realms of paradise,[115]

---

112. Prudentius now turns to the fate of souls after judgment, starting with the eternal punishment of the damned, for whom immortality means eternal punishment.

113. In Hesiod's *Theogony*, Tartarus emerges after Chaos and Gaea (earth); it is a dark place in the depths of the earth. Later writers asserted that various monsters and enemies of the gods were imprisoned there; for Roman writers, it was where sinners were sent for punishment. Prudentius here conflates the underworld of Greek and Roman myth with Christian notions of hell.

114. Because the soul is imperishable, God has to devise punishments that are immortal to keep her in continual torment. The tortures both foster (*foveo*, "to foster, nourish") and gnaw (*carpo*, "to pluck, graze, devour, gnaw") the material substance, *materia*, of the soul. The Latin is *materiam sine fine datam*, literally, "matter given without end." *Materia* means "matter, stuff, nutritive matter." The phrase echoes, and occupies the same metrical place in the line as, Jupiter's famous pledge to Venus that he has given empire without end to the Romans: *imperium sine fine dedi, Aen.* 1.279.

115. It is unclear whether Prudentius identifies paradise with heaven or shares the belief of many of his contemporaries that paradise was a place where the just souls waited until the final resurrection. See Delumeau 2000, 26–31 for a discussion of paradise as a place of waiting, with extensive citations from early Christian writers.

God's majesty, endowed with knowledge of
the future, has allotted very different   1115
rewards for spirits pure and free of any
sin, who didn't turn around to look
upon the ruins of Gomorrah, but
with eyes averted, as is right, they turned
their backs upon the dark and looming dangers   1120
of our wretched world.[116]
                    These souls are first
uplifted to the stars in easy flight,
from whence the soul that animated Adam
after God had shaped him. For because
the weight of life no longer drags her tender   1125
nature down toward earth, nor impedes it
with iron fetters,[117] she cuts her path and glides
swiftly through the heavy atmosphere
and, like a glowing spark, she rises far
above the heaven whence she came, despising   1130
the prison house of clay where she was exiled.
Returning to her rightful home,[118] the soul
is swept into the arms of Faith, her white-
haired, darling nurse, who gently soothes her as
she tells in plaintive tones the sufferings she   1135
endured since taking up her lodging in
the body. Resting on a crimson couch,
she tastes the sweet perfumes exhaled from ever-
blooming flowers, and from the roses strewn
about her feet she drinks ambrosial dew.   1140
Across the great divide, smoke rises from the
wealthy denizens of hell: they are
so thirsty! They could drink entire rivers,
as much rain as the heavens could unleash.

---

116. The just souls, likened to Lot, who did not turn to look at Sodom, ascend to heaven. In what follows, Prudentius envisions this ascent as a return to the soul's rightful home, and casts the just soul as returning from exile.

117. Prudentius draws on the Platonic tradition that viewed the body as the prison house of the soul, and the attendant myth that the soul has fallen from a purer state. Mastrangelo (2008, 132–34) discusses Prudentius's adoption of Platonic and Neoplatonic ideas about the soul's fall and bondage, and its need to flee the body.

118. The Latin uses the word *postliminium*, a technical term for "the resumption of civic rights held in suspension during exile, capture, etc., on one's return" (*OLD*); it reinforces both the legal imagery that permeates the conclusion of the poem and the Neoplatonic imagery of the soul exiled or imprisoned in the body.

They beg her just to wet her finger and lift it   1145
to their mouths to quench the surging flames, but she
says no.[119]
      Don't be surprised to find that both
guilty souls and innocent can clearly
see each other despite the yawning gulf
that separates their homes: the just deserts   1150
of each in turn are noted across the great
abyss the axis of the sky marks off
from middle earth.[120] You would be wrong to judge
the powers of souls according to the limits
of human eyes, which are surrounded by   1155
a shining covering like a glassy barrier;
the substance gels within and forms a mirror
that impedes the mobile windows of the eye
by covering it with moisture. You don't think
that souls have eyes that shed big rounded tears   1160
with vigor, or shaggy eyebrows bristling all
around, or eyelids for protection, do you?
They have a keen gaze—not, like ours, a tiny
pupil, but a fire that leaps across
the misty zones and penetrates the darkness.   1165
Nothing made of iron, nothing solid
blocks their glance: the mists of night, the blackening
clouds give way, as does the universe's
rounded vault spread out before them. The
spirit's vision does not merely pierce   1170
the void of space: its gaze can penetrate
the mountain ranges lying in its path,
and thrust as far as Ocean's edges and the
farthest shores of Thule, while glancing swiftly
at Tartarus.
               It's true that to our mortal   1175
sight all color perishes beneath the night
and shapes are wiped out in the hours of darkness.
But do those who've lost their limbs and bodies
also lose the power to know familiar

---

119. Refreshed by ambrosia and reclining in her flowery bed, the just soul refuses to help the souls suffering in hell.

120. Prudentius returns to the theme of vision. It is noteworthy that the spectacle of these sufferings of the damned appears to be part of the reward of the just souls, just as the sight of the rewards of the just souls increases the suffering of the damned.

things? Are they lost and wandering? No.[121] 1180
The shape and color of the atmosphere
around the souls remains the same forever,
whether their deeds in life have brought them
in the end to the left- or right-hand path.
Ever-changing time does not transform 1185
or vary their allotted fates: whatever
that fate, it lasts forever: the ages
unroll in one universal progress.

    You have noticed how the wakeful mind
of those asleep in the dewy, quiet night 1190
often perceives remote and distant places,
and sends its gaze through fields and stars and seas.
Do you doubt that souls who have the power
of sight are also able to penetrate
things hidden from the body's eyes?[122] The soul, 1195
indeed, does not leave the living body
before death, nor flee in exile from the hearth
of flesh and blood; she does not set herself
free from her home inside our hearts and drive
our life away, but from her seat inside 1200
the body, she looks on everything with keen
eyes: wherever she has turned the sharp
gaze of her mobile nature, she sees, with nothing
hindering her sight, the world spread out
beneath her, and deep within the heavy earth, 1205
the lowest regions of hell. The earth, indeed,
lies in her path of sight, but does not block
her vision; but even if she turns her face
to the starry firmament, no intervening
object slows the fiery gaze of that 1210
unsleeping soul, though heavy clouds pile up
and veil the darkened heaven with fleecy black.

    Just so the gift of sleep once fell upon

---

    121. This is the last occurrence of the imagery of the lost traveler in the poem. After the soul has shed the shackles of the body, for better or for worse, her fate is certain and her wanderings are over. Gnilka (2000, 8–15) makes a strong argument that H. 1180–88 (Lat. 887–91) are an interpolation, suggesting that the lines on the invariability of the souls' shape and color disrupt the argument.

    122. The theme of vision, introduced in line 82 (Lat. 58) and following, culminates in this section, which describes the keen vision of the soul, the revelatory vision of the apostle John, and the view that the just and unjust souls have of one another across the gulf that divides paradise from hell.

the apostle John, while he was still among us,
not yet released from flesh and blood. It loosed him, 1215
albeit briefly, from his flesh, and he,
now free to see, beholds the secrets hidden
in the silent future, his eyes reviewing
the years laid out before him and the days
to come.[123] He sees the host of angels ready, 1220
armed for the world's immediate destruction,
hearing with his ears the gloomy blast
of trumpets heralding the end of the world.
He saw these things before his death, while trapped
inside the prison of the flesh; his soul 1225
was absent for a moment, not withdrawn
forever. Won't the animating breath
take note of everything much better without
the body, when the garment of the flesh
is laid to rest inside the chilly grave? 1230
Our faith is certain that the gloomy world
below is lit by blazing furnaces
that burn polluted souls for centuries
in the eternal flame, and that these souls
are seen by the poor whose home is far away 1235
across that great divide, and that, despite
the distance, the golden gifts and shining crowns
belonging to the just are visible
to souls submerged in seas of pain. And this
is why the guilty spirit, sadly wailing 1240
in her desolation, is presented
to the happy soul that dwells in paradise,
healed of her dreadful sores and pains! Each one
sees in turn the fate the other earned.

O God, father of all, giver of our 1245
souls, O Christ our God whose lips breathed forth
the one and only Spirit, I am guided
by your governance; I draw my life
from you, my ruler; with you as judge I tremble,
and yet with you as judge I hope that you 1250

---

123. Prudentius here refers to the book of Revelations, also known as the Apocalypse of John. It was widely read in the fourth century, though there was some dispute as to whether it should be included among the canonical books of the Bible.

46]   *THE ORIGIN OF SIN*: AN ENGLISH TRANSLATION

will pardon what I do, although my deeds
and words might be unworthy of your pardon.[124]
Although what I deserve is evil, when
my soul takes leave forever of her host,
my body, built of nerves and skin and blood   1255
and gall and bones, whose loving arms, alas!
seduced by pleasure, she cannot bear to leave—
when that unhappy hour has closed these eyes
and wailing mourners lay my corpse to rest,[125]
when my naked soul at last can see   1260
with her own eyes—Good Judge, I beg that then
you grant her greater gifts than I have earned.
May she never have to know a thief
as mad and cruel, as terrible in face
and voice as he who wants to drag me   1265
stained as I am with sin, and throw me headlong
into caves of darkness, and there extort
in full the payment, down to the last penny,
that I owe for such a sinful life.

The Father's treasure-house has many mansions,[126]   1270
O Christ, in many different places. I
do not seek a home among the blessed:
let the sacred troop of heroes dwell there,
all those men who scorned the world's riches
and sought instead your wealth; and may virgins   1275
who had the strength to castrate their desires
dwell there always in the flower of youth.
For me, it is enough if I don't see
the face of any fiend of hell, and if

---

124. This is the culmination of the legal imagery that is part of the symbolic structure of the *Hamartigenia*. Prudentius imagines God as his judge in the Last Judgment, with his soul as the defendant, much as Eve appeared as defendant in her sole appearance in the poem.

125. *Conclamata iacebit/materies* (Lat. 944–45): An important phrase. More literally, "my material being, much mourned, will be laid out." The material part of the poet, his body (*materies*) will be laid out (*iacebit*) and subject to ritual mourning (*conclamata*). The verb *conclamo* means "to call out together," either in triumph or in mourning for a corpse.

126. John 14:2: "In my Father's house are many mansions." Prudentius uses the words *thesaurus*, "treasure-house," and *habitatio*, "dwelling." He may be drawing on Ambrose, *De bono mortis* 10, where Ambrose equates the "habitations" (*domitacula*) of 4 Ezra 7:23 with the *mansiones* of John, envisioning them as a storehouse (*promptuarium*) of souls, where they can await the Last Judgment (Delumeau 2000, 26). Like Prudentius, Ambrose describes the fates of just and unjust souls, and the additional punishment suffered by the unjust souls as they gaze at the rewards enjoyed by the souls of the just.

Gehenna's greedy flame does not consume   1280
my soul, plunged deep inside the fiery furnace.
But if my body's fall requires this fate,
then let the gloomy flames devour me
in cavernous Avernus. Yet grant at least
that the fire be slow and mild, exhaling   1285
gentle vapors, and that its heat become
a mellow warmth and lose its fury. Let others
glory in boundless light and crowns that bind
their temples; as for me, this is my prayer:
may my punishment be light and clement.[127]   1290

127. After the striking contrast he has drawn between the eternal punishment of the guilty and the rewards of the just souls, Prudentius ends his poem with a prayer for a third way for himself—a gentle punishment. The "others [that] glory in boundless light" and wear crowns are the martyrs whom he celebrates in his collection of hymns, *On the Crowns* (*Peristephanon*). The final line of the poem, *at me poena levis clementer adurat*, contains a punning reference to the poet, whose full name is Aurelius Prudentius *Clemens*. Etymological wordplay was taken seriously in antiquity, and Prudentius was particularly fascinated by it. In his allegorical poem, *Psychomachia*, Prudentius has his personified Virtues and Vices enact the literal meanings of their names; similarly here, he hopes that he, the poet *Clemens*, will be treated with clemency by God.

An Interpretive Essay

INTRODUCTION

HERE ARE TWO WAYS of looking at a poem:

> A poem should be palpable and mute
> Like a globed fruit
> . . . .
> A poem should not mean
> But be
> (ARCHIBALD MACLEISH, "Ars Poetica")

> [T]he theory
> Of poetry is the theory of life,
> As it is, in the intricate evasions of as,
> In things seen and unseen, created from nothingness,
> The heavens, the hells, the worlds, the longed-for lands.
> (WALLACE STEVENS, "An Ordinary Evening in New Haven," XXVIII)

Macleish's claim that a poem should not "mean" but "be" is profoundly paradoxical. How can a poem, an artifact of language, exist without performing language's primary function, signification? Of what would such a poem consist? From the point of view of an early Christian reader, Macleish's poem would be beyond understanding—available, perhaps, to be glimpsed in the imagination like a fruit gleaming, tantalizingly, on the highest branch of a tree, but forever out of reach, like the apple that Sappho describes:

> All alone a sweet apple reddens on the topmost branch,
> high on the highest branch, the apple pickers did not notice it,
> they did not truly forget it, but they could not reach it.
> (Fr. 105)

That fruit, out of reach, not really noticed but never truly forgotten, haunts the poetry of Prudentius. He shared the early Christian view that language is fallen, and that the prelapsarian world, in which human language once reflected the unity of being and meaning that is the attribute of the divine Word, is forever lost. The "fair Fruit," as Milton calls it, that first opened Eve's eyes to the knowledge of good and evil, has made a poem like Macleish's "globed fruit"—a poem that does not *mean* but *is*—an impossibility. Unlike God's eternal "I AM," a poem in human language cannot "be." It is doomed instead to strive for meaning, to signify through what Stevens calls "the intricate evasions of as."[1] We might think of Prudentius's poetry as an expression of his perception of human language as a trap in which the divine "is" is always unobtainable and the human "as" is always inadequate.

The *Hamartigenia* is an exploration of the problem of sin, which for Prudentius, as I argue in the pages that follow, is inseparable from the fallen state of language and the fruit of that fall. In the *Hamartigenia* Prudentius pursues a number of interrelated themes: orthodoxy and heresy, similitude and difference, understanding and misinterpretation, blindness and sight, fruitful creativity and sterile duplication. He ties all of these oppositions to the basic problem of the fall: man, created as the *imago Dei*, the likeness of God, has become, through his own will, *unlike* the God who is his origin. Like Milton, who retells the same tale on a heroic scale in *Paradise Lost*, Prudentius wrestles with the enigmatic pattern of likeness and unlikeness that is man.

Paradise Lost, indeed, has proved to be a useful text against which to read the *Hamartigenia*, despite the vast differences in scope, scale, narrative, and tone of the two poems, and I will occasionally be turning to it to illuminate the *Hamartigenia* (and sometimes vice versa). The parallels between the two poems are extensive and enlightening, and have not, to my knowledge, been explored in any depth. Milton had certainly read Prudentius, and drew on the *Hamartigenia*'s vivid and original portrayal of the devil in his portrait of Satan.[2] My focus in this book is on the *Hamartigenia,* not on Milton, but it is striking and intriguing to see how much Prudentius's systematic, thematic employment of visual language and imagery foreshadows Milton's, and how both writers engage in elaborate, often enigmatic forms of wordplay at significant thematic moments in their poems.

Of course, as is often the case with similes and comparisons, the differences between the two poems are as revealing as their similarities. Any reader of Milton will come away from Prudentius's text astonished by the near absence of Eve from the poem, and by the *Hamartigenia*'s fierce misogyny. Absent too is the radiant beauty of so much of Milton's poem, the sensuous joy in creation that comes across so strongly in his account of Paradise. Like Milton, Prudentius is a brilliant poet with a strikingly vivid command of language, but the world of the *Hamartigenia* is not that of Milton's lost Paradise: rather, it is the world of Milton's Hell, dark and treacherous. In it the beauties of nature feature only as traps for our perverted senses.

Paradise Lost has an irresistible teleological narrative trajectory that propels us onward. It ends not with an ending, but with the beginning of a new journey, fraught with difficulty but overseen by Providence:

> The World was all before them, where to choose
> Thir place of rest, and Providence thir guide:
> They hand in hand, with wandring steps and slow,
> Through *Eden* took thir solitary way.
> (*PL* 12.646–49)

The *Hamartigenia*, on the other hand, is curiously and, for the twenty-first-century reader, frustratingly static. Its narrative structure is based on tableaux rather than plot, and its many oppositions are never finally resolved. It ends not with the hopeful assertion that Providence will be our guide, but with a prayer that the poet's guilty soul might suffer only mild torments in hell.

Finally, although Milton sometimes struggles with the nature of his creativity, even verbally associating himself with Satan and with Sin at one point, he ultimately does not doubt his own role as a creator. Prudentius's view of his own poetry is much more ambivalent in the *Hamartigenia*. Especially in this poem, he takes the fallen nature of language seriously. Although he embraces and asserts a typological view of Christian history that looks forward to the redemption of Adam's sin, and although, as I have argued previously, he undoubtedly takes enormous pride in his own poetic mastery, in this poem about sin and its consequences, he presents himself as less than confident that he has escaped the traps and snares of language in the creation of his own text.

My interpretation begins with a discussion of ways of reading late antique literature, and then moves to an overview of Prudentius's poetics before turning to the particular text of the *Hamartigenia*. My purpose in both the translation and the reading of the *Hamartigenia* that follows is to equip the reader to engage imaginatively with Prudentius's unfamiliar but fascinating poetics. His language is both *figural*, in that it assumes a typological view of Christian history (that is, the belief that the events of the Old Testament "shadow forth" the events revealed by the New Testament and that history itself will culminate in the unveiling [apocalypse] of truth), and *figurative*, in that it very self-consciously makes its meaning through *figurae verborum*, through tropes and textual figures. Far from being mere verbal ornament, these rhetorical figures are fundamental to Prudentius's poetic project. As I hope to demonstrate, the best way to understand this difficult but rewarding text is to figure out and figure forth the figures that constitute it.[3] The *Hamartigenia* offers insights into late antique ideas about sin, justice, gender, violence, the afterlife, and language. It is also a complex and sophisticated poem by a writer whose poetic innovations had an enormous impact on the development of the European literary tradition.[4] This study, then, is a reading and contextualization of the *Hamartigenia*, beginning with the preface and proceeding through the poem to its conclusion.

Prudentius

Reconstructing the biographies of ancient writers is necessarily an uncertain enterprise because of the lack of reliable evidence. Prudentius provides us with just enough information to sketch out a rough picture of his life.[5] We know his name: he refers to himself by name (*Prudentium*) at *Peristephanon* 2.582, and the manuscripts indicate that his full name was Aurelius Prudentius Clemens.[6] He came from northeastern Spain, the Roman province of Hispania Tarraconensis, probably from the city of Calagurris on the Ebro River. What little we know of his chronology comes from the only two poems of his that can be firmly dated: the preface to his collected works (405 CE) and the *Contra Symmachum* (402–3 CE). From these we know that Prudentius was born in 348, and died sometime after 405, the year he wrote his preface. Prudentius is not mentioned in Jerome's *De viris illustribus,* which suggests (though it does not prove) that he had not yet written, or not circulated, his poems at the time Jerome was writing (392–93). It is probable, then, that most of Prudentius's poems were written over the period of roughly a decade before 405, during the reigns of his contemporary, the Spanish emperor Theodosius I, and Theodosius's son, Honorius.

What Prudentius tells us about his life is highly schematic, almost generic: he was educated in grammar, rhetoric, and law; he had a successful career in public service and received two appointments as provincial governor (he does not name the provinces, nor specify his rank), followed by some sort of position in the imperial court (probably under Theodosius; see Palmer 1989, 25n1). We know from his other poems that he had spent time in Rome and probably traveled a good deal. We know nothing about his family, whether he was married, or whether he had children. Literary analysis of his work demonstrates that, in addition to his formidable knowledge of his classical poetic predecessors, he was well aware of the work of other poets of his day, including Ausonius and Claudian, two poets with connections to the imperial court, and perhaps Paulinus of Nola as well.[7]

From the preface to his works, it seems that Prudentius had a conversion experience some time in middle age. It is reasonable to conjecture (though it is only conjecture) that he retired from his administrative career and devoted the rest of his life to forging a new identity as a Christian (perhaps a Christian contemplative) and a poet. Such a move—a turn away from secular life toward a life of religious devotion—was certainly not uncommon in the fourth and fifth centuries. In addition to the most famous convert of them all, Augustine of Hippo, Paulinus is another example of an aristocrat who withdrew from secular affairs to take up a Christian life. After spending some time in retreat at his own estates, he became a Christian ascetic and was particularly devoted to Saint Felix of Nola.[8] It is not clear from the preface whether all of Prudentius's poetry dates from the period subsequent to his withdrawal from public life, nor is there any evidence of where Prudentius settled down after his retirement, though Roberts, following Fontaine, plausibly suggests that he withdrew to his own estate in Spain and composed most of his surviving poetry there.[9] His poetic project was ambitious: "Nothing less than to give expression in his poetry to the mental, spiritual, and material world of the late fourth-century Roman Christian" (Roberts 1993, 3). Prudentius, then, was a well-educated, well-connected, successful member of the late Roman elite, a man fully engaged with the politics and culture of his times, and with his faith.

The Roman world experienced enormous cultural change in the course of the fourth century. After the grim economic collapse and political instability of the third century, the reforms instituted by Diocletian and the consolidation of power and military success of Constantine and his heirs resulted in economic recovery and a concomitant cultural revival. But even as state revenues stabilized and the central bureaucracy reorganized, the gap between rich and poor increased dramatically, and the basis for the feudal economy was laid, as wealthy estate owners acquired more and more wealth, cities declined in population, and formerly independent peasants were forced to become virtual slaves of the estate owners. The senatorial class, which had lost much of its institutional power by this time, now grew in wealth and regained its political clout. In this period Christianity moved from being recognized as a religion by Constantine to becoming the only state religion under Theodosius, a development that changed the nature of Christianity as much as it changed the nature of the empire. "In such times history itself is up for grabs, available to be claimed by whatever side wins the political, religious, and intellectual battles. In the fourth century, Christians were winning those battles and thus staking their claim to a particular view of history."[10]

I. WRITING IN CHAINS

THE LITERATURE of the fourth century reflects the dynamism and upheaval of the time. The third century appears to have been a cultural wasteland for Latin literature, remarkable for the paucity of literature, especially poetry, that has survived. In the fourth and fifth centuries, the floodgates opened: old genres were revived and new ones created. After the silence of the third century, the voices of men like Julian and Augustine, Ausonius and Claudian, Prudentius and Ambrose, Jerome and Ammianus emerge. Rhetoricians, grammarians, editors and commentators, philosophers, and historians scrutinized and revitalized many classical genres, while the rapid Christianization of the empire led to new forms of Christian literature, including the sermon, the hymn, scriptural exegesis, the saint's life, and autobiography. And yet, amid this cultural ferment, as Mastrangelo (2009, 313) has argued, there appears to have been a significant erosion of the cultural authority of classical poetry for the cultured elite of the period, as many of the philosophical, ethical, and political functions of poetry were taken over by the new genres of patristic prose and the devotional hymn:

> While the church fathers were appropriating and recasting issues such as the relationship of myth to history, the construction of political identity, and the definition of the good life, they were also dismantling pagan poetry's claims to pronounce on these questions and thus eroding poetry's political, social, and ethical relevance. This disenfranchisement of poetry as a purveyor of truth marginalized the practice of poetry in the Roman Christian context. Roman Christian poets thus began from a disadvantageous position in which poetry's claims to truth had been dismissed.

As the classicizing philosophy that had dominated the Second Sophistic gave way to Christian theologians bent on verifying the truth of the biblical text and converting souls, sermons, exegesis, and doctrinal treatises became the most influential genres; the more complex classical poetic genres such as tragedy, heroic and national epic, lyric, and epigram faded in importance. Increasingly, Christians placed pagan rhetoric, philosophy, and poetry in opposition to the Christian search for truth. Lactantius gives an indication of the scorn that philosophy, rhetoric, and poetry evoked in the mind of the Christian reader: "Philosophy, oratory, and poetry are all pernicious for the ease with which they ensnare incautious souls in beguiling prose and the nice modulations of poetical flow. They are honey, hiding poison."[1] Lactantius inverts Lucretius's famous dictum that philosophical verse was like honey smeared on a cup of medicine to make it more palatable. For Lactantius, honeyed verse is instead a trap, within which lies not medicine but poison (a metaphor Prudentius adopts, as we will see below). This anxiety about poetry's distance from the truth, about its essential fictionality, was widespread among Christian thinkers; the most sustained critique of poetry on these terms is Augustine's dismantling of Vergilian epic in *The City of God*. The complex intermingling of myth, history, divine machinery, and human history that characterized the epic tradition was reduced by Augustine to a stark contrast between truth and lies.[2] The consequences of such thinking for the literature of the fourth century were profound. For Christian writers, poetry was of marginal interest—poets are virtually absent from the *Chronica* of Eusebius and the *De viris illustribus* of Jerome and Gennadius. A new Christian poetry developed, featuring the genres of of biblical epic, didactic epic, and hymns, and privileging the functions of praise and didacticism over all others. This poetry was to a large extent circumscribed by and harnessed to an ideological program:

> As a result, each genre of poetry appears to have a definable (authorial) function that translated into specific and instrumental effects on the audience. This suggests that fourth-century poetry was produced in an effectively circumscribed political environment where the church, the imperial government, the authors, and readers collectively possessed to an unprecedented degree the same ideological and literary assumptions.[3]

Prudentius and his contemporaries, Claudian and Ausonius, appear to be writing their classicizing verse at a moment when it was losing its cultural capital, which may explain why their verse is not mentioned by patristic writers. Prudentius stands out for the intensity of his engagement with Rome's literary history, political success, and cultural legacy. Above all, through his use of typology, Prudentius revives the ethical, historical, and political functions of poetry, and connects that poetry directly to the reader.[4] In the *Psychomachia*, for example, the formation of the individual soul is linked with the stability of the nation-state of Rome as well as with the narratives of the Old Testament and the future of the church. Even as classical poetry was rapidly losing its cultural capital, Prudentius reimagined Roman epic, drawing from both Vergil and Lucretius, to form a new master narrative for the Roman Christian reader. But, as the *Hamartigenia* demonstrates, his poetic accomplishment was not an easy achievement, and his attitude toward his own poetic program was not free of the anxieties over poetry and rhetoric that characterized his age.

Reading Late Antique Poetry

In this interpretive essay I follow what Patricia Cox Miller calls "the logic of a text's figuration," exploring new dimensions of the poem through a focus on ornaments and figures, textual devices that delighted late antique readers but which tend to be opaque to modern readers. Prudentius's use of language and rhetorical figures is intense, sometimes difficult, often startling; the *Hamartigenia* offers many instances of "the image that deforms or changes how one apprehends a text's meaning rather than conforming to habituated modes of understanding."[5] Grasping the way such images function, tracing the chain of associations that links the various textual figures together, will guide our steps along the path toward understanding the poem. It is not a straight and narrow path: as Prudentius, who returns again and again in his poems to the figure of the lost and lonely traveler, says, "So many crossroads loom before us, trodden smooth . . . and we encounter hidden bypaths on the way / where here and there the paths entwine" (*Apoth. praef.* 7–10). The pursuit of such thematic images and figures through the twining pathways of the *Hamartigenia* will, I hope, open up an obscure but rewarding text to new readers, enhance the understanding of Prudentius's often dark and always intricate poetics, and further advance the study of the late antique poetic imagination.

Much late antique poetry is complex, formal, and experimental, sometimes dauntingly so. Even the prose writers of the period exuberantly deploy striking techniques, including allusion, repetition, patterns of alliteration, and vivid description. Catherine Chin, in an intriguing discussion of the role of grammatical theory and practice in the creation of Christian readers, notes that reading in late antiquity was shaped by a grammatical tradition that relied on the *interruption* of narrative flow as part of the process of creating meaning for the reader. She cites two techniques fundamental to teaching grammar in late antiquity: the quotation of earlier texts and the making of lists (a device not limited to the grammarians; it is frequently found in late antique poets).

> Both of these gestures are at once destructive and productive, in that they tend to break up narrative sequence, or interrupt flows of argument, and to introduce expansion. Illustrating a grammatical point with a line of Virgil both interrupts the grammarian's voice and expands the point into another text; the quoted line is likewise interrupted and expanded to include grammatical meaning. Lists of words, for example of verb conjuga-

tions, similarly both interrupt the flow of grammatical argument and expand it through illustration. These are techniques that have important effects, as they are deployed by late ancient gramarians in the construction of a Latin literary tradition.[6]

It is helpful in considering the digressive, allusive, ekphrastic style of late antique writers to bear in mind that the disruption of the narrative flow that characterizes their texts mirrors the way that people were taught to read. As Chin succinctly puts it, "The basic technique for approaching Latin reading was verbal fragmentation: *grammatica,* as Sidonius Apollinaris tells us, *dividit."*[7] And division, as we shall see, is a major theme of the *Hamartigenia.*

In his influential book *The Jeweled Style: Poetry and Poetics in Late Antiquity,* Michael Roberts compares the distinctive style of late antique poetry to the visual arts of the period, and demonstrates the strong parallels between poetry and contemporary mosaics. Both rejoice in repetition, formal patterning, relations of parallelism and antithesis, avoidance of the representational, and comprehensiveness. The eye is continually enticed by detail, and appreciation of the craftsmanship and design is an integral part of the experience of the artwork. Roberts takes as one example the procession scenes in the nave of the Basilica of Sant' Apollinare Nuovo in Ravenna. In the lower zone there is a procession of saints. The figures are similar in size, costume, and bearing, but each figure is distinct, differentiated by details such as hairstyle, facial features, the design of his crown, and his attributes. Roberts compares such procession scenes to the poetic catalog (a device much loved by late antique poets, which lists individuals of a particular type and gives two or three distinguishing features to each) and to literary descriptions of crowd scenes in which subgroups are differentiated by various actions and designated by characteristic formulas such as *pars . . . pars . . . , hi . . . alii.*[8] A good example of the latter is Claudian's description of the death of Rufinus (emphasis mine):

> *hi* vultus avidos et adhuc spirantia vellunt
> lumina, truncatos *alii* rapuere lacertos.
> amputat *ille* pedes, umerum quatit *ille* solutis
> nexibus; *hic* fracti reserat curvamina dorsi;
> *hic* iecur, *hic* cordis fibras, *hic* pandit anhelas
> pulmonis latebras. spatium non invenit Ira
> nec locus est odiis.
>   (*In Ruf.* 2.410–16)

> *Some* tear at his greedy face and his eyes still flashing with life; *others* tear his arms out by the roots and carry them off. *Over there* a man cuts off a foot, another shakes a shoulder free from its shredded joints. *Right*

here one unhinges the curved ribs from his cracked spine, *one* lays bare his liver, *someone else* explores the gasping caverns of his lungs. Rage can find no space, there is no place for hatred.

In this passage Roberts notes how the reader's attention is drawn from one section of the crowd to another by the formal, highly patterned language (note, for example, the anaphora, alliteration, and the ascending tricolon in the phrase *hic iecur, hic cordis fibras, hic pandit anhelas pulmonis latebras*).[9] This aesthetic is far removed from classicism (though certainly not without its precedents in classical literature), and makes its own demands on the reader or viewer, as Roberts notes:

> The poets of late antiquity employ patterns of verbal parallelism, synonymy, or enumeration . . . thus distracting from the representational content of a passage, as conveyed by its syntactic structure. Like the mosaics, the poetry, at its most extreme and characteristic, draws attention to formal properties at the expense of the referential in a fashion that is disconcerting to the classically oriented reader. It delights in abstract complexity and assumes a similar delight in its audience. (ROBERTS 1989, 85)

Although Roberts captures well the exuberant delight in formal properties that characterizes Claudian's poetry in particular, and late antique poetry in general, he does not remark here on the dynamic at play between the figured language and the extreme violence of the description. Jennifer Ballengee (2009, 10), however, has insistently raised the question, "What does it mean for a text to use torture as a literary and rhetorical *figure*? What responsibility does this incur for the reader?" The patterned, "jeweled" style creates a startlingly vivid image of brutal dismemberment that reflects a fascination with pain and torture that is characteristic of the late Roman world and very much a part of the early Christian imagination.[10]

Scholarship on late antique and medieval thought has brought to the forefront the vital importance of image, metaphor, and sign, "the figurative sensibility that is a distinctive feature of many texts of this period."[11] I would extend Roberts's important insight that "the poetry of the period draws attention to formal properties at the expense of the referential" to say that, while the pleasures of late antique poetry may come at the expense of the *referential*, they do not therefore come at the expense of *meaning*. Late antique writers do not use language and imagery as "perfect, transparent media through which reality may be presented to the understanding,"[12] but rather as vehicles to enable readers to generate their own meaning from a text.

Essential to understanding how Prudentius and other late antique poets compose their poems is recognizing the importance of visualization in their conception of how audiences are affected by speech and writing: ekphrasis and enargeia are key concepts. Ekphrasis in antiquity meant something much broader than its modern definition (the vivid presentation in words of an artwork). Ancient rhetorical treatises define it as "a speech that brings the subject matter vividly before the eyes."[13] Though most of the technical discussion of ekphrasis comes from rhetorical treatises whose concern was with oratory, it was a commonplace that in addition to orators, writers of prose and poetry had to master the craft of ekphrasis and be able to place a subject before the eyes of their audience (Homer, Thucydides, and Vergil were the acknowledged masters of ekphrasis). Enargeia, or vividness, is essential to successful ekphrastic writing, as is verisimilitude or likeness to reality. The goal of ekphrasis is to make listeners or readers into spectators so that they see the subject in their mind's eye. Words are a vehicle for transmitting the mental image (the *phantasia* or *visio*) of the speaker to the mind, or inner eye, of the audience. Quintilian (*Inst.* 6.2.29) addresses this process:[14]

> What the Greeks call *phantasiai* (let us call them "*visiones*") are the means by which images of absent things are represented to the mind in such a way that we seem to see them with our eyes and have them present before us. Whoever has really grasped them will have a powerful effect on the emotions.

Visualization was closely linked to memory: there is a great emphasis on visual images in rhetorical treatises on techniques for memorization. Rhetoricians relied on striking mental images to order and help them recall the content of their speeches, and the practice of rhetoric trained Romans "to visualize the unseen as if it were actually present. Visions (*visiones*), induced by powerful verbal representations, so stirred the emotions and stimulated the imagination that complex scenes could manifest themselves with convincing, vivid immediacy before the mind's eye."[15]

An Aesthetics of Memory

Mary Carruthers has discussed the relevance of this visual model of memory to an analysis of Prudentius's strikingly figural poetic style.[16] The function of ornament in a picture or a text is, precisely, to make things memorable, since memory provides the mind with matter that intellect can work with. Carruthers's discussion of Prudentius's technique in the preface to his miniature epic, *Psychomachia* (*The Battle in the Soul*), is especially helpful in demonstrating how ornaments of different sorts (e.g., etymology, biblical allusion, and epitome) combine to fix the text in the reader's mind. The *Psychomachia* is the first sustained personification allegory in Latin literature. Its plot unfolds in an abstract landscape, and the action consists of first a series of combats between the personified Virtues and their evil opposites, and then a description of the Virtues' entrance into a new temple constructed by Faith and Concord, modeled on a number of biblical passages.[17]

The hexameter poem opens with an iambic preface whose purpose is to provide an interpretive model for the reader. Carruthers comments:

> From the start of its preamble, *Psychomachia* functions as a mnemonic gathering place, a "common place" into which a number of stories are collated. Recollection works through associational chains; the formation of these is a core technique of Prudentius' story-telling.... Prudentius calls his texturized retelling of the story of Abraham and Lot "haec linea" that he has "praenotata," "sketched out first" (before his main story) "as a model... which our life should resculpt in due measure."... *Linea* is used here as a synonym of *ratio*, the mental schemes and schedules that Augustine found, along with images and notations of emotions, among the things in his memory. (CARRUTHERS 1998, 144–45)

In reading a text like the *Psychomachia* or the *Hamartigenia*, we should keep in mind that the narrative structure (such as it is) is a schema to help us organize and transfer to our own memories the linked associations assembled by the writer, rather than a plot to follow as we would the plot of a heroic epic like the *Aeneid* or a novel like *Bleak House*.[18] The *Psychomachia*'s longevity and widespread influence in European art and literature attests to Prudentius's success in creating a simple background scheme (the plot: seven battles between a virtue and her opposite vice followed by the victory celebration and foundation of the temple of Wisdom) into which he has gathered related material (ornament of different sorts, including biblical exempla, classical and biblical allusions, lengthy speeches, and similes) associatively linked both to its place in the plot and to underlying patterns of signification across the poem. Carruthers cites as an example Prudentius's use of biblical stories:

> So when Lust is slain by Chastity, her victory speech "collates" Judith and Holofernes, the "virgin immaculate" who bore Christ, and the Whore of Babylon shut into hell. This kind of "chain-making" or *catena* is familiar to all medievalists, from innumerable examples in both Latin and vernacular literatures. I want to emphasize its basis in *memoria*, "gathering" associations into a "place." (CARRUTHERS 1998, 147)

The ornaments used to furnish a particular "place" in the scheme of the poem are chosen not only for their appropriateness to their setting but also for their ability to reverberate intra- and intertextually, creating another kind of image chain linked by verbal or visual imagery. Thus the figure of Judith, slayer of Holofernes, recalled in some detail in the combat between Chastity and Lust, is evoked by association later in the poem when Patience, assisted by Hope, cuts off the head of Pride and holds it up in triumph.[19]

The pictures of harsh Judith standing over the blood-soaked, bejeweled bed of Holofernes (*Psychomachia* 58–65) and of Patience "tempering her joy with a friendly expression" as she receives the sword from Hope and decapitates her enemy (*Psychomachia* 271–83) are vivid examples of enargeia, the art of word-painting, the ability to appeal to "the eyes of the mind," as Quintilian describes it (8.3.62) and create "rerum imago quodammodo verbis depinguitur," "an image of things painted, in a way, by words." Such vivid, mind's-eye images do not necessarily facilitate reading (a fact often disapprovingly noted by scholars of late Roman literature, who chafe at what appear to be unnecessary digressions). Rather, like the textual allusions and lists of the grammarians cited by Chin, they disrupt and expand the reading process, arresting the mind of the reader or listener, requiring attention and encouraging the creation of a mental picture that can be fixed in memory and then recalled at will.

Prudentius is particularly effective at creating vivid, memorable images that appeal to all the senses—too effective, indeed, for many modern readers, who might prefer not to have quite so many violent images impressed upon the mind.[20] In her study of late antique attitudes toward torture and truth, Grig remarks that "Prudentius's poetry is known for the baroque effect produced by the layering of the improbable, the impossible and the merely nasty."[21] In reading his poetry, as Grig's article demonstrates, it is important to think through rather than dismiss "the merely nasty" and the ways in which violent suffering is both celebrated and deployed as a means of shaping the reader's mind and soul.[22] Carruthers, commenting on the "extreme" battle scenes of the *Psychomachia*, summarizes his technique as follows:

> Prudentius' images are painted for the mind's eye. Effort is made not to overwhelm the student with detail: the narrative details are few but they are particularly vivid and specific. This accords with a basic technique for making such images: one must be careful not to overwhelm the mental eye with an excess of images. And those one has must be extreme, "eye-catching" of course, but also fully *synesthetic*, a fully realized sensory experience that includes recreated sound (the screams and cries and battle trumpets) and taste (chiefly of blood and crushed bone) and odor (vomit and blood but also crushed violets) and touch (chiefly pain).... These pictures stick in the mind, not as "concepts" or "objects" but as *an inventory* of synaesthetic, syncretic memory cues, to be drawn upon, drawn out from, and *used* for constructing new work. (CARRUTHERS 1998, 148; her emphasis)

Building on the work of Carruthers and others, in *The Medieval Theatre of Cruelty: Rhetoric, Memory, Violence* Jody Enders argues that ancient rhetorical theories of mnemonics are implicated in a violent dynamic. As many scholars have noted, ancient writers link the discovery of mnemonic technique to violent death (and commercial transaction) in the story of the poet Simonides.[23] The *ars memoriae*, in this anecdote, originates in violence and in the reciprocal communal need to commemorate the dead.[24] Through a *technē* (his ability to recall figures within an architectural space) Simonides was able to restore order to a community disrupted by violence—violence that appears to the participants in the anecdote to be accidental, but seems to the reader to have been a form of divine vengeance upon the patron who refused to pay Simonides the full price for his poem. And violence inheres in other Roman discussions of mnemonic technique. The *Rhetorica ad Herennium* teaches us that one way to make a mental image that will be easy to recall is to deform it or stain it with blood, as Enders notes:

> Even in the celebrated Pseudo-Ciceronian invocation of the *imagines agentes*, there inheres an unmistakably violent subtext as the author oscillates between beauty and ugliness, formation and deformation, betraying a preoccupation with *disfigurement*: "if we somehow *disfigure them* [aut si qua re *deformabimus*], as by introducing one stained with blood or soiled with mud or smeared with red paint, so that its form [*forma*] is more striking, or by assigning certain comic effects to our images, for that too will ensure our remembering them more readily" (*RAH* III.37).... The potential assignment of "certain comic effects" to disfigured, bloodied bodies might eventually have fallen under the rubric of the "silly spectacles" Hugo of St. Victor would go on to condemn. But there is nothing silly about staining the mind's *dramatis personae* with blood to enhance their evocative value.[25]

The rhetorical strategy that late antique writers employ is the product of a technique that involves using visually striking memory images, including the violent, the comic, and the comically violent; and the epistemological system within which they wrote was one that encouraged readers and viewers, as Enders (1999, 71) puts it, "to aestheticize both figuration and disfiguration." Prudentius's lasting popularity stems in part from his successful deployment of this ekphrastic technique. The visually, often synesthetically arresting verbal images that Prudentius created in the *Psychomachia* were drawn on, drawn out from, and used throughout the Middle Ages and beyond. One of the first nonbiblical works to be illustrated, the poem gave rise to a host of moral allegorical texts, and to the rich visual tradition of illustrations and paintings of the battles between the Vices and the Virtues.[26]

But the emphasis on the visual that Roberts, Carruthers, Enders, and Webb all, in their different ways, stress must not be separated from the fundamental importance of language and signification in the late antique imagination overall, and in Prudentius's poetry in particular. Patricia Cox Miller elegantly describes what she terms "poetic imagination" in *The Poetry of Thought in Late Antiquity*:

> My own quest for the late ancient imagination has focused on theories of interpretation and language as well as on texts that, whether implicitly or explicitly, use images not as mere reflections of reality but as vehicles that generate meaning and, in so doing, transform the reader's perception at the same time as they alter the conditions of meaning. The authors of the texts considered here did not use images simply as ornaments or rhetorical embellishments that could be discarded as secondary to their arguments. Rather, images were constitutive of the insights of such texts.[27]

Late antique writers *thought figuratively*, and were explicitly aware of the figurative nature of their discourse, Miller argues. The emphasis on figuration arises in part from the view, shared by Christians and Neoplatonists, that language is a series of signs and words open to multiple interpretations. As Origen put it, "I think each word of divine scripture is like a seed whose nature is to multiply diffusely. . . . Its increase is proportionate to the diligent labor of the skillful farmer or the fertility of the earth."[28]

But the dazzling fertility of the word creates its own anxieties: How to reconcile the unity of the Logos, the Word that is also God, with the multiplicity of discourse? Are divine Logos and human language irreconcilably different? If language is inherently polysemous and ambiguous, how can one ever be sure an interpretation of a text, let alone a sacred text, is correct? What is the proper role of rhetoric in a culture that more and more relies on powerful public performances by its priests and bishops, but at the same time feels under assault by the seductive appeal of popular dramatic performance and oratorical displays? These questions are fundamental to Prudentius's approach to the subject of the origin of sin, for language and sin are, as we shall see, inextricably linked in his thought.

Reading Prudentius

Prudentius's poetry is difficult to characterize. He wrote in various meters and genres:[29] hymns to the martyrs (the *Peristephanon*), lyric (the *Cathemerinon*), epigram (*Dittochaeon*), epic (the *Psychomachia*), and didactic or apologetic (the *Apotheosis* and the *Hamartigenia*). He tends to set his poems in a temporal no-man's-land, so they are at once free from the constraints of politics and yet engaged with contemporary issues.[30] In some of Prudentius's hexameter poems, the issues raised are abstract and fiercely rational. The *Apotheosis* is an account of the incarnation of Christ, written, apparently, in response to various heretics who questioned the nature of the Trinity, and against the Jews. The *Psychomachia*, as we have seen, depicts the battle within the soul between the Virtues and the Vices. All of Prudentius's works reflect the poet's own struggle with the problem of language, an issue of primary importance in the *Hamartigenia*. And so, before turning to the *Hamartigenia*, it is useful to focus on Prudentius's views on language. His deployment of particular poetic effects in the *Psychomachia*, his best-known and most experimental work, affords the easiest introduction.

The *Psychomachia*'s allegorical structure arises directly from Prudentius's view of language, a view generated by his theology, as Marc Mastrangelo has argued. Citing Pelikan's work that shows that in patristic texts allegory is an expression of an apophatic theology—in other words, it is a strategy developed in reaction to a belief that human reason and human language are incapable of comprehending and expressing the reality of the godhead[31]—Mastrangelo argues that "the *Psychomachia* posits the linguistic puzzle of how to describe God and the soul and responds with a series of typologies that express interpretations of biblical texts and Christian dogma.... Allegory formed from typological interpretation of the Bible makes it possible for the poet to communicate ideas that are incommunicable through normal object or referent language."[32] He cites as a summary of Prudentius's basic negative theological point this statement from *Apotheosis*:

nam mera maiestas est infinita nec intrat
obtutus aliquo ni se moderamine formet.
   (*Apoth.* 26–27)

For pure majesty is infinite, and does not enter
our vision unless it takes on some moderating figure.

In the opening of *Apotheosis*, the moderating figure that will allow us to grasp the nature of the Trinity is Prudentius's retelling of the biblical account of the visit of a triple-formed angel to Abraham's tent, an angel Prudentius identifies as Christ. The typological allegory of the angel, Mastrangelo says, "is the positive meaning produced in response to the epistemological problem that apophatic language raises."[33]

The epistemological problem that language raises is profound, and is enacted in Prudentius's deep and complex poetry. His poems are all, despite their varied subjects, highly polished, self-reflexive experiments that test the limits of human language.[34] Mastrangelo has elegantly analyzed the didactic methodology and aim of the *Psychomachia*, revealing a poem whose radical purpose is to change the soul of the reader "through inner inspection of her thoughts and desires through the memory and choice of proper typological connections." In the *Hamartigenia*, too, Prudentius intends to shape the soul through memory and typology. My analysis of the *Hamartigenia* is very much in accord with Mastrangelo's conclusion that for Prudentius, "poetry must give knowledge of God and the soul's relation to God, both of which sit beyond normal, rational, human understanding."[35] Prudentius's deployment of historical typology in his poems is, as Mastrangelo has argued, his attempt to move beyond the problems generated by the perceived failure of language and enable his poetry to communicate knowledge beyond human understanding.

I argue, however, that the *Hamartigenia*—as perhaps befits a poem whose topic is sin and its consequences—puts its emphasis on the dark side of the problem of human language, and raises troubling questions about whether what poetry "must" do is in fact possible in a fallen world. The poem is deeply preoccupied with the limits of language, in particular, with its excessive polysemy. Prudentius in many ways prefigures later medieval writers such as Chaucer and Jean de Meun, who display "the late Gothic ability to maintain contradicting attitudes and to derive aesthetic pleasure from the tension of unresolved conflicts."[36] John Fyler, discussing the Ovidian irony and skepticism that characterize Chaucer and Jean de Meun, remarks that "when the two poets resist or undermine the dominant Augustinian paradigm of language, they may seem surprisingly or even implausibly modern" (2007, 52). The powerful typological paradigm that underlies Prudentius's poems has tended to obscure the "implausible modernity" of his radically skeptical, deconstructive use of language. But it is precisely the tension between the unifying paradigm of the transcendent Logos and the irresistible multiplying energy of postlapsarian language that lies at the heart of Prudentius's poetry, and that this book aims to recover.

Sed ubique lingua pollet

For early Christian thinkers, human language is marked by its radical separation from the divine Logos. One response to this postlapsarian problem was the development of strategies of figural reading, which John Dawson (2002, 216) summarizes thus:

> The overwhelming presumption of classical Christian figural reading ... is that the Christian Bible is read Christianly when it is seen to depict the ongoing historical outworking of a divine intention to transform humanity over the course of time.... Moreover, Christian figural readers insist that the history of Israel, Jesus of Nazareth, his immediate followers, and the Church are all somehow ingredients in this overarching divine intention. That intention and its outworking in history are regarded as alternately clear and obscure, reliable and unpredictable. Figural readers turn to the text of the Bible for clues and models useful for unraveling as much as they can of what they think they discern as the mysterious working of God in the lives of people over time. What is always ultimately at stake is the reality and the proper characterization of a divine performance in the material world of space and time, a performance that defines the personal, social, ethical, and political obligations of Christians in the present, as well as their stance toward past and future.

68] AN INTERPRETIVE ESSAY

In Prudentius's poems, the Bible indeed offers clues and models useful for unraveling the mysterious working of God, but whether the individual human soul can or will successfully interpret them is never certain. This uncertainty is the consequence of sin, the subject of the *Hamartigenia*. In the postlapsarian world, the ontological connection between signifier and signified is shattered. Not only is the human word sundered from divine meaning, but it also has a tendency to generate in us improper meanings that deceive us into incorrect interpretation. For Prudentius, the problem of sin cannot be separated from the problems of signification and interpretation. He infuses his poetry with linguistic play that highlights the problematic nature of language.

One device by which the fissure between words and their meanings can be highlighted with economy is in wordplay that pits different meanings of a word against one another. While such wordplay occurs throughout Prudentius's poetry, his play on the different meanings of the key word *lingua* (language, tongue, or speech) is especially relevant to our discussion, for, as we will see, the tongue plays a crucial role in the *Hamartigenia*. In both the *Peristephanon* and the *Psychomachia*, Prudentius makes a point of placing the physical and the abstract meanings of *lingua* in heightened juxtaposition through vivid, violent imagery. In *Pe.* 13, a hymn on the martyrdom of Saint Cyprian of Carthage, Prudentius makes the point that the persuasive rhetoric of Saint Cyprian lives on, despite his death. This is an unremarkable sentiment, but the surreal language in which Prudentius couches it puts special emphasis on the tongue as a body part, and refuses to let the physical meaning of *lingua* be superseded by the abstract (italics added):

> Punica terra tulit quo splendeat omne quidquid usquam est,
> inde domo Cyprianum, sed decus orbis et magistrum.
> est proprius patriae martyr, sed amore et ore noster;
> incubat in Libyae sanguis, sed ubique *lingua* pollet.
> *sola superstes* agit de corpore, *sola obire nescit*,
> dum genus esse hominum Christus sinet et vigere mundum.
>   (*Pe.* 13.1–6)

The Punic earth bore him to make everything everywhere shine.
Cyprian's home is there, but he is the glory and teacher of the whole world.
He is his own land's martyr, but love and language make him ours;
his blood broods over Libya, but his tongue has power everywhere—
his tongue, the only survivor of his body, the only part that knows not how to die,
as long as Christ allows the race of men to live and flourish in the world.

In a parallel passage from *Peristephanon* 10, the longest and in many ways the strangest of Prudentius's hymns to the martyrs, Prudentius inverts the scenario played out by Cyprian: whereas Cyprian loses all of his body *except* his tongue, which keeps on talking, the martyr Romanus loses his tongue in a grotesque act of torture. Nevertheless, like Cyprian's tongue, Romanus keeps on talking: he launches into the longest of all the speeches attributed to martyrs in the *Peristephanon*.[37] Once again, the literal meaning of *lingua* is played against its equally common metaphorical meaning, language. As Ballengee (2009, 107) argues:

> The removal of Romanus' *lingua* emphasizes the literality of his speech—that is, its rhetorical ambivalence or undecideability. The poetic language of the poem, which allows such a rhetorical, metonymic trope to remain unresolved, allows both meanings to exist simultaneously. In other words, the ambiguity of Prudentius's poetic language (*lingua*) maintains the possibility of more than one meaning at once.

Wordplay reveals language's inability to limit itself to a single, stable meaning, and this inability is systematically enacted by the personified characters of Prudentius's *Psychomachia*, the battle between the Virtues and the Vices.[38] Once again, Prudentius uses the tongue as the emblem of the unbridled dissemination of meaning. Georgia Nugent points out that "just as on the narrative level the poem unmasks from time to time the myth that *virtus* and *vitium* are neat polarities, so linguistically *virtus* is not irrevocably fixed as one stable term in a polar opposition, but can mediate between virtue and vice, expressing the powers of either" (Nugent 1985, 71). The slippage in meaning that occurs on a narrative level in the *Psychomachia* is a central preoccupation of that text (one that Prudentius attempts to circumvent, as Mastrangelo argues, through the strategic deployment of historical typologies). James Paxson examines Prudentius's deployment of the trope of personification in the *Psychomachia*, and finds the emphasis on the physical embodiment of the Virtues and Vices of particular semiotic interest. He sees the frequent descriptions of tongues, lips, mouths, and teeth in the *Psychomachia* (in which faces are shattered with dismal regularity) as particularly significant: "The mouth (along with the larynx which modulates the breath) is the seat of the power of language. As organs, the mouth and the eyes constitute a sign of the face. And the face (*prosopon*) thematized is the signature of prosopopeia" (Paxson 1994, 142).

While Paxson draws attention to the symbolic importance of the destruction of the face, Georgia Nugent has similarly drawn attention to the ways that the Vices meet their various deaths: six of the seven die by being strangled or having their throats cut. Nugent links this pattern of "death by the throat" to their gender.

Noting the multiplicity of models available for violent death in Latin literature, she suggests that the lack of variety, the obsessive repetition of attacks to the throat in the poem is deeply rooted in classical culture's concept of the female body. In Greek tragedy, strangulation is a favorite form of death for women because it seals in death the female's dangerously open body, and this is a widespread cultural pattern in antiquity, as Nicole Loraux has shown.[39] "Supporting this pattern of thought," notes Nugent, "is the homology of oral with vaginal orifices which conceptually links woman's speaking or ingesting mouth with sexual availability and/or voraciousness. If woman is, by nature, excessively open, at least she can be 'shut up.'"[40] Or can she? As we will see below (esp. chapter 6), the drive to contain female sexuality and reproduction is an important element in the scheme of the *Hamartigenia*.

Nowhere in the *Psychomachia* is the imagery of the destruction of the face and the attack on the throat more blatant than in the climactic defeat of the Vice Discordia. She represents deceit, disguise, and instability of all sorts; she appears in disguise and wounds her opposite, the Virtue Concordia. Once captured, she reveals her name and character in a speech that evolves around a series of disturbing plays on words (emphasis added):

>   "*Discordia dicor*,
> cognomento Heresis; *Deus* est me *discolor*," inquit,
> "nunc minor aut maior, modo duplex aut modo simplex,
> cum placet, aerius et de phantasmate visus,
> aut innata anima est quotiens volo ludere numen.
> praeceptor Belia mihi, domus et plaga mundus."
>   (*Psy.* 709–14)

> "I am called Discord. My other name is Heresy. My God is variable—
> sometimes small, sometimes huge, sometimes two, sometimes one.
> When I wish, he seems like an airy phantom,
> or when I want to play tricks with divine power, he is the inborn soul.
> Belial is my teacher, the world is my territory and my home."

The punning echoes of her own name in the first few lines of the speech (*Discordia dicor . . . deus . . . discolor*) suggest that speech itself is a form of Discordia. She calls attention to her own facility with wordplay when she boasts of her ability to define God as she wishes. She calls this playing (*ludere*) with his divinity (*numen*), and her boast comes immediately after she includes *Deus* among the plays she makes on her own *nomen*.

Discordia, in fact, in her excessive self-confidence in her own verbal powers and her playful ability to manipulate meaning, seems like the foremother of a character from a much later work of fantastically figured fiction: Humpty Dumpty, the original egghead (who shares Discordia's fate of utter disintegration). Here we see him explaining to Alice the relative merits of birthday versus un-birthday presents:

> "As I was saying, that seems to be done right—though I haven't time to look it over thoroughly just now—and that shows that there are three hundred and sixty-four days when you might get un-birthday presents—"
> "Certainly," said Alice.
> "And only one for birthday presents, you know. There's glory for you!"
> "I don't know what you mean by 'glory,'" Alice said.
> Humpty Dumpty smiled contemptuously. "Of course you don't—till I tell you. I meant 'there's a nice knock-down argument for you!'"
> "But 'glory' doesn't mean 'a nice knock-down argument,'" Alice objected.
> "When I use a word," Humpty Dumpty said in rather a scornful tone, "it means just what I choose it to mean—neither more nor less."
> "The question is," said Alice, "whether you can make words mean so many different things."
> "The question is," said Humpty Dumpty, "which is to be master—that's all."
> Alice was too much puzzled to say anything, so after a minute Humpty Dumpty began again. "They've a temper, some of them—particularly verbs, they're the proudest—adjectives you can do anything with, but not verbs—however, I can manage the whole of them! Impenetrability! That's what I say!" (LEWIS CARROLL, *Through the Looking-Glass*, chapter 6)

Like Humpty Dumpty, who freely admits that the result of his interventions with language is "impenetrability," Discordia is surprisingly open and frank for a character who represents deceit and who first appears disguised as a Virtue. Just as Humpty Dumpty lays bare the arbitrary nature of language and undermines Alice's unthinking assumption that words have a fixed meaning, so Discordia makes the radical move of using her speech to undermine language by revealing its arbitrary nature. Her punning, polysemous discourse destabilizes language.

Precisely because Discordia represents the destabilizing nature of language, the Virtues attempt quite literally to "fix" her, appropriating her divisive power for their own uses. The character, who begins by metaphorically representing multiplicity and fragmentation, ends up being physically ripped apart, as the Virtues' attempts to control the dissemination of meaning are represented in the narrative as attacks on the body of the Vice. After Discordia has delivered her punning speech, Fides (Faith), the Virtue most concerned with policing the language of truth, immediately steps in to put an end to this threat to meaning by blocking her words, closing off her throat with a javelin, and transfixing Discordia's tongue, the instrument of ambiguity, with her spear:

> non tulit ulterius capti blasphemia monstri
> Virtutum regina Fides, sed verba loquentis
> impedit et vocis claudit spiramina pilo,
> pollutam rigida transfigens cuspide linguam.
> (*Psy.* 715–18)

> Unable to endure the captive monster's blasphemies
> any longer, Faith, Queen of Virtues, cut off Discordia's
> words as she spoke, closing off her vocal chords with a javelin,
> transfixing her polluted tongue with a rigid spear.

But this attempt to stop the monster's tongue from its reckless dissemination of meanings does not entirely succeed. Instead of fixing Discordia to the spot and containing her once and for all, the Virtues, in an unbecoming frenzy of rage (like Humpty Dumpty's verbs, these Nouns seem to have a temper), dismember her and disperse her remains through three realms: earth, sea, and sky. How are we to interpret this death? Is it a triumph of virtue?

There are compelling reasons to argue, as Roberts and James do, that there is nothing discordant in the depiction of Discordia's death. According to the principle of *lex talionis* that underpins the Roman legal system, dismemberment perfectly suits the divisive nature of *Discordia*, and enacts the meaning of her name:

> It would be a misreading of the passage to regret the apparent savagery of Heresy's fate. While it is natural to be touched by the mutilation of a human being—Hector, for instance, in the *Iliad*—it is inappropriate to feel the same sympathy for an allegorical personification such as Heresy. Heresy's fate is fit and proper punishment, not cruel and unusual savagery. Just as Heresy, otherwise named *Discordia* (709–10), tears apart the Christian church, so her body is torn apart in appropriate retribution. The punishment corresponds to the *lex talionis*, that the punishment should fit the crime.[41]

Paula James similarly argues against seeing any incongruity in the violent actions of the Virtues: "Prudentius would surely not have seen his rerouting of the arena spectacle as a risk-taking venture. The message was intended to be unequivocal. The Vices were condemned criminals and really did deserve to die."[42]

But Prudentius's text is no more unequivocal than it is univocal. The dismemberment of the Vice is *more* than an appropriate retribution—so much more that it has the disconcerting effect of shifting the reader from pondering a sober assessment of the evils of Heresy to focusing on the absurdly excessive actions of the one-dimensional personified abstractions who populate the battle lines on both sides of the poem.⁴³ Prudentius, like Ovid, is a master of this sort of destabilizing humor; the excesses of the Virtues here are no more (and no less) absurd than the grotesque conceit of Cyprian's tongue continuing to preach long after the saint himself has moved on to his heavenly reward, or the hyperphallic image of the prelapsarian Satan as an erect serpent (*H.* 197–200), or the fraught humor that characterizes the interchanges between martyrs and persecutors in the *Peristephanon*.⁴⁴

The black humor of the dismemberment scene destabilizes the narrative armature of the *Psychomachia* by drawing the audience's attention toward the way the text dismantles its own rhetorical structure. As Paxson shows, Prudentius, through the extreme description of the physical dismemberment of Discordia, calls attention to his use of figured language, in this case the trope of personification. For the face, *prosopon,* is the image behind the term prosopopoeia, as Paul de Man puts it:

> We can identify the figure . . . of prosopopeia, the fiction of an apostrophe to an absent, deceased, or voiceless entity, which posits the possibility of the latter's reply and confers upon it the power of speech. Voice assumes mouth, eye, and finally face, a chain that is manifest in the etymology of the trope's name, *prosopon poein,* to confer a mask or a face (*prosopon*).⁴⁵

Personification allegory, which Prudentius was the first to employ throughout an entire narrative, is akin to prosopopoeia in that it is a device that gives voice and actional status to an abstract fictional entity. This trope draws attention to the polyvalence of language, for it ostentatiously reveals the fictional status of all narrative characters. In the *Psychomachia*, Prudentius overtly deconstructs his own trope through the violent battle scenes between the Virtues and the Vices, exposing the operation of the figure and thus dismantling it.⁴⁶

Mastrangelo takes a different approach to the issue of the violent deaths of the Vices in the *Psychomachia*. He argues that "the use of violence in the *Psychomachia* serves a wider and deeper poetic purpose than hitherto acknowledged."⁴⁷ Prudentius adapts language and ideas from Epicurus and Lucretius in his descriptions of the violent deaths of the Vices. Specifically, he refers to the Epicurean idea that the soul is diffused throughout the body and dissipates into nothingness when the body dies, as Lucretius argues at *DRN* 3.455–58:

> ergo dissolvi quoque convenit omnem animai
> naturam, ceu fumus, in altas aeris auras,
> quandoquidem gigni pariter pariterque videmus
> crescere, et ut docui, simul aevo fessa fatisci.

> Therefore it is fitting that the whole nature of the soul dissolves also, into
> the high breezes of the air, since we see that it is born at the same time
> and grows at the same time, and as I have taught, it grows tired,
> exhausted by age, at the same time.

For the Epicurean Vices, soul and body are mortal and subject to destruction by violent penetration. Conversely, the Virtues reflect the immortality of the soul that adheres to Christian teachings and is rendered impregnable.[48] A binary opposition is constructed, in which the Vices and the soul dominated by vice behave in an Epicurean way, that is, they are penetrated, break up, and are dissipated, while the Virtues and the soul dominated by Christian virtue are protected and unharmed. Mastrangelo's argument, firmly grounded in the language and imagery of the *Psychomachia*, significantly improves our understanding of the poem—indeed, it suggests the need for a much more comprehensive assessment of Prudentius's use of Epicureanism, and of *De rerum natura* in particular, in his poetry.

Mastrangelo's exposition of the philosophical roots of Prudentius's construction of the Virtues and the Vices does not, I believe, negate Paxson's important point, which is that the *Psychomachia* enacts a symbolic dismantling of its own master trope, personification. There is a definite tension between the doctrinal point Prudentius expresses through his engagement with Epicurean teachings on the soul and the rhetorical devices he uses to expound it. On the one hand, on the level of symbolic allegory, Prudentius takes on Lucretius by turning the death of the Vices into a parodic exemplum of the Epicurean doctrine of the dissolution of the soul, and by deploying his impregnable Virtues to represent the immortality of the Christian soul. On the other hand, Prudentius's punning, polysemous, recombinant verse technique bears a strong resemblance to Lucretius's atomistic text, a text that enacts Epicurean doctrine at the level of the word, the syllable, and even the letter.

But Prudentius's view of language was also shaped by other philosophical theories of language. Jeffrey Bardzell, in his analysis of the battle between Concordia and Discordia, reads the episode as reflecting a tradition of Stoic language theory:

> The Stoics posit a binding between the rational *logos* of the cosmos and all of the bodies within it, a binding that Christians embrace by replacing God for the cosmos. Discordia and Concordia can both be seen as reflecting aspects of this cosmic binding: for though the Stoic cosmos is guided by the divine *logos*, assent to the many false impressions that are a part of the human experience leads to error. Discordia is the force behind the problems of signification manifested in impressions, while Concordia is the force that asserts the underlying unity that is really there according to both Stoic and Christian doctrine, even if we fail to perceive it. As long as

we are bound to the limitations of human knowing, *Discordia and Concordia unfortunately imply one another,* two intensional aspects of the human experience of the bond that connects us to God and the universe. (emphasis added)[49]

As we will see, a similar tension between the limited nature of human language and perception and the ungraspable divine Logos underlies the *Hamartigenia* as well.

2. FIGURING IT OUT

ON THE ORNAMENTS AND FIGURES of the *Hamartigenia* rested the burden of generating meaning in the mind of the active Roman reader. We will explore those ornaments and figures in what follows, in the hope that through the process of figuring out the figures in the text, the contemporary reader will be better equipped both to follow the logic and to enjoy the linguistic virtuosity of the poem. As the *Hamartigenia* is neither a well-known nor a transparent text, a brief summary of its narrative scheme may be helpful to readers unfamiliar with the poem.

Reading the *Hamartigenia*

Like Prudentius's other hexameter poems, the *Hamartigenia* appears in the manuscripts under a Greek title and features a preface written in a different meter from that of the poem itself (iambic preface followed by hexameter poem).[1] The main topic of the poem is the origin of sin in the universe and its consequences; it is framed as a refutation of the heresy of Marcion, a second-century-CE thinker who preached a dualistic theology.[2] The preface describes Cain's murder of Abel and associates that crime with heresy in the church and the fallen state of humanity, in which flesh is pitted against spirit. The poem proper begins with an apostrophe to Cain, who is castigated as a "divider of God" (this is, on the face of it, a surprising charge against Cain, who shows no dualist tendencies in Genesis, but Prudentius has already identified Cain with Marcion, the dualist heretic, in the preface) and accused of having double vision.[3] Prudentius next asserts the unity of God and rejects any division of the Godhead (1–173; Lat. 1–123). He describes the apostasy of the devil, with a vivid description that identifies him as the biblical hunter Nimrod (Nebroth), and names him the fountainhead of sin (173–280; Lat. 124–205). From there, Prudentius addresses the effects of sin on the universe; human transgressions and the corruption of the five senses; and, in a miniature

Psychomachia, the attack of Satan and the vices against humanity. The souls under attack by the vices are compared to the Jews who, led by Moses out of Egypt and by Joshua across the Jordan into the Promised Land, nevertheless keep backsliding into sin (280–657; Lat. 206–505). Arguing that God cannot be the originator of evil and that man cannot blame his nature for sin, Prudentius provides two exempla of the origin of sin: a graphic description of the breeding habits of vipers, and the biblical tale of David and Absalom. He then describes Adam's original sin, for which, he argues, man's free will, not God, is responsible (658–957; Lat. 506–722). To illustrate the central concept of free will, he sets out a series of vivid exempla: the biblical stories of Lot and his wife fleeing the cities of the plain; Ruth's loyalty to her mother-in-law Naomi (957–1051; Lat. 722–88); a parable of two brothers at a crossroads (1051–70; Lat. 788–803); and a simile describing the fates of a flock of doves, a few of whom fly to heaven, but most of whom fall victim to a snare with poisoned food and are unable to take flight (1071–95; Lat. 804–23). The poem culminates with a vision of the fates of souls after judgment: the damned are condemned to worms, torture, and flames, while the saved return to a heaven filled with delights, one of which is the pleasure of watching the torments of the damned (1096–1244; Lat. 824–931). It ends with a prayer for clemency for the poet's own soul (1245–90; Lat. 931–66).

As Catherine Conybeare (2007) has pointed out, the *Hamartigenia,* though a written text, assumes the rhetorical markers of an oral text, using apostrophe (direct address to the reader or to a character in the poem), prosopopoeia (having imaginary characters speak or act), and first-person interventions by the narrator. This "feigned orality" reflects the pervasive influence of rhetorical performance for Christians and non-Christians alike in late antiquity.[4] Throughout most of the poem, the poet/narrator is ostensibly addressing an interlocutor, who occasionally is presented as responding in direct dialogue. The dialogue is heavily one-sided, however; the brief interventions of Marcion are answered with a torrent of verbiage from the narrator asserting orthodoxy.[5] The addressee is a heretical thinker from the second century CE: Marcion, the son of the bishop of Sinope in Pontus, who expounded one of the forms of dualism so popular in late antiquity.[6] Marcion believed that there were two gods: the god of the Hebrew scriptures, who was a creator god associated with matter, which is imperfect; and the god of the New Testament, a good god, entirely immaterial, who sent his son to redeem mankind from the creator. Believing that the material world is at best imperfect, he rejected both the notion of the resurrection of the body, which, he argued, had no place in the kingdom of heaven, and the institution of marriage, which produces more creatures subject to the inferior creator god.[7]

It is highly unlikely that Prudentius thought that Marcionism per se presented a clear and present danger to orthodox Christianity. The controversy over Marcion's teachings had largely disappeared by the late fourth century. Manichaeism was a much greater contemporary threat, and the poem seems to address dualist heresies in general as much as Marcionism in particular. Indeed, Catherine Conybeare has persuasively argued that Prudentius's use of biblical quotation in the *Hamartigenia* is directly related to contemporary debates about Manichaeism. The central problem of the poem is as much an issue for Manichaeans as it was for followers of Marcion: What is the origin of sin and evil? How can they exist if God is indeed omnipotent and benevolent? The logical response of the dualists is that, in fact, a good God could not and would not have created evil, so we must assume the existence of two gods, one good, one evil. The *Hamartigenia* struggles to refute this notion.

Prudentius's response to these arguments is as much exegetical and figural as it is philosophical or doctrinal. In other words, while both Marcion and Prudentius rely on the authority of scripture, Prudentius's refutation of dualism depends on his way of reading that scripture. Marcion is central to the overall design of the poem because he could represent the dangers of dualist theologies *and* because of his interpretative methodology, which was literal and reductionist. With his refusal to reconcile the apparent conflicts embedded in the Bible and his wholesale rejection of most of the canonical books of both the Jewish and the Christian scriptures, Marcion initiated the process of canon formation: the identification of a restricted list of books thought to have a privileged relation to divine authority and truth.[8] "Sacred story had become sacred book," Patricia Cox Miller observes. "Marcion's sense of authority, rooted as it was in theological content and a conception of 'original' or pristine meaning, was adopted some forty years later by Irenaeus of Lyons, who, although he did not accept Marcion's version of the New Testament canon, nevertheless accepted the *idea* of canon that Marcion initiated."[9] It is important that Prudentius's rejection of Marcion appears to be focused at least in part on his literal and restrictive approach to reading and interpretation. This is of key importance, for reading and interpretation are crucially linked to the ability to distinguish right from wrong, and thus to appropriately exercise free will. In her study of reading in the *Hamartigenia*, Catherine Conybeare points to the importance of reading as an interpretative and ethical act in the poem:

> Prudentius engages explicitly with no books other than holy scripture. And he brings into play no clear metaphors of the book: for example, Christ is never represented simply as the gospel incarnate. Yet the *Hamartigenia* is profoundly and constantly concerned, not with doctrine as something rightly spelled out . . . but with reading: with reading as an interpretative act, and hence as an ethical one; with the right and wrong motivations for reading; and with the results of right reading. Prudentius counters Marcion and related heresies not with direct refutation, but with *illustrative subterfuge*: the poem enacts in its construction the sort of figural reading which by its very nature renders the two testaments of the Bible indispensable to each other. (emphasis added)[10]

Conybeare's point, that the *Hamartigenia*'s concern throughout is with reading as an interpretative act, and with the results of right and wrong reading, is key to interpreting the poem. Correct interpretation leads the soul to discern right from wrong, and thereby to choose proper over improper action.

Marcion follows in the tradition of addressees of didactic verse, from Perses, castigated by his brother Hesiod, to Memmius, whom Lucretius tried so strenuously to educate. In the *Hamartigenia*, Marcion is cast in a particular role, the role of a bad reader whose interpretation needs the constant correction supplied by the poet. One of the ironies of this poem is that by adopting this adversarial structure—the opposed pair of Prudentius and Marcion is only one of a series of polar opposites—Prudentius creates a polarized text that reflects the dualist view of the world that he strives so hard to refute.

Before the Beginning

Concern with right reading manifests itself immediately in the *Hamartigenia*; it is the subject of the poem's preface. Prefaces were evidently an important tool for Prudentius: as we have noted, he introduces each of his hexameter poems with one. As is the case for the *Psychomachia*,[11] the preface of the *Hamartigenia* sets forth an epitome (which, as Carruthers points out, is "an ornament of contraction") of a biblical story, and follows it with an exegesis that ostensibly serves as an interpretive model to assist the reader in interpreting not just the opening figure but the *Hamartigenia* as a whole.[12] The story begins in medias res with two brothers performing a sacrifice:

> Fratres ephebi fossor et pastor duo,
> quos feminarum prima primos procreat,
> sistunt ad aram de laborum fructibus
> Deo sacranda munerum primordia.
> hic terrulentis, ille vivis fungitur;
> certante voto discrepantes inmolant,
> fetum bidentis alter, ast alter scrobis.
> Deus minoris conprobavit hostiam,
> reiecit illam quam paravit grandior.
>   (*H. praef.* 1–9)

> Adolescent brothers, a digger and a shepherd—the two
> born first to the first of women—
> set on the altar firstfruits of their labor,
> offered up as holy gifts to God.
> One offers earth's crops, the other living things.
> In conflict, they make rival pledges:

> one the young of a sheep, the other the yield of his trench.
> God approved the victim of the younger brother
> and rejected what the older had acquired.

The brothers, at first unidentified, are described as youths (*ephebi*), one a farmer (*fossor*), the other a shepherd (*pastor*). They are the first sons (*primos*) of the first of women (*feminarum prima*). They offer a sacrifice to God, the fruits of their labor (*laborum fructibus*), a sacrifice that reflects the nature of their professions: the farmer gives the fruits of the earth, the shepherd offers up a living sacrifice. The sacrificial moment brings with it fatal rivalry: the offerings are contentious as the brothers try to distinguish themselves through the act of sacrifice. The younger offers a lamb, the elder the produce of the earth (marked as inferior by Prudentius's use of the word *scrobis,* literally "ditch," a word that carries the negative connotations of one of its common meanings, "grave"). God approves the sacrifice of the younger, but rejects that of the elder brother. This tale of two brothers is, of course, the story of Cain and Abel, as we learn when the voice of God identifies Cain by suddenly shouting a rebuke: "Cain, quiesce!" (*H. praef.* 11). Cain sacrifices improperly to God, and in his rage and jealousy at God's acceptance of Abel's sacrifice, he kills his brother. Prudentius, in an ostentatious act of exegesis (*agnosco nempe quem figura haec denotet*) that links heresy to this paradigmatic crime, compares Marcion's improper division of the Godhead into two with Cain's improper sacrifice, and interprets the murder of Abel as symbolic of Marcion's destruction of the soul. The preface ends with Cain celebrating a triumph over the death of his brother's soul (*Cain triumphat morte fratris halitus, H. praef.* 63).

Certain thematic ideas that originate in the preface recur throughout the poem, most notably division, imitation, reproduction and its consequences, deception, and the notion of being lost or astray. As Rosemarie Taddei has suggested, one of Prudentius's main reasons for opening with the sin of Cain is his desire "to emphasise the idea of division ... which he finds in the Septuagint version of the story."[13] In the Septuagint, as in the Vetus Latina, the reason Cain's sacrifice is rejected is that he divided it improperly.[14] In Prudentius's account, the voice of God warns Cain that properly offering without dividing the sacrifice according to divine law would lead to sin:

> vox ecce summo missa persultat throno:
> "Cain, quiesce! namque si recto offeras,
> oblata nec tu lege recta dividas,
> perversa nigram vota culpam traxerint."
>   (*H. praef.* 10–13)

> Look! A voice resounds from the throne on high:
> "Cain, be still! If you rightly make your offering

and yet do not divide it up correctly,
your perverted gifts will bring black guilt."

What would constitute proper division is not stated, nor is there any explanation of what is improper about Cain's division.[15] By identifying Marcion with Cain, he implies that Cain's improper division of the sacrifice foreshadowed Marcion's division of God into two deities, making him a precursor of heretics who espouse a dualist interpretation of the Old and New Testaments. Improper division of the sacrifice leads to jealousy that culminates in fratricide, the most radical form of division within human society. There is a long-standing exegetical tradition associating Cain with walling cities, dividing land, and developing weights and measures. Josephus says that Cain "changed, by his invention of weights and measures, the simplicity with which men previously lived, their life innocent because of their ignorance of such things; and he turned magnanimity into cunning artifice and corruption."[16] Augustine (*De civ.* 15.5 and 15.8) identifies Cain as the first city builder. Boundaries, cities, weights and measures all exemplify division, and the distance of fallen humanity from the perfect prelapsarian unity of Eden.[17]

Interpreting the Figure

Prudentius's interpretation of the Cain and Abel story is unusual and sets him apart from the mainstream of exegesis.[18] In contrast to the arbitrariness of God's rejection in the *Hamartigenia*, Milton makes it very clear why Cain's sacrifice was not accepted by contrasting Cain's "unculled" offering of what was to hand with Abel's careful selection of the best of his flock:

> A sweatie Reaper from his Tillage brought
> First Fruits, the green Eare, and the yellow Sheaf,
> Uncull'd, as came to hand; a Shepherd next
> More meek came with the Firstlings of his Flock
> Choicest and best.
>   (*PL* 11.434–38)

Milton's account of the story of Cain comes close to the end of the poem, when the angel Michael removes from Adam's eyes the film "which that false fruit that promised clearer sight / Had bred," and shows him visions of man's future. Prudentius, on the other hand, deliberately places Cain's sin at the beginning of the *Hamartigenia* so that it stands as the exemplary original sin within the narrative framework of the poem. This is out of line with the narrative chronology of Genesis, in which the sin of Eve and Adam precedes the account of the sin of Cain, and the chronological peculiarity underscores the importance of the story. Immediately after recounting Abel's murder, Prudentius draws attention to the process of reading and interpreting it, in a passage that seems to go out of its way to ensure that the reader arrives at a proper interpretation:

> ergo ex futuris prisca coepit fabula
> factoque primo res notata est ultima,
> ut ille mortis inchoator rusticus
> insulsa terrae deferens libamina
> Deumque rerum mortuarum deputans
> rastris redacta digna sacris crederet,
> viventis atrox aemulator hostiae.
> agnosco nempe quem figura haec denotet,
> quis fratricida, quis peremptor invidus
> prave sacrorum disciplinam dividat,
> mactare dum se vota censet rectius.
>   (*H. praef.* 25–35)

> So the ancient story began with things yet to be,
> and the last things were marked out by that first deed,
> when the crude farmer who invented death
> brought his bungled, unsalted offerings of earth,
> and thinking God a god of lifeless things,
> believed the yield of his hoe worth offering
> in his dark envy of the living victim.
>   I recognize, of course, whom this figure implies,
> the killer of his brother, the jealous slayer,
> who perversely divides holy doctrine
> and reckons his own offerings more just . . .

This story sets up a template for reading the *Hamartigenia*, but it is a complicated template. As Mastrangelo (2008, 48) notes, this passage reverses the typological relationship, so that stories of the past *originate* in the events of the future: "The future, constructed as a set of ideologically fixed points in time (e.g., the Incarnation and Last Judgment), causes the stories of the past to exist as history."

Mastrangelo suggests that part of this passage, lines 25–26, should be read in dialogue with two other passages in which Prudentius uses the word *fabula*. The first is from the *Apotheosis*, in which Prudentius accuses a Manichaean interlocutor of imagining that all of human history, right up to the present day, is nebulous and illusory: *Omne quod est gestum notus auferat inritus, aurae / Dispergant tenues. Sit fabula quod sumus omnes!* (*Apoth.* 1017–18). ["Everything that has been done the South wind carries off in vain, / the light breezes disperse. All we are is a story!"] The second is from *Pe.* 9, in which a church attendant asserts the veracity of the events depicted in a painting of the martyrdom of Saint Cassian—a schoolmaster stabbed to death by the pens of his own pupils:

> aedituus consultus ait: "quod prospicis, hospes,
> non est inanis aut anilis fabula.
> historiam pictura refert, quae tradita libris
> veram vetusti temporis monstrat fidem."
> (*Pe.* 9.17–20)

> When asked, the doorman said, "What you look at, guest,
> is no old woman's empty story. The picture relates
> the history which, handed down in books,
> shows the true faith of old times."

Mastrangelo argues that Prudentius, in these passages, expands the typical fourth-century meaning of *fabula* (a tale that is false or untrue) and uses it to mean "literary storytelling," which he constructs as the proper vehicle for salvation history. "Taken together, these three texts suggest that the true stories of individual human beings are typological in nature. This constitutes the core of Prudentian history. A human life is a story that is typologically connected to the past.... The concept of typology is at the core of Prudentius' thinking" (Mastrangelo 2008, 48). Such a Christian typological view of sacred scripture and scriptural history is fundamentally positive, one that sees the new law brought into being by Christ as both superseding and completing the law of the Old Testament.

Complicating this typological schema, which is fundamental to Prudentius's view of Roman and Christian history, is his view of language, a view succinctly summarized in a review of Fyler's 2007 study of post-Augustinian theories of veiled language in the works of Dante, Chaucer, and Jean de Meun:[19]

> Telling the same story [i.e., the story of Christian universal history] in terms of the fate of language ... offers a very different and much more somber perspective. Without renouncing the dialectic between the old law and the new, the linguistic perspective roots itself firmly in the material world of biblical—and contemporary—history. For this reason, it does not stress the positive figures of the Fall and its aftermath but invokes rather the negative dynamic of the old law. This antifigural movement effectively models itself on the duplicitous language introduced by Satan in his seduction of Eve: diabolical eloquence previews the ambiguous, veiled language of the fallen world.

Similarly, throughout the *Hamartigenia* an optimistic typological scheme stands in uneasy tension with a fundamentally apophatic view of language and interpretation.[20] This is evident even in the preface, which confidently asserts a clear reading of the story of Cain and Abel. "I recognize, of course, whom this figure implies," says the narrator, *agnosco nempe quem figura haec denotet*. But the very intrusion of the narrator is evidence of the need to guide the reader to a proper interpretation of the text—it points, that is, to the possibility of misinterpretation.

At this point, the text identifies Marcion as Cain, and then goes on to present an allegorical reading of the story of Cain in which Cain represents Flesh, who attacks Spirit (Abel) in a passage that introduces several images that permeate the *Hamartigenia*:[21]

> natura cuius fraude floret fertili
> fecunda fundens noxiorum crimina,
> animaeque vitam labe carnis enecat.
> caro in sororem tela mentem dirigit,
> mens in cerebro ventilatur ebrio,
> ex quo furores suculentos conligit
> madens veneno corporis lymphatico.
> Deum perennem findit in duos Deos,
> audet secare numen insecabile.
> cadit perempta denegans unum Deum,
> Cain triumphat morte fratris halitus.
>   (*H. praef.* 53–63)

> Its nature flourishes with fertile fraud,
> pouring from her womb the teeming sins of guilty men,
> and kills the life of the soul through the fall of flesh.
> Flesh turns her shafts against her sister, Mind;
> Mind fans the flames within the drunken brain,
> where she gathers potent passions,
> drunk with Flesh's maddening poisons.
> Eternal God she splits into two; she dares
> divide the Godhead indivisible.
> Murdered, she falls, denying God is one.
> Cain triumphs in his brother Spirit's death.

The warring brothers Cain and Abel are figures for Flesh (*Caro*) and Spirit (*Mens*), here personified as warring sisters. Failure to comprehend divine unity results in divisiveness on many levels: the separation of spirit from flesh within the individual; societal strife, as represented by Cain's murder of Abel; heresy within the church. This closing figure creates a matrix of ideas (deception, madness, reproduction, division, and death) that will be further explored in the poem itself.

3. SEEKING HIDDEN TRUTH

BY OPENING THE *Hamartigenia* with a typological allegory and guiding us toward its correct interpretation through personification allegory, Prudentius draws attention to the process of figural reading. But as is the case with the *Psychomachia,* whose preface also opens with a biblical exemplum that is interpreted for us (the story of Abraham), it turns out that more complex modes of figural reading than the one provided in the preface will be required. As the *Hamartigenia* progresses, the process of interpreting signs becomes less and less clear-cut, as Prudentius presents his argument through different figures—analogy, allusion, simile, exempla—whose ambiguity and complex interrelationships suggest the infinite ability of signs to generate meaning, and the concomitant difficulty of arriving at a right reading.[1]

The Allegory of the Sun

The first major figure of the poem sets forth a model of interpretation taken from the natural world. Refuting the heretical notion that there are two gods, Prudentius offers as counterargument the analogy of the sun, which we are to view analogically as a visible sign of the innate unity of God (the sun is *unicus*) as well as the Trinity (the sun is also *triplex*):

> idcirco specimen posuit spectabile nostris
> exemplumque oculis, ne quis duo numina credat
> . . . .
> una per inmensam caeli caveam revolutos
> praebet flamma dies, texit sol unicus annum;
> triplex ille tamen nullo discrimine trina
> subnixus ratione viget, splendet, volat, ardet,

motu agitur, fervore cremat, tum lumine fulget.
   (H. 67–68, 70–74)

He placed this symbol right before our eyes,
a visible proof that shows that we should not
place our faith in two divine powers: . . .
. . . .
one sun alone weaves the year together
from the days, and yet it is threefold,
reliant on three qualities without
distinction: light and speed and heat. Its speed
propels it; heat provides its warmth, and light
its radiance.
   (H. 92–94, 97–102)

Marcion's claim that there are two gods is refuted by an analogy, a hermeneutic model. As Gosserez (2001, 42) says, "The text of the *Hamartigenia* effectively provides, besides a refutation of immanence and dualism, a definition of metaphysical allegory. It provides a justification of the figurative knowledge of God that one can derive from the contemplation of the sun."[2] Contemplation of the sun leads us to a comprehension of the unity of God and the nature of the Trinity through a process of analogical thinking. This process is a corrective to Marcion's excessively literal interpretative method, and is based on the notion that the natural world itself is a sort of book, a set of signs given by God for us to interpret. Prudentius's use of the analogy of the sun is multilayered.[3] Plato is one important source, as Prudentius signals by a sophisticated allusion: in line 84, he states that "we have the privilege of seeking hidden truth in proximate things" (et datur occultum per proxima *quaerere verum*). This echoes a famous line from Horace's *Epistle* 2.2: "atque inter silvas Academi *quaerere verum*" ("to seek the truth amidst the groves of Academe"), in which Horace is recalling his own study of philosophy.[4] Thus Prudentius's quotation from Horace points the reader toward Platonic philosophy, though as we will see below, the phrase "*quaerere verum*" has scriptural resonances as well.[5]

The Platonic passage that is most relevant here is from book 7 of *The Republic*, where Socrates narrates the analogy of the cave, in which the rational part of the soul undergoes a pilgrimage that takes it from the darkness of the cave to a vision of truth, and then must return to the darkness of the cave, forever transformed by its glimpse of reality. In that extended allegory, Socrates describes prisoners inside a cave who are unaware that there is a world outside. They believe that the fire burning inside the cave is the sun, and that the shadows of things outside projected on the walls of the cave are real. Socrates asks his interlocutor, Glaucon, to imagine the state of mind of one of them who is suddenly exposed to the world outside the cave:

> —At first, he'd see the shadows most easily, then images of men and other things in water, then the things themselves. Of these, he'd be able to study the things in the sky and the sky itself more easily at night looking at the light of the stars and the moon, than during the day, looking at the sun and the light of the sun. . . . Finally he'd be able to see the sun, not images of it in the water or some alien place, but the sun itself, in its own place, and be able to study it.
> —Certainly.
> —And at this point he would infer and conclude that the sun provides the seasons and the years, governs everything in the visible world, and is in some way the cause of all the things that he used to see. (*Rep.* 7.516a–b, trans. GRUBE and REEVE)

This allusion is especially significant because it refers the reader to a passage in which the process of analogical interpretation is clearly laid out and instantiated. Socrates first relates his allegory to Glaucon, then leads him through a process of reasoning based on it, and finally (lest there be any chance for misinterpretation) provides his own interpretation:

> This whole image, Glaucon, must be fitted together with what we said before. The visible realm should be likened to the prison dwelling, and the light of the fire inside it to the power of the sun. And if you interpret the upward journey and the study of things above as the upward journey of the soul to the intelligible realm, you'll grasp what I hope to convey. . . . In the knowable realm, the form of the good is the last thing to be seen and it is reached only with difficulty. Once one has seen it, however, one must conclude that it is the cause of all that is correct and beautiful in anything. (*Rep.* 7.517b–c, trans. GRUBE and REEVE)

In her study of the imagery of light in the works of Prudentius, Laurence Gosserez reveals the centrality of the metaphor of the allegory of the sun to Prudentius's thought. Prudentius's use of allegory reflects, she argues, far more than the definition of allegory provided by Quintilian ("an extended metaphor"—citing van Assendelft, 1976, 18):

> It restores a vision of the world, the fundamental unity of which it is the reflection. The structure of Prudentius' imaginary is entirely oriented toward this center. The representation of the center thereby acquires a metapoetic

function at the same time as a metaphysical one. The sun is not only the image of God, it is "the metaphor of metaphorization," the reference to the absolute referent of all language, and the inscription of the transcendent radiance of the Logos across degrees of dissimilarity. (GOSSEREZ 2001, 41)

For Gosserez, Prudentius's view of language is essentially centripetal: the poet "is only deciphering the figure that Providence has already imprinted in nature and in his heart. Symbolism and realism are not exclusives, but correlatives" (Gosserez 2001, 42). Certainly the allegory of the sun, modeled on the allegory of the cave from Plato's *Republic,* seems to suggest an unproblematic relationship between symbol and reality.

But despite the way in which the master trope of the sun is presented as providing a positive model of interpretation in the *Hamartigenia,* the interpretation of the analogy of the sun remains problematic, as its use by Augustine demonstrates. Augustine held to a physics of vision that posited that a ray of light, projected through the mind of the viewer, literally touches its object and thus physically connects the viewer to the object. Reciprocally, the visual ray prints the object on the soul of the viewer—indeed, citing the chameleon and the fetus, shaped by what its mother looks upon, Augustine argues that even the body can be shaped by what it looks upon. As Margaret Miles shows, for Augustine, the *possibility* of spiritual vision exists through divine illumination, but divine illumination is not enough. The viewer must take the initiative to train his vision. Augustine, in fact, used the metaphor of the sun to illustrate the *weakness* of the human eye and the eye of the soul, which must be carefully trained in order to see the truth, as Miles argues:

> Just as the bodily eye requires the most strenuous exercise and strengthening before it can see strongly illuminated objects, so the eye of the mind requires intensive exercise and training before it can see—even momentarily—eternal truth.... [In *De trinitate*] Augustine acknowledges no automatically "healthy and vigorous" eye. The agenda of *De trinitate* is the careful, steady drawing of a cumulative understanding of the Trinity. Even though, at the beginning of the effort, the Trinity's "own light seemed to be present around us, still, no trinity appeared to us in nature, for in the midst of that splendor we did not keep the eye of our mind fixed steadily upon searching for it ... because that ineffable light beat back our gaze, and the weakness of our mind was convinced that it could not yet adjust itself to it" (15.6.10). (MILES 1983, 131)

Optical Illusions

Like Augustine, Prudentius draws a strong connection between the capability of the soul and vision, which, as both Gosserez and Taddei have demonstrated, is a dominant motif throughout the poem. In his presentation of the analogy of the sun, Prudentius, again like Augustine, expresses doubt about the efficacy of human vision, which he links metaphorically to anxiety about proper interpretation. Immediately after the magnificent description of the sun and its powers, Prudentius introduces a note of doubt: Is analogy appropriate? Can anything be compared to God? Indeed, what appears to be the triumphant conclusion to his exegesis of the allegory of the sun—that the appearance of one sun in the sky is a transparent symbol of the unity of God—is immediately qualified by another analogy: Marcion, who believes in two gods, is like a man who sees two suns. This would appear to be a self-evident impossibility, since there is only one sun, but it is, Prudentius demonstrates, quite possible—not because there actually *are* multiple suns, but because our perception can be distorted by different factors, so that we perceive two where there is only one:

> nemo duos soles nisi sub glaucomate vidit,
> aut, si fusca polum suffudit palla serenum,
> oppositus quotiens radiorum specula nimbus
> igne repercusso mentitos spargit in orbes.
> (H. 85–88)

>   No man has ever seen
> two suns, unless he sees them through a cataract
> that veils his eyes, or a dusky mantle spreads
> across the clear heaven and makes it blush,
> when clouds block shafts of light, reflect their fire,
> and scatter them into counterfeited orbs.
> (H. 118–23)

The source of the anonymous man's double vision is physical and external—it is caused either by cataracts or an optical effect of light reflected off of clouds—the parhelion, or sun dog. The effect is caused when rays of the sun penetrate clouds of ice crystals; the refracted rays produce what look like mock suns or halos, a phenomenon noted by Aristotle (*Met.* 3.2.372a) and mentioned by numerous Roman writers.[6] Cicero, indeed, uses a discussion of the parhelion to start the dialogue in *De republica* 1. Countering arguments that the study of nature is irrelevant to those concerned with governing the state, Philus makes the case that the microcosm of human society reflects the macrocosm of the cosmos:

> Scipio was asking me, replied Philus, what I thought of the parhelion, or mock sun, whose recent apparition was so strongly attested.
> *Laelius.* Do you say then, my Philus, that we have sufficiently examined those questions which concern our own houses and the Commonwealth, that we begin to investigate the celestial mysteries?
> And Philus replied: Do you think, then, that it does not concern our houses to know what happens in that vast home which is not included in walls of human fabrication, but which embraces the entire universe—a home which the Gods share with us, as the common country of all intelligent beings? (CICERO, *Rep.* 1.13, trans. YONGE)

The example of the parhelion thus offers an example of deceptive optical illusion, but within a context (the passage from *De republica*) that suggests that the interpretive principle of analogical interpretation is operative. But as Prudentius is quick to point out, more disturbing distortions of vision can be caused by the mind:

> est glaucoma, aciem quod tegmine velet aquoso,
> libera ne tenerum penetret meditatio caelum
> neve Deum rapidis conprendat sensibus unum:
> spargitur in bifidas male sana intentio luces,
> et duplices geminis auctoribus extruit aras.
>   (*H.* 90–94)

> Each mind is shrouded over with its own
> opaque atmosphere: a cataract
> with watery veil dulls our keen gaze, blocks
> the flow of our freed contemplation's thrust
> up into heaven's softness, and obstructs
> our rapid senses' comprehension that
> our God is One. And our malfunctioning sight
> fractures the image, strives to follow two
> sources of light, and builds a pair of altars
> to twin creators.
>   (124–33)

This "cataract" that obscures our inner sight is a result of the Fall; Prudentius balances this discussion of the limits of mortal sight and understanding with a lengthy discussion of the keen vision of the liberated soul, freed from the limitations of the flesh, near the end of the poem. In this description of the viewer afflicted with double vision, Prudentius may be drawing on Vergil's description of Dido as she descends into madness and despair.[7] Dido is described as "weary of gazing at the vault of the sky" (*taedet caeli convexa tueri*, *Aen.* 4.450). She sees dreadful omens on the altars and is haunted in her sleep by nightmares:

> Eumenidum veluti demens videt agmina Pentheus,
> et *solem geminum* et duplicis se ostendere Thebas;
> aut Agamemnonius scaenis agitatus Orestes
> armatam facibus matrem et serpentibus atris
> cum fugit, ultricesque sedent in limine Dirae.
>   (*Aen.* 4.469–73)

> She was like Pentheus, stripped of his mind, seeing armies of Furies,
> Seeing the sole sun double, and Thebes in a duplicate presence;
> Like Agamemnon's child, driven mad in a drama: Orestes
> Fleeing his mother who's armoured with flames and with dark hissing serpents
> While, at the door of the palace, avenging Furies sit waiting.

In the simile, Vergil compares the dreaming Dido to two characters from the tragic stage: Pentheus, who in his madness sees two suns and two Thebes, and Orestes, whose guilt leads him to see his mother in the guise of a Fury. There are several layers of unreality in this passage, which conflates different kinds of illusions: simile, stage, dreams, and madness.

Orestes' disturbed vision was a stock example in Stoic philosophical discussions of *phantasiai*. The Stoics distinguish between mental images derived from perception of real objects or from reasoning (*kataleptikai phantasiai*), from illusions not derived from reality, such as dreams or hallucinations. Orestes' vision of the Furies was adduced as an illustration of the latter.[8] Rhetoricians, however, make no such distinction between types of mental images and make no judgment about the truth of the image or its relation to reality. Ps. Longinus (15.2) refers, apparently favorably, to Orestes' vision of the Furies in his discussion of enargeia: "Here the poet saw the Furies himself and compelled the audience to almost see what he imagined (*ephantasthē*)." Webb (2009, 97) notes that this claim that the poet must have seen the Furies himself relies "on the assumption that the poet himself worked by creating mental images that he then expressed in words . . . and that these same words can therefore allow the reader to access and share this image." Moreover, for rhetoricians and poets, the images do not have to be derived from real things or reason to be effective: they merely have to be "like truth" for the audience to seem to see them.[9]

Prudentius has set out a clear interpretative model for his poem: the visible universe is a sign that, when properly interpreted, will lead the soul to an understanding of God; by analogy, we are led to conclude that the text is a sign that will lead us to a similar understanding. Similarly, in Plato's allegory of the cave the text moves from illusion to understanding: the prisoner is led from the shadowy cave to the light of day, and Socrates is there to provide an on-the-spot exegesis for Glaucon. But even in the *Republic*, the prisoner in the cave does not attain a permanent state of enlightenment. When he moves from the cave into the sun, he is blinded by the light. Later, forced to return to the cave so he can report his experience to the other prisoners, he is blinded by the darkness. As Andrea Nightingale puts it, "The philosopher must accept the condition of blindness as the precondition of philosophical insight. He goes blind in order that he may see. The activity of metaphysical contemplation does not, then, offer a 'god's-eye view,' i.e., the simultaneous and panoptic vision of all things" (Nightingale 2004, 104).

Parvorum speculo

In between the analogy of the sun and the metaphor of the man with double vision, Prudentius interjects himself into the text to ponder the process of comparison and analogy, in a passage that reveals the inadequacy of human understanding:

> non conferre Deo velut aequiparabile quidquam
> ausim, nec Domino famulum conponere signum:
> ex minimis sed grande suum voluit Pater ipse
> coniectare homines, quibus ardua visere non est.
> parvorum speculo non intellecta notamus,
> et datur occultum per proxima quaerere verum.
> (H. 79–84)

> I wouldn't venture to compare any
> thing to God as if it were His equal,
> nor think a sign, His servant, to be His peer.
> But the Father Himself has willed that we
> deduce that He is great from smaller things,
> since we are not allowed to see or visit
> higher things. But looking in a mirror,
> we see in smaller things the images
> of what our minds can't comprehend, and He
> has granted us to search for hidden truth
> in the closest things.
> (H. 108–18)

This is a key passage in the poem. Prudentius moves from the analogy of the sun (on which no man can gaze without being blinded) to the metaphor of the mirror,[10] a progression that collates two famous passages from Saint Paul. In Romans 1:20, Paul argues that we come to know invisible things from visible evidence: *invisibilia enim ipsius a creatura mundi, per ea quae facta sunt intellecta, conspiciuntur.* ("For since the creation of the world His invisible attributes are clearly seen, being understood by the things that are made.")[11] And in 1 Corinthians 13:12, Paul uses the metaphor of the mirror to express the limitations of human understanding as opposed to the understanding of the soul after death: *videmus nunc per speculum in aenigmate tunc autem facie ad faciem nunc cognosco ex parte tunc autem cognoscam sicut et cognitus sum.* ("For now we see through a glass, darkly; but then face to face: now I know in part; but then shall I know even as also I am known.") *Per speculum in aenigmate*, translated by the King James Version as "through a glass darkly," literally means "through a mirror, in an enigma."

An *aenigma* is a riddle; it is also, as Augustine reminds us, a figure of speech, classified by some as a form of allegory.[12] It works through similitude and obscurity. Donatus defined it thus:

> Aenigma est obscura sententia per occultum similitudinem rerum, ut *mater me genuit, eadem mox gignitur ex me*, cum significet aquam in glaciem concrescere et ex eadem rursus effluere.
>
> Enigma is a statement that is obscure because of a hidden likeness of things, e.g., *my mother gave birth to me, she herself soon is born from me*, which means that water solidifies into ice and then flows back out of it.[13]

As Cook notes, an *aenigma* is a concealed likeness, a closed or hidden simile. A simile asserts that X is like Y; an *aenigma* makes the simile into a question: What is X like? Like all metaphors, an *aenigma* can provide pleasure and enlightenment, according to Aristotle: "For the mind seems to say, 'How true it is! but I missed it.' ... And clever riddles are agreeable for the same reason; for something is learnt."[14] Augustine, in his discussion of the Corinthians passage, offers a riddle from scripture as his example of the word's meaning: "An enigma is, to explain it briefly, an obscure allegory, as, e.g., 'The horseleech had three daughters,' and other like instances."[15] From the small riddle of the horseleech's daughters, Augustine moves quickly to larger enigmas (*De trin.* 15.9, emphasis added):

> Accordingly, as far as my judgment goes, as by the word glass he meant to signify an image, so by that of enigma any likeness you will, but yet one obscure, and difficult to see through. While, therefore, any likenesses whatever may be understood as signified by the apostle when he speaks of a glass and an enigma, so that they are adapted to the understanding of God, in such way as He can be understood; *yet nothing is better adapted to this purpose than that which is not vainly called His image.* Let no one, then, wonder, that we labor to see in any way at all, even in that fashion of

seeing which is granted to us in this life, viz. through a glass, in an enigma. For we should not hear of an enigma in this place if sight were easy. And this is a yet greater enigma, that we do not see what we cannot but see. For who does not see his own thought? And yet who does see his own thought, I do not say with the eye of the flesh, but with the inner sight itself? Who does not see it, and who does see it? Since thought is a kind of sight of the mind; whether those things are present which are seen also by the bodily eyes, or perceived by the other senses; or whether they are not present, but their likenesses are discerned by thought; or whether neither of these is the case, but things are thought of that are neither bodily things nor likenesses of bodily things, as the virtues and vices; or as, indeed, thought itself is thought of . . . or whether it be even evil, and vain, and false things that we are thinking of, with either the sense not consenting, or erring in its consent. (trans. HADDAN)

Though chronology precludes Prudentius having read *De trinitate*, Augustine's discussion nevertheless sheds light on Prudentius's use of the passage from Corinthians at this point in his argument. Augustine implies that humans are uniquely suited to understanding likenesses, *similitudines*, because we ourselves are made in the image of God. Man, because he is himself an image, has an inherent understanding of the process of similitude. At the same time, however, because man is an image, he is utterly unlike the divine Original he strives to comprehend (*De trin.* 15.11):

But this perfection of this image is one to be at some time hereafter. In order to attain this it is that the good master teaches us by Christian faith, and by pious doctrine, that "with face unveiled" from the veil of the law, which is the shadow of things to come, "beholding as in a glass the glory of the Lord," i.e., gazing at it through a glass, "we may be transformed into the same image from glory to glory, as by the Spirit of the Lord," as we explained above. When, therefore, this image shall have been renewed to perfection by this transformation, then we shall be like God, because we shall see Him, not through a glass, but "as He is," which the Apostle Paul expresses by "face to face." But now, who can explain how great is the unlikeness also, in this glass, in this enigma, in this likeness such as it is?

Augustine links Paul's use of *aenigma* to the process of reading scripture typologically, argues Eleanor Cook:

The Hebrew Scriptures are read as if they were "under the veil," to repeat Paul's expression. In typological terms, the Hebrew Scriptures become the Old Testament by this reading, wherein they shadow forth what stands clear in the New Testament. This is the first stage of seeing by means of a clearer *speculum* or mirror and in a less obscure enigma. The second stage will come at the end of time.... Augustine is emphatic that *aenigma* is a trope having to do with unlikeness as well as likeness. Rhetorical reading trains us to read how X is like *and unlike* Y.[16]

Through Augustine's explication of Paul's text it becomes easier to discern Prudentius's transitions as he moves from the analogy of the sun to the figure of the mirror to the man with distorted vision to Marcion's false doctrines. The clarity of the interpretive model laid out in the analogy of the sun gives way to the figure of the mirror and the search for hidden truth through enigmatic likeness. Pauline theology lays out an enigma that is what Cook (2006, 64–66) calls a masterplot: "Enigma, in the Pauline sense, holds as in a nutshell the Christian history of the world and time; its resolution points to eternity.... This kind of enigma will end in revelation, in light, in the dispersal of cloud, in the clarifying of the obscure, in the straightening of the labyrinthine." The masterplot tells us how the story will end—Prudentius does not need a plot in the *Hamartigenia* because his readers already know it. But while faith can look forward to revelation, the individual, encumbered with the consequences of sin, cannot see what will happen to his own character, so to speak, as the universal plot unfolds, and has no certainty that he can correctly decipher the signs that could lead him out of the maze.

Seeking truth through the interpretation of signs carries with it the possibility of misinterpretation. Just as our unreliable senses can lead us to misperceive the natural world, like the man who sees two suns, so our inherently imperfect understanding can lead us to an improper interpretation of scripture, like the dualist argument that there are two gods that Prudentius (deploying the rhetorical figure prosopopoeia) puts in the mouth of Marcion in lines 154–72 (Lat. 111–23)—an argument, as we will see in the next chapter, that Prudentius uses all of his rhetorical resources to counter, but which proves diabolically difficult to contain.

4. FALLING INTO LANGUAGE

MARCION'S SPEECH INTRODUCES the poisonous notion that the Creator God is responsible for evil:

"unus," ais, "tristi residet sublimis in arce,
auctor nequitiae, scelerum Deus, asper, iniquus,
qui quodcumque malum vitioso fervet in orbe
sevit, et anguino medicans nova semina suco
rerum principium mortis de fomite traxit."
  (H. 111–15)

"One sits on high," you say, "inside a grim
citadel: the author of wickedness,
the god of vices, harsh, unjust, who sowed
whatever ills ferment in this corrupted
globe. Imbuing his new spawn with snaky
poison, he struck the spark of our beginning
from death's combustible matter."
  (H. 154–60)

This insidious notion evokes a strong counteroffensive on Prudentius's part. In one of the poem's gestures of feigned orality, the narrator responds directly to Marcion:

haec tua, Marcion, gravis et dialectica vox est,
immo haec attoniti phrenesis manifesta cerebri.
  (H. 124–25)

  This voice
—oppressive, dialectical—is yours

Marcion; it's proof of the psychosis
of your stricken brain.
(H. 172-75)

Prudentius uses the Greek term *dialectica* to associate Marcion with the dialectic reasoning typical of ancient philosophy. In the dialectical process, truth is approached through a series of arguments and counterarguments; a favorite strategy of Socrates, who relied on this method, was to look for inconsistencies in his interlocutor's argument. Rational argument, logic, has led Marcion to a false conclusion, what Prudentius calls a *phrenesis manifesta*, obvious madness.[1] The true identity of Marcion's Creator God cannot be derived through the logic of dialectic. It must be derived through faith, and that is the gist of Prudentius's response. Rather than refuting Marcion's logic through argument, he asserts instead the collective knowledge of the faithful: "We know a father / of sin exists; we also know that he / is not a god at all" [*novimus esse patrem scelerum, sed novimus ipsum / haudquaquam tamen esse Deum*] (H. 175-77; Lat. 126-27).

Prudentius has used the rhetorical devices of prosopopoeia (giving Marcion a voice) and apostrophe (responding in propria persona to Marcion's speech) to present Marcion's argument as part of a dialectic process, *as if* the two were participating in a philosophical dialogue. Prudentius's adoption of the form, but not the substance, of dialectic, and his attribution of a *dialectica vox* to his heretical straw man may be seen as part of what Simon Goldhill (2009, 7) suggests is a general tendency in late antiquity for Christianity to move "towards hierarchy, with a commitment to certainty and the repression of difference ('heresy') as it increases its power as the religion of the Empire," and to be increasingly resistant to dialogue.[2]

Naming the Devil

After Prudentius has intervened in an apostrophe to establish the true identity of Marcion's god, he turns to ekphrasis, presenting the devil in an elaborately detailed and vivid description:

> quin immo gehennae
> mancipium, Stygio qui sit damnandus Averno,
> Marcionita Deus, tristis, ferus insidiator,
> vertice sublimis, cinctum qui nubibus atris
> anguiferum caput et fumo stipatur et igni,
> liventes oculos subfundit felle perusto
> invidia inpatiens iustorum gaudia ferre.
> hirsutos iuba densa umeros errantibus hydris
> obtegit et virides adlambunt ora cerastae.

ipsa manu laqueos per lubrica fila reflexos
in nodum revocat, facilique ligamine tortas
innectit pedicas nervosque in vincula tendit.
ars olli captare feras, animalia bruta
inretire plagis, retinacula denique caecis
indeprensa locis erranti opponere praedae.
   (H. 127–41)

                    No, he is damned
to servitude in hell, condemned to live
in Stygian Avernus—Marcion's God,
severe and grim, a treacherous betrayer,
his head erect, his snaky brow surrounded
by somber clouds, dense-wrapped in smoky flame.
Envy, who cannot stand to see the joys
of just men, fills his bruised and spiteful eyes
with burning gall. The roving snakes that crowd
his mane cover up his bristling shoulders,
while crested bright-green serpents lick his face.
With his hand he coaxes coils of twisted
cord in snares, and weaving tangled fetters
in easy knots, he stretches nets for traps.
It is his art to capture wild creatures,
to lie in wait for beasts, to set his snares
for wandering animals in hidden places,
undetected.
   (H. 177–94)

Prudentius is the first writer of biblical epic to portray the devil as an anthropomorphic creature rather than as the serpent of Genesis, setting a precedent that would culminate in Milton's charismatic Satan.[3] He endows this creation with significant attributes. Envy, *Invidia*, who can't endure the sight of the joys of the just, has filled his eyes with burning gall, giving him an extreme version of the flawed vision Prudentius described earlier.[4] His mane of twisted snakes associates him not only with the serpent of Genesis and with the writhing, vicious vipers described at length later in the poem, but with the petrifying figure of Medusa as well—*anguiferum caput* echoes Ovid's description of the head of Medusa at *Met.* 4.741, where Perseus gently lays the decapitated head on a cushion of seaweed so as not to bruise it as he washes his hands of her blood.[5] The writhing serpents are succeeded by coils and twists of ropes that serve as nets and snares. Prudentius's devil is a master of cunning intelligence, *metis*. His nets and snares associate him with the perils of sophistic language, just as his spokesman, Marcion, has been accused of possessing a *dialectica vox*.[6]

Thirteen lines into the description, the devil has his attributes—clouds, fire, serpents, nets, and snares—but no name. The strategy of withholding the name of a hero is common in epic, beginning with the *Odyssey*, where the *andra . . . polutropon* (*Od.* 1.1), "the man of many ways," who is the subject of the Muse's song, is not named until *Od.* 1.20. In the *Hamartigenia*, Prudentius identifies the unnamed devil typologically with the biblical figure Nebroth (Nimrod):

> hic ille est venator atrox, qui caede frequenti
> incautas animas non cessat plectere, Nebroth,
> qui mundum curvis anfractibus et silvosis
> horrentem scopulis versuto circuit astu,
> fraude alios tectisque dolis innectere adortus,
> porro giganteis alios luctando lacertis
> frangere, funereos late exercere triumphos.
>   (H. 142–48)

>   This one, this is Nimrod
> the savage hunter, one who never rests
> from punishing the careless souls of men
> with ceaseless slaughter. Cunningly, he circles
> the earth with its craggy peaks and tufted forests
> and winding labyrinthine paths, to trap
> some by fraud and hidden tricks, to wrestle
> others to the ground with his giant arms,
> and spread his deadly triumphs far and wide.
>   (H. 194–202)

Nimrod makes a brief appearance in Genesis 10:8–12: "Cush was the father of Nimrod, who grew to be a mighty warrior on the earth. He was a mighty hunter before the Lord; that is why it is said, 'Like Nimrod, a mighty hunter before the Lord.' The first centers of his kingdom were Babylon, Erech, Akkad and Calneh, in Shinar." Though a shadowy figure in the Bible, Nimrod grew to be an important figure in the exegetical tradition. He was associated with the giants, the offspring of the sons of heaven and the daughters of man, of Genesis 6 (hence his giant arms, *giganteis . . . lacertis*, 147).[7] Philo allegorically explains that giants represent those who honor earthly things more than heavenly ones: "For in truth he who is zealous for earthly and corruptible things always fights against and makes war on heavenly things and praiseworthy and wonderful natures, and builds walls and towers on earth against heaven. But those things which are [down] here are against those things which are [up] there. For this reason it is not ineptly said, 'a giant before (*enantion*) God,' which is clearly in opposition to the Deity. For the impious man is none other than the enemy and foe who stands against God."[8] Elsewhere Philo explains that Nimrod's name means "desertion," *automolēsis*, and says that he led the sons of the earth to surrender to the flesh, i.e., to desert God.[9] This explanation fits with the Jewish etymology of his name, from *mrd*, "rebel," and it is easy to see how Nimrod was identified with the rebellious king of Babylon, of whom Isaiah says, "How art thou fallen from heaven, O Lucifer, son of the morning! How art thou cut down to the ground, which didst weaken the nations! For thou hast said in thine heart, I will ascend into heaven, I will exalt my throne above the stars of God.... Yet thou shall be brought down to hell, to the sides of the pit." As early as the second century, this Lucifer was identified with the serpent of Genesis and with Satan, who first appears in the book of Job as "the adversary" or "prosecutor," an identification that was commonplace by Prudentius's day.[10]

Significantly for the *Hamartigenia*, there is a strong tradition associating Nimrod with linguistic confusion. His status as a hunter led him to be associated in the Jewish exegetical tradition with snares and sin: "He would trap men by their tongues and say to them: Depart from the laws of Shem and cling to the laws of Nimrod."[11] Augustine reflects a common tradition when he says that Nimrod was the builder of the Tower of Babel, where the language of men was confounded, so they could not understand one another's speech (Genesis 11).[12] As we will see, the association of the devil with linguistic confusion is of key importance in the *Hamartigenia*; this is one reason why Prudentius identifies Marcion's god not with Satan or Lucifer but with Nimrod, the master of snares and traps who is responsible for the loss of natural language. In addition, Nimrod was believed to be the first worshipper of idols, which would make him a logical prototype for Marcion, the archetypal heretic.[13]

When Prudentius counters Marcion's *dialectica vox* by asserting his true knowledge of Marcion's god (*novimus ... novimus*, line 126), his revelation turns out to be that Marcion's god is Nimrod. He does not use the name that we might expect, "Satan." However, the name Satan is suggested in the text through etymologizing wordplay. The most common derivation of Satan's name is from a Semitic root meaning "to be hostile toward, to accuse"; it carries the meaning of "adversary" or "prosecutor." There is an alternative etymology in Job 1:7, where Satan is first named in the Old Testament: "And the Lord said to Satan: 'From where do you come?' So Satan answered the Lord and said, 'From going to and fro on the earth, and from walking back and forth on it.'" The Hebrew verb used for "going to and fro" is from the root *šuṭ*, "to wander": according to this meaning of his name, Satan is "the Wanderer." As Prudentius's Nimrod, master of linguistic confusion, circles the earth on labyrinthine paths, he is revealed as a linguistic wanderer, living up to one etymology of "Satan," his true but suppressed name.

This complicated play of concealment and revelation of the devil's name is a striking feature of *Paradise Lost* as well. When Milton introduces the devil, he explicitly makes a puzzle out of his identity, introducing him not with his name, but with a question:

> Who first seduc'd them to that fowl revolt?
> Th' infernal Serpent; he it was, whose guile
> Stir'd up with Envy and Revenge, deceiv'd
> The Mother of Mankinde...
> (*PL* 1.33–36)

Instead of "Satan," Milton introduces "th' infernal Serpent," whose name is not revealed until line 82: "the Arch- Enemy, / And thence in Heav'n call'd Satan." As John Leonard argues, "There are some ways in which 'Satan' is the most questionable name in the poem."[14] For similar reasons, Milton was interested in the figure of Nimrod, who appears in *PL* 12 not identified as the devil, as he is in the *Hamartigenia*, but as the "mightie Hunter" and builder of the Tower of Babel:

> A mightie Hunter thence shall he be styl'd
> Before the Lord, as in despite of Heav'n,
> Or from Heav'n claming second Sovrantie;
> And from Rebellion shall derive his name.
> (*PL* 12.33–36)

The tyrant Nimrod and his followers build Babel to "get themselves a name" (12.45); it is ironic, then, that Milton never uses the "name" Nimrod. The angel Michael speaks the meaning of his name (Rebellion), but not the name itself. He also avoids naming Babel, calling it instead "Confusion":[15]

> Forthwith a hideous gabble rises loud
> Among the Builders; each to other calls
> Not understood, till hoarse, and all in rage,
> As mockt they storm; great laughter was in Heav'n
> And looking down, to see the hubbub strange
> And hear the din; thus was the building left
> Ridiculous, and the work Confusion nam'd.
> (*PL* 12.56–62)

Milton's treatment of the names "Nimrod" and "Babel"—concealing them, yet revealing them through their etymological meanings—is a form of enigmatic wordplay that illuminates the confusion that results from the loss of natural language. In creating this enigma about names, he follows in the footsteps of

Prudentius, who also significantly represses the devil's name. "Satan" is not simply postponed in the *Hamartigenia*, it does not appear at all in the poem, or indeed anywhere else in Prudentius's work.[16]

Seeing and Saying: Satan and the Fall of Language

Before the Fall of Adam comes the rebellion of Satan. Although created good, the devil turns to evil of his own free will when he becomes jealous of man:

> sed factus de stirpe bonus, bonitatis in usum
> proditus et primo generis de fonte serenus,
> deterior mox sponte sua, dum decolor illum
> inficit invidia stimulisque instigat amaris.
> arsit enim scintilla odii de fomite zeli
> et dolor ingenium subitus conflavit iniquum.
> viderat argillam simulacrum et structile flatu
> concaluisse Dei, dominum quoque conditioni
> inpositum, natura soli pelagique polique
> ut famulans homini locupletem fundere partum
> nosset et effusum terreno addicere regi.
> (H. 184–94)

>   And even he was good
> at first, and meant for goodness, clear and bright
> from the first beginning of his being.
> Soon, though, of his own free will he sank
> into evil, when Envy, that discolored
> creature, infected him and spurred him on
> with bitter pricks and goads. For a spark of hate
> struck by Envy, caught and blazed, and sudden
> anguish ignited his impatient mind.
> He had seen a simulacrum, fashioned
> of clay and warmed to life by God's own breath
> and given dominion over earth; he saw
> all of nature—earth and sky and ocean—
> had learned to pour forth harvests, and to give
> her riches liberally for the use of man,
> the earthly ruler.
> (H. 250–65)

Envy kindles a spark of hatred in the once serene angel. Given the central importance of the metaphor of sight in the poem, it is significant that Satan's fall is caused by envy, *invidia*, which in Latin is closely linked with the verb *video*, "to see." *Invideo*, the verb from which *invidia* is derived, means literally "to look askance at." Satan's *invidia* is kindled when he sees (*viderat*) the newly created man, who is described as a *simulacrum*, an imitation or copy, and his vision is skewed when he gazes jealously at man, a created being, instead of directing his eyes properly to God, the Creator.[17] His jealous gaze at man leads to the fallen angel's metamorphosis:

> inflavit fermento animi stomachante tumorem
> bestia deque acidis vim traxit acerba medullis,
> bestia sorde carens, cui tunc sapientia longi
> corporis enodem servabat recta iuventam,
> complicat ecce novos sinuoso pectore nexus,
> involvens nitidam spiris torquentibus alvum.
> (H. 195–200)

>   The savage beast swelled up,
> his heart disturbed by sour anger, and drew
> upon the strength within his acid marrow.
> Once he was a stainless creature: upright
> wisdom kept his tall young body free
> of knots. But look! In sinuous curves he coils
> himself in new complexities, and bends
> his shining belly in sliding spirals.
> (H. 265–72)

Satan undergoes a vivid transformation, poisoning himself from within with his own bile. Once kept straight by his wisdom (*erecta sapientia*), he develops the characteristic coils of a snake, in a scene later imitated by Milton.[18] In *Paradise Lost*, Satan had coils even before he lost his upright posture, but they were folded up on top of him:

> not with indented wave,
> Prone on the ground, as since, but on his reare,
> Circular base of rising foulds, that tour'd
> Fould above fould, a surging Maze; his Head
> Crested aloft, and Carbuncle his Eyes;
> With burnisht Neck of verdant Gold, erect
> Amid his circling Spires that on the grass
> Floated redundant....
> (PL 9.496–503)

Man's upright posture was conventionally associated with his superiority over the other animals, which gaze at the ground while man looks at the heavens. Satan's loss of erect posture thus marks his new distance from the divine. In the *Hamartigenia* this distancing from the divine culminates in the last step in the transformation of Satan, which immediately follows his loss of upright posture: the trifurcation of his tongue.

> simplex lingua prius varia micat arte loquendi
> et discissa dolis resonat sermone trisulco.
>   (*H.* 201–2)

>   His tongue,
> once single, now is treacherously split,
> and flickers with the art of varied speaking,
> its fissured words reechoing.
>   (*H.* 272–75)

His tongue, which had been single, *simplex,* before, now splits. Skilled in the art of eloquence, *arte loquendi,* it utters "fissured words," *sermone trisulco,* a phrase that echoes Vergil's description of a snake with a similarly three-forked tongue at *G.* 3.349 (*arduus ad solem et linguis micat ore trisulcis*), in a passage of great symbolic significance in the *Georgics.* As Richard Thomas suggests in his commentary (ad loc.), the snake in the *Georgics* is associated with the fiery heat of the Dog Star, which brings the destruction of crops, and it directly precedes a catalog of diseases culminating in the plague of Noricum, which signifies the destruction of the pastoral world and the ruin of the farmer's labor. In the symbolic scheme of the *Georgics,* the snake is the physical embodiment of the plague (*pestis acerba boum,* G. 3.409); his presence threatens the whole pastoral world with destruction. Prudentius keeps the georgic symbolism here: his serpent also introduces disaster to the natural world. But this serpent delivers his venom not through his fangs but through his *lingua,* which, as was the case with the irrepressibly verbal Saint Cyprian, carries the meanings of both the physical organ, "tongue," and that which the tongue produces, "language."

Natale caput vitiorum

The splitting of the devil's tongue has great symbolic importance: it is, Prudentius tells us, the fountainhead, *natale caput,* of all vices:

> Hinc natale caput vitiorum, principe ab illo
> fluxit origo mali, qui se corrumpere primum,
> mox hominem didicit nullo informante magistro.
> ultimus exitium subverso praeside mundus
> sortitur mundique omnis labefacta supellex.
>   (*H.* 203–7)

> And hence
> the origin, the source, the fountainhead
> of sin! The origin of evil flowed
> from that prince first: not needing any teacher
> he first discovered how to ruin himself,
> and soon he ruined man. The world—with all
> the earth's resources undermined, and man,
> its guardian, corrupted—met its doom.
>   (H. 275–82)

The splitting of the tongue, and the consequent corruption of language, is thus emphatically placed *at the origin* of human sin. No teacher other than Satan is required to corrupt man, and once man has been turned away *(subverso)* from God, the whole of creation falls with him *(mundus labefacta supellex)*. It is significant that this moment, when the devil's sin results in linguistic division, is followed immediately by the poem's first extended simile. If language were in its prelapsarian state, similes, like any other form of analogy, would not be necessary; language would be a transparent medium through which we would perceive reality. But since our experience of language is postlapsarian, analogy and other forms of figuration become necessary evils, as Prudentius has indicated through the analogy of the sun and the metaphor of the mirror. They convey meaning, but are both dangerous and unreliable, like the world after the end of the golden age.

The simile compares Satan to a highwayman robbing an unwary traveler. The image of the devil as a highwayman or robber was common in Christian literature.[19] Particularly relevant to the *Hamartigenia*'s simile are contemporary exegeses of the parable of the Good Samaritan:

> A certain man went down from Jerusalem to Jericho, and fell among thieves, who stripped him of his clothing, wounded him, and departed, leaving him half dead. Now by chance a certain priest came down that road. And when he saw him, he passed by on the other side. Likewise a Levite, when he arrived at the place, came and looked, and passed by on the other side. But a certain Samaritan, as he journeyed, came where he was. And when he saw him, he had compassion. (LUKE 10:30–33)

According to the interpretations of Ambrose and Augustine, the traveler is Adam; Jerusalem stands for Paradise; Jericho is either the mortal realm or the moon, which represents the mortal realm; the brigands are the devil and his henchmen, and the Good Samaritan is Christ. Thus the parable of the Good Samaritan is a version of the story of the fall of Adam and prefigures his redemption.[20] The simile of the robber is part of an image chain that links together a number of travelers in the poem: the Good Samaritan, Adam driven from Paradise, the Jews wandering in the wilderness, Lot and his wife fleeing from Sodom, Ruth and Naomi, the unnamed brothers at the crossroads, the exiled soul returning to her country, and the poet himself who prays that at the hour of death he will not be waylaid by fierce robbers. The traveler beset by dangers on the road is a familiar figure in Prudentius's other poetry as well. In the preface to his *Apotheosis*, in fact, it is introduced as the master trope for the whole poem, used to describe the difficulties of correct interpretation of doctrine in the face of heretical teachings.

> Est vera secta? te, Magister, consulo.
>   rectamne servamus fidem?
> an viperina non cavemus dogmata,
>   et nescientes labimur?
> artam salutis vix viam discernere est
>   inter reflexas semitas.
> tam multa surgunt perfidorun conpeta
>   tortis polita erroribus,
> obliqua sese conserunt divortia
>   hinc inde textis orbitis.
> quas si quis errans ac vagus sectabitur
>   rectum relinquens tramitem,
> scrobis latentis pronus in foveam ruet,
>   quam fodit hostilis manus,
> manus latronum, quae viantes obsidet
>   iter sequentes devium.
>   (*Apoth. praef.* 1–16)

> Are we on the true path?[21] Teacher, I consult you.
>   Are we preserving the right faith?
> Or are we not enough afraid of snaky teachings,
>   and already falling without knowing?
> It's almost impossible to discern
>   the narrow path of salvation amid these tortuous paths.
> So many crossroads, worn slippery from the twisted
>   wandering steps of those who betrayed the faith,
> rise up to meet us; so many oblique side paths multiply
>   this way and that, in woven coils.
> If someone, wandering and lost, will follow them,
>   deserting the right path,
> he will fall headlong into the pit of a hidden trap
>   dug by the enemy's hand,[22]
> by a band of robbers who attack
>   travelers who follow the wrong track.

The metaphor of the soul's journey from the visible to invisible reality through study and contemplation was a familiar one in Neoplatonic literature—one that Augustine corrects in *De doctrina* by asserting that the journey can be accomplished only by goodness of works and character, not by study, and only through the mediation of Christ, who is at once the destination and the path of the soul's journey.[23] In the *Apotheosis* passage Prudentius focuses on the perils of the journey, explicitly linking the coils and toils of deceptive language—the "snaky teachings" of the heretics—with the twisting labyrinth of interconnected roads that confuses the traveler, who tries vainly to discern the right path, and the robber who preys on him. Here it may be useful to compare Jerome's use of the figure of the reader as traveler, which Catherine Chin (2007) has analyzed. In three letters written in Bethlehem to Paulinus of Nola, Jerome uses "the language of travel in order to create an imagined Christian landscape, visible, however, only through the mediations of fragmented literary texts" (Chin 2007, 102). He compares Paulinus's study of scripture to journeys made by famous figures of antiquity: Plato to Sicily, Apollonius to India, Pythagoras to Egypt, Paul to Jerusalem. Chin argues that Jerome conceives of the material to be learned as the space into which the reader travels: "Jerome's conflation of reading and travel serves fundamentally to suggest the goal of an ideal Christian space enclosed in texts" (Chin 2007, 105), what Chin calls a Christian utopia. Jerome's strategy, however, presents him with a problem: different readers may map different paths into the ideal Christian space and arrive at the wrong meaning. His concern over this possibility emerges in letter 53.7, where he castigates those who "juxtapose otherwise incongruous passages in order to make up their own meanings, as if this were some great thing, and not the faultiest teaching method of all, to distort the meaning and to force the reluctant scriptures to their bidding." Chin argues that in order for Jerome to cast Christianity as a utopian space where a traveler might arrive, he must also imagine that travelers journeying toward it might get lost. As a scriptural exegete, he "must chart specific interpretive paths rather than claim that all ways lie open" (Chin 2007, 109).

The Unwary Traveler

In the *Hamartigenia* too, the traveler must make his or her way warily along the paths of interpretation. Prudentius develops this theme in relation to the devil as the poem moves from Satan's acquisition of his twisting coils and split tongue to the figure of the highwayman preying on an unwary traveler:

> non aliter quam cum incautum spoliare viantem
> forte latro adgressus, praedae prius inmemor, ipsum
> ense ferit dominum, *pugnae nodumque moramque*
> quo pereunte trahat captivos victor *amictus*
> iam non obstanti *locuples* de corpore praedo,

sic homini subiecta domus, ditissimus orbis
scilicet in facilem domino peccante ruinam
lapsus erile malum iam tunc vitiabilis hausit.
    (H. 208-15)

No different from a thief who chances on
a careless traveler, to rob him: first
unmindful of the spoils, he stabs the master
(the struggle is slow and difficult), and then,
victorious, he strips the spoils from
the unresisting corpse that's made him rich.
Just so the mansion under man's dominion,
the rich and fruitful earth, fell easily to ruin
when its master sinned and, prone to sin
already, drained to the dregs its master's evil.
    (H. 283-92)

In this simile, the robber is the devil; his victim, the unwary traveler, is man.[24] The phrase *pugnae nodumque moramque,* used to describe the traveler, is an allusion to Abas, a Latin ally of Aeneas, the first to fall victim to the young Italian warrior Lausus in *Aeneid* 10.[25] The context—heroic combat on the battlefield—is somewhat incongruous for the Prudentius passage: far from meeting the traveler honorably on the battlefield, as Lausus meets Abas, the highwayman catches him unawares and ambushes him. The relevance of the allusion lies not so much in the battle scene as in the figure of Abas, who appears earlier in *Aeneid* 10 as the second in the catalog of Etruscan allies of Aeneas:

una torvus Abas: huic totum insignibus armis
agmen et aurato fulgebat Apolline puppis.
    (*Aen.* 10.171-72)

   Fierce Abas is sailing alongside,
His unit all fitted out with elaborate armour, his vessel
Glistening in light with its figurehead wrought as a gilded Apollo.[26]

Abas and his men are singled out for the richness of their arms and their ship, whose figurehead is a golden image of Apollo. In addition to his own men, Abas leads a contingent of men from Elba, characterized by the wealth of its mines. The allusion to Abas associates Prudentius's traveler with a figure of great wealth, and thus underscores the richness of the raiment, *amictus,* stolen by the highwayman.

A parallel passage in the *Psychomachia* helps explain the significance of the clothing stolen by the devil in his figurative guise as the highwayman. Pride (Superbia) relates the importance of the Vices' influence on humanity by claiming credit for the fact that Adam clothed himself in skins: "And venerable Adam put on a garment of skins—naked to this day, had he not followed my teachings" (*pellitosque habitus sumpsit venerabilis Adam / nudus adhuc, ni nostra foret praecepta secutus, Psy.* 226–27). Adam's original nakedness followed by his acquisition of clothing, as Mastrangelo (2008, 101) puts it, "exegetically translates to before and after the Fall, paradise and the world of suffering, immortality and mortality." Man's decision to clothe himself is the first visible sign of sin.[27] If Adam's primitive clothing is a mark of the original Fall, rich clothing is a mark of further degradation, as Prudentius will make explicit later in the poem, in his discussion of the vices of women and effeminate men.[28]

Many of the terms that Prudentius employs in the robber simile are terms that associate the theft with rhetorical ornament. The world that falls as a result of man's sin is described as *supellex* in line 207, a word that means "furnishings" or "outfit," but which was commonly used as a rhetorical term to describe mental furniture or rhetorical ornament, often disparagingly.[29] Prudentius uses the word at *Pe.* 11.130 as well, in a context that explores issues of interpretability and deceptive language.[30] *Amictus*, "cloak," can also be used figuratively to mean rhetorical ornament,[31] just as the related verb *amicio* can mean "to clothe with words" (see *OLD*, s.v. *amicio* 3). And *locuples*, the word that describes the successful highwayman, has a root meaning of "rich" or "ample," and was used specifically to describe a rich or copious rhetorical style.[32] In short, the corruption of the created world that results from man's fall and from Satan's original sin *also* represents the theft of rhetoric from man, both its richness and its power to conceal now appropriated by the devil. The use of this "original simile," the first such figure in the *Hamartigenia*, to describe the results of original sin reenacts man's loss at the level of the text, for a simile by its very nature represents a replacement or supplementation of an absent original by a substitute.

Thus the appearance of Satan introduces the first sustained simile in the *Hamartigenia*, a simile that reveals the failure of language to represent truth directly. From the simile of the highwayman, the text then turns to the topos of the corruption of the material world, symbolized by the advent of threats to agriculture. The appearance of the figure of the robber has triggered a universal catastrophe:

Then it was that the malignant land
from its infertile soil bore hybrid crops
and flimsy burrs and weeds, and spoiled the grain
with useless straw. Now savage lions learned
to kill the shepherd and drain the guiltless cattle
of blood, and rip apart with savage jaws
young bulls already broken to the yoke.
The wolf, too, irked by plaintive bleating, burst

boldly into crowded pens at midnight. Skill,
experienced in cruel stratagems,
stained every beast, and craft honed twisted senses
keen: although a wall surrounds a blooming
garden, or thick hedgerows guard the vineyard,
the devastating locust will devour
the budding plants, and wild birds attack
and scatter clustered grapes.
  (H. 293–308; Lat. 216–29)

Once the cosmic bonds that maintain order in the universe are ruptured, nature runs riot. Even the orderly progress of time is disrupted. In Prudentius's anachronistic narrative sequence, the advent of Satan is immediately followed by the corruption of the natural order, symbolized by the weeds in the fields, the herdsman threatened by lions, the sheepfold attacked by wolves, and locusts and birds destroying the garden, despite the fact that Adam and Eve have not even appeared in the text yet and humanity has not yet moved from the effortless joy of paradise to the toil of human agriculture.[33]

The trigger for this cosmic collapse is man, whose life, says Prudentius, provides a negative exemplum. Man and the created universe are typologically linked; the fall of man sets the pattern for the fall of the creation:

exemplum dat vita hominum, quo cetera peccent
vita hominum, cur quidquid agit Vesania et Error
suppeditant, ut Bella fremant, ut fluxa Voluptas
diffluat, inpuro fervescat ut igne Libido,
sorbeat ut cumulos nummorum faucibus amplis
gurges Avaritiae, finis quam nullus habendi
temperat aggestis addentem vota talentis.
Auri namque Fames parto fit maior ab auro.
inde seges scelerum, radix et sola malorum,
dum scatebras fluviorum omnes et operta metalla
eliquat Ornatus solvendi leno Pudoris . . .
  (H. 250–60)

    It's human life that gives
the pattern for the world's sin—human life!
Madness and Error stimulate our actions,
causing Wars to rage, and Pleasure to flood
the world, and Lust to burn with filthy fire,
and hungry Greed to suck down heaps of coins
with gaping jaws. No limit of possessing

slows Greed from adding hope for more and more
to money she's amassed. The thirst for gold
grows when gold's acquired. Hence a harvest
of woes, sole root of evil, while Ornament,
a pimp for dissipated Honor, pans
for gold in rushing streams and digs for hidden
ores . . .
   (H. 333–46)

As we saw in the allegory of the sun at the opening of the *Hamartigenia*, where nature provides the sun as a sign that reveals the nature of God, exempla from the natural world are theoretically able to lead man from confusion to truth. Here, after the intrusion of the devil into the text has introduced an interpretive crisis, the poem reveals the terrifying negative aspect of the typological relation between man and the natural world. Rather than setting the pattern that leads the world toward truth, man's exemplum unleashes the forces of madness and error (*vesania et error*). The interpretive model held up earlier in the poem through the analogy of the sun is inaccessible to the postlapsarian traveler wandering the paths of error.

5. UNDER ASSAULT

> *Remove their swelling epithetes thick laid*
> *As varnish on a Harlots cheek ...*
>
> MILTON, *Paradise Regained*

IN THE *HAMARTIGENIA*, cosmic collapse leads immediately to a condemnation of women's greed and vanity, epitomized by cosmetics, and of the inappropriate clothing and disgraceful behavior of effeminate men. Although it makes little sense chronologically or causally, there is nevertheless a logic to the way in which Prudentius moves directly from describing the corruption of the cosmos to describing the sin of excessive adornment. *Kosmos* is the Greek word for order or arrangement, and *cosmetics*, inappropriate adornment, are man's perversion of God's creative ordering of the universe. As we will see, the excesses of which women and effeminate men are accused are thematically related to the issues of figuration and interpretation raised by the simile of the robber and by man's status as a perverted exemplum for the universe.

Leading Prudentius's parade of human vices is the made-up woman (who, according to Tertullian's *De cultu feminarum*, is a living exemplum of Eve).[1] Tirades against feminine cosmetics are a commonplace of the Roman literary tradition, particularly in satirical and moral works, and the topos has been well analyzed by Amy Richlin and Victoria Rimell.[2] As Ovid demonstrates in his *Medicamina faciei feminae*, cosmetics could be associated with culture and refinement. *Mundus muliebris*, the legal term for women's equipment (personal property allowed to women), may be derived from *mundus* meaning "sky, universe, or world," just as the Greek root *kosm-* in cosmetics is derived from *kosmos*, the word for "universe." These words associate cosmetics with the pleasing order of the universe. *Cultus*, meaning "cultivation" or "culture," represents the process of taming the natural world and bringing it to a pleasing level of refinement. Ovid programmatically associates *cultus* with the agricultural processes of plowing, weeding, and grafting in *Medicamina* 1–10. Rimell, discussing the overlap between the allied projects of agricultural cultivation, the cultivation of feminine beauty, the imposition of imperial culture, and art, says of these lines:

Cultivation is empire's project, and in Ovid's opening lines, woman represents a colonized barbarian territory or one of many exotic imports to be processed by civilizing artistry: the didactic *discite* (line 1) soon slips into steely sounding reporting (*cultus humum sterilem Cerealia pendere iussit/munera*, "Cultivation ordered the sterile earth to yield the gifts of wheat," 3–4). We don't need to put a great deal of pressure on these lines to imagine that it is *she* that is to be plowed into shape, then dipped and dyed like a raw fleece (*vellera saepe eadem Tyrio medicantur aeno*, 9); that *her* sterile "field" is to be violently weeded of "devouring briers" *(mordaces interiere rubi,* 4): and that the bitter juices of *her* fruit are destined to be sweetened by intensive farming. Her pulchritude, we are later told, will be violently despoiled by age (*formam populabitur aetas,* 45), calling for surgery at the hands of Rome's craftsmen, who will carve her up into bite-sized titillations (*sectile deliciis ... ebur,* 10).[3]

In the opening of the *Medicamina*, the woman's body is like a wild field, needing cultivation. In the third book of the *Ars amatoria*, Ovid associates the body cultivated by makeup with the beauty of modern Rome and its splendid architecture. But Ovid elevates makeup to the level of high culture in order to mock traditional values: as Rimell says, the *Medicamina* is "Ovid's most explicit and concentrated packaging of a twisted moral code, which not only privileges contrivance and novelty over primitiveness and tradition, but also markets *cultus* as a means to *improve* and emancipate nature." For Ovid, makeup is an *ars* that closely resembles his own poetic *ars*, working with raw material that requires enormous labor to refine and transform, and standing for masquerade and mutability.

In most Roman discussions of the topic, however, makeup is associated not positively with art and agriculture, but negatively with medicine and poison.[4] Tertullian puts a Christian spin on the topos in his *De cultu feminarum*: he blames woman (placing Eve firmly at the origin of sin in the very first sentence of the treatise) for a host of ills that plague humanity, and ascribes the invention of women's adornment to fallen angels who mated with the daughters of men.[5]

In the *Hamartigenia*, contemplation of cosmic collapse, spurred on by man's negative exemplum, leads seamlessly to the subject of cosmetics, and the first woman to appear in the text, usurping Eve, is generic Woman (*femina*, H. 265), elaborately adorned and made-up. Prudentius castigates her for the vice of excessive ornament, beginning with an attack on her jewelry and ending with condemnation of her makeup:

> nec enim contenta decore
> ingenito externam mentitur femina formam
> ac, velut artificis Domini manus inperfectum

> os dederit, quod adhuc res exigat aut hyacinthis
>   pingere sutilibus redimitae frontis in arce,
> colla vel ignitis sincera incingere sertis,
> auribus aut gravidis virides suspendere bacas,
> nectitur et nitidis concharum calculus albens
> crinibus aureolisque riget coma texta catenis.
> taedet sacrilegas matrum percurrere curas,
> muneribus dotata Dei quae plasmata fuco
> inficiunt, ut pigmentis cutis inlita perdat
> quod fuerat, falso non agnoscendo colore.
> haec sexus male fortis agit, cur pectore in arto
> mens fragilis facili vitiorum fluctuat aestu.
>   (H. 264-78)

> For Woman, not content with natural beauty,
> puts on borrowed glamour; she even binds
> the pearly stones from seashells in her gleaming
> hair, or plaits her braids with golden chains,
> as if the hand of God, the master craftsman,
> had left her face unfinished, so she had
> to decorate her brow with woven sapphires,
> wind blazing gems around her flawless neck,
> or weight her ears with dangling emerald stones.
> It would be dull to run in detail through
> the sacrilegious efforts made by married
> women, who stain with dye the gifts with which
> God endowed their forms. Makeup now
> destroys the former beauty of their skin,
> unrecognizable beneath its coat
> of false color—but that's the weaker sex.
> Within the narrow confines of her breast
> a tide of sins batters her fragile mind.
>   (H. 350-67)

Unlike some of his predecessors in invective against woman, Prudentius's main concern here is the deception inherent in the use of makeup rather than its capacity to lead men astray into adultery. His woman indulges in necklaces, tiaras, hair ornaments, and—worst of all—makeup, which is distressing because it renders her skin unrecognizable (*non agnoscenda*). *Ornatus* is deceptive, whether it adorns a woman or a text. Unlike the *figura* of Cain and Abel, which Prudentius interpreted with such confidence in the preface (*agnosco nempe quem haec figura denotet*), the face, *figura,* of the made-up woman is impossible to read.[6]

In interpreting this passage in the light of Prudentius's overall concern with figuration, it is helpful to keep in mind that many of the terms used to describe feminine adornment in this passage and in earlier diatribes overlap with terms taken from rhetoric. In the realm of rhetoric, figural ornament, like women's makeup, is both potentially useful to create *munditia* (elegance) and dangerous if applied to excess. Cicero discusses the proper application of *ornatus* in the *Orator*, at the beginning of a section on figured language, and employs the metaphor of made-up women to explain the difference between appropriate and inappropriate adornment:[7]

> For just as some women are said to be more beautiful when unadorned—this very lack of ornament becomes them—so this plain style gives pleasure even when unembellished: there is something in both cases which lends greater charm, but without showing itself. Also all noticeable ornament, pearls as it were, will be excluded; not even curling-irons will be used; all cosmetics, artificial white and red, will be rejected; only elegance and neatness will remain. . . . He will be modest in his use of what may be called the orator's stock-in-trade. (*supellex*). For we do have after a fashion a stock-in-trade, in the stylistic embellishments (*ornamentis*), partly in thought and partly in words.[8]

Excessive ornamentation leads to a rhetorical style that is highly suspect, and one that Roman writers characterize in terms that suggest gender slippage. Seneca, in particular, offers a clear-cut example of the association between excess in rhetoric and effeminacy in his vivid description of the rhetorical style of the famous Maecenas, which he compares with Maecenas's effeminate dress, hairstyle, and gait.[9]

This gender slippage is evident in Prudentius as well. His text moves immediately from a condemnation of women's cosmetics to an attack on pathic homosexuals and eunuchs, who supply another example of *cultus* put to bad use. As men, their function is to rule and govern woman:[10]

> quid quod et ipse caput muliebris corporis et rex,
> qui regit invalidam propria de carne resectam
> particulam, qui vas tenerum dicione gubernat,
> solvitur in luxum? cernas mollescere cultu
> heroas vetulas, opifex quibus aspera membra
> finxerat et rigidos duraverat ossibus artus,
> sed pudet esse viros . . .
>   (H. 279–85)

And what about the fact that Man—the head
of a woman's body, the king who rules the small

and fragile creature carved from his own flesh,
he who rules the tender vessel with
his governance—is also dissipated
in hedonism? Look at the aging athletes,
softened by good living, men to whom
the Maker gave hard bodies and strong limbs
scaffolded by bones. Yet they're ashamed
of being men . . .
   (H. 368-77)

The language of the passage reflects the confusion generated by effeminate men, whose collapsing of gender categories through their improper imitation of women (an imitation achieved by means of woman's emblem, ornament) is not only castigated but also reflected in the text. The description of the feminized male falls into three clauses: he is the *caput muliebris corporis,* "the head of the woman's body," who rules *invalidam propria de carne resectam particulam,* "the small and fragile creature carved from his own flesh," and who governs the *vas tenerum,* "the tender vessel," with his judgment. Each of these phrases exemplifies a collapse of categories on a linguistic level. As the *caput muliebris corporis,* man is the head in the metaphorical sense of "ruler," but if one takes the phrase more literally, it would suggest that the body of the effeminate male is already feminized: his head is on the body of a woman.[11] The second and third phrases also suggest gender confusion on a grotesquely graphic level. Given the context—Prudentius is castigating effeminate men and eunuchs—the words "small and fragile creature carved from his own flesh" bring to mind severed testes, and this connotation is strengthened by the next phrase, *vas tenerum,* for *vas* is a commonly used term for the penis.[12] Thus each term that ought to describe the proper relation between the sexes (male as head, woman as body; male as king, woman as his subordinate; male as governor, woman as weak vessel) also carries within it another level of meaning in which men are marked as effeminized and castrated.[13]

Images of looseness, limpness, and flowing ruin the integrity of the hard male body as Prudentius continues his attack, drawn from the long tradition of diatribes against *luxus* in the Latin tradition. He singles out textiles as the emblem of the effeminate male's excessive ornament:[14]

   quaerunt vanissima quaeque
quis niteant, genuina leves ut robora solvant.
vellere non ovium, sed Eoo ex orbe petitis
ramorum spoliis, fluitantes sumere amictus
gaudent et durum scutulis perfundere corpus.

additur ars, ut fila herbis saturata recoctis
inludant varias distincto stamine formas.
(H. 285-91)

[They] chase whatever vanities
will make them beautiful, and foolishly
dissolve their native strength. Flowing robes
delight them—robes not made of wool from sheep
but culled from the spoil of Oriental trees,
and diamond shapes and checkered patterns ripple
when they flex their muscles. They invented
the art of steeping threads in dye to make
figures in different-colored fibers.
(H. 377-85)

Weaving, whether of garlands or fabric, is a metaphor ubiquitously associated with the creation of literary texts in antiquity, and Prudentius uses it frequently of his own craft.[15] In this passage, however, Prudentius associates the art of weaving with poison (*fila herbis saturata recoctis*), in words that recall *Georgics* 2.458-66, a passage that condemns various aspects of urban living, including the customary morning *salutatio,* garments embroidered with gold, bronzes, dyed fabric, and perfumed oil.[16] In both passages, the language used for the dying of wool is suggestive of poison and of makeup *(herbis saturata recoctis; fucatur lana veneno)* and in both the verb *inludo* is used to describe elaborate embroidery, but also to suggest that the act of embellishing is inherently deceptive and unnatural.[17]

Performance Anxiety

Prudentius's feminized man, with his flexible limbs and flowing, patterned robes, is not simply a stock character from satire and moral invective. From the details Prudentius describes, it is likely that he intends us to understand a pantomime dancer, a figure that provoked deep anxieties in antiquity, especially in Christian writers. Pantomime dancers were solo performers who acted out stories from mythology through gesture and movement. Although they themselves performed in silence, they were accompanied by a chorus of singers and musicians. The invention of pantomime was attributed to two Greeks, Pylades and Bathyllus, who introduced it during the reign of Augustus. As Ruth Webb notes, "In its wordless communication it was truly an international art form, fitting the ambitions of the new Principate."[18] Pantomime performers wore masks with closed mouths (as opposed to the open-mouthed masks of tragedy and the unmasked performance of mime actors); wore ankle-length silk robes, often elaborately embroidered with gold; and, as Cassiodorus tells us, they played all the roles in a performance piece: "The same body represents Hercules and Venus, presents a woman in a man's body, makes a king and a soldier, shows an old man and a young man, so that this varied art of imitation would make you think that in a single person there were many people."[19] *Anthologia latina* 100 describes a pantomime dancer in terms that emphasize gender confusion and the playing of multiple roles:

> mascula femineo declinans pectora fluxu
> atque aptans lentum sexum ad utrumque latus,
> ingressus scenam populum saltator adorat.
> . . . .
> tot linguae quot membra viro, mirabilis ars est
> quae facit articulos ore silente loqui.
>
> Bending his masculine breast with feminine flow, and suiting his pliant torso to either sex, the dancer enters the stage and salutes the crowd. . . . He has as many tongues as he has limbs: it's an amazing art that makes his gestures speak while his mouth is silent.

Webb's analysis of performance culture in late antiquity explores the ways in which the pantomime's "signifying body" was read by late antique audiences. Pantomime evoked strong emotions, ranging from the passionate admiration of devoted fans to the loathing and fear of many Christian writers. The theater, with its enhanced visual display, was for the Christian a particularly dangerous place, a place where the soul was exposed to assault through the senses. The idea that the senses were gateways through which the soul could be attacked appears explicitly in Prudentius's contemporary John Chrysostom, who describes the soul of the young boy as a city to be ruled over by watchful parents:

> Suppose that the outer walls and four gates, the senses, are built. The whole body shall be the wall, as it were, the gates are the eyes, the tongue, the hearing, the sense of smell, and, if you will, the sense of touch. It is through these gates that the citizens of the city go in and out; that is to say, it is through these gates that thoughts are corrupted or rightly guided.
> (JOHN CHRYSOSTOM, *On Vainglory and the Education of the Young*, 27)[20]

Of all the senses, Chrysostom says, the most dangerous is sight, which is

> another gate, fairer than those others but difficult to guard, beautiful. It has many little postern gates and not only sees but is seen if well fashioned. Here strict laws are needed, the first being: *Never send thy son to the*

theater that he may not suffer utter corruption through his ears and eyes.
(*On Vainglory*, 55–56)

The eye was conceived of as active rather than passive; the ray it emits physically touches the object it views. Viewer and viewed were connected; the external object had the power to enter the viewer's mind—hence the danger of sight to Chrysostom. As Miller puts it, the act of seeing could be dangerous because "the eye could wither, devour, and de-soul the object of its gaze" (Miller 2005, 30). Augustine, railing against the "lust of the eye," identifies public performances as places where the eye is exposed to addictive pleasures: "What evils vulgar, shameless curiosity causes, the lust of the eyes, the avid craving for frivolous shows and spectacles, the madness of the stadiums, the fighting of contests for no reward" (*Serm.* 313a.3).[21]

Prudentius follows a similar train of thought: he moves from the description of the pantomime-like effeminate male, weakened by self-indulgence, to a description of the dangers of the five senses, whose frailty leaves us unable to distinguish appearance from reality:

> omnia luxus habet nostrae vegetamina vitae,
> sensibus in quinque statuens quae condidit auctor.
> auribus atque oculis, tum naribus atque palato
> quaeritur infectus vitiosis artibus usus;
> ipse etiam toto pollet qui corpore tactus
> palpamen tenerum blandis ex fotibus ambit.
> pro dolor! ingenuas naturae occumbere leges
> captivasque trahi regnante libidine dotes!
> perversum ius omne viget, dum quidquid habendum
> omnipotens dederat studia in contraria vertunt.
> (H. 298–307)

> The Creator
> placed our vital powers in our senses:
> self-indulgence now controls all five!
> The use we make of ears and eyes, of nose
> and palate, is ruined by vice: even touch,
> which rules all of our body, now solicits
> the sensuous caress of heated lotions.
> Oh, what anguish! Nature's laws lie low,
> her captured dowry dragged behind the tyrant
> Lust. Perverted justice prospers; every
> thing that God Almighty gave to men,
> they twist to different ends.
> (H. 392–403)

Like Chrysostom, Prudentius employs the imagery of a city under siege in his description of the assault on the soul through the path of the senses: our perceptions, which he calls the gifts or dowries of nature, are described as captive women dragged behind their conqueror, Lust (*captivasque trahi regnante libidine dotes*, *H.* 305). And, like Chrysostom and Augustine, he fixes on the image of the theater, and uses theatrical vocabulary, to epitomize the dangers that enter the soul through the eye:

> idcircone, rogo, speculatrix pupula molli
> subdita palpebrae est, ut turpia semivirorum
> membra theatrali spectet vertigine ferri,
> incestans miseros foedo oblectamine visus?
> (*H.* 308–11)

>   I ask you,
> was the watchful pupil set below
> the delicate lid in order to pollute
> its sight with gross delight, or watch the foul
> bodies of transvestites swept away
> by floods of stage emotion?
> (*H.* 403–8)

The "foul bodies of transvestites," *turpia membra semivirorum*, that he singles out here again recall the pantomime dancer who appears often in Christian discourse "as a figure for the waves of passion that sweep through and undermine the individual" (Webb 2008, 204). The pantomime dancer's seductive fluidity, his ability to transform his identity and gender, and his power to evoke violent emotion in his audience make him a perfect emobdiment of the anxieties about identity and integrity that clearly underlie the *Hamartigenia*. And through the figure of the dancer, Prudentius returns once more to the vexed question of representation, for it is the dancer's uncannily perfect representation of other people, his mastery of mimesis, that lies at the heart of his disturbing power. There are two main senses of mimesis: reenactment, and the reproduction of the appearance of a thing in a different medium. As Webb argues,

> The two are never entirely separable and are liable to bleed into one another, allowing theatrical *mimesis* to be understood as a defective copy, particularly when it involved the stylized enactment of pantomime.... These are men pretending to be women so therefore they are (from an antitheatrical point of view) defective, uncategorizable, and unnatural. But the potency of mimesis also means that the spectator of the pantomime is consequently at risk of being infected by this very indeterminacy. (WEBB 2008, 190)

The ability to distinguish appearance from reality is, therefore, vital to maintaining the integrity of the soul, a point Prudentius makes at the conclusion of his exposé of the dangers of the senses:

> felix qui indultis potuit mediocriter uti
> muneribus parcumque modum servare fruendi,
> quem locuples mundi species et amoena venustas
> et nitidis fallens circumflua copia rebus
> non capit, ut puerum, nec inepto addicit amori,
> qui sub adumbrata dulcedine triste venenum
> deprendit latitare boni mendacis operto.
> (H. 330–36)

> The man who is able to find the golden mean
> is happy—the man who can with moderation
> enjoy the gifts he has been given, and use
> them sparingly. The rich appearance of this
> world, its lovely charm, the overflowing
> abundance of its glittering toys cannot
> trick or capture him as if he were
> a child, cannot enslave him to a love
> unsuitable, if once he has discovered
> beneath the sweet appearance of a seeming
> good the deadly poison that lurks inside.
> (H. 431–41)

Praise of moderation and the golden mean is, of course, a widespread literary topos in antiquity. Prudentius engages in particular with Lucretius, who similarly praises moderation of appetite at the opening of *De rerum natura* 2. Prudentius signals his interest in Lucretius through an allusion to a famous line of Vergil's *Georgics*, "*felix qui potuit rerum cognoscere causas.*" Vergil's fortunate man who understands the causes of nature is almost certainly a reference to Lucretius, and perhaps signals, through the evocation of the didactic genre, the therapeutic nature of Prudentius's didactic verse.

In this passage Prudentius conflates two famous Lucretian images—the child terrified by the dark, and the child tricked into drinking his medicine by means of honey smeared on the rim of his cup. In the opening to *DRN* 2, Lucretius compares men caught up in the pursuit of pleasures and wealth and ensnared by fear of death to a child afraid of the dark:

> nam vel uti pueri trepidant atque omnia caecis
> in tenebris metuunt, sic nos in luce timemus

inter dum, nihilo quae sunt metuenda magis quam
quae pueri in tenebris pavitant finguntque futura.
hunc igitur terrorem animi tenebrasque necessest
non radii solis neque lucida tela diei
discutiant, sed naturae species ratioque.
   (*DRN* 2.55–61)

For we, like children frightened of the dark,
Are sometimes frightened in the light—of things
No more to be feared than fears that in the dark
Distress a child, thinking they may come true.
Therefore this terror and darkness of the mind
Not by the sun's rays, nor the bright shafts of day,
Must be dispersed, as is most necessary,
But by the face of nature and her laws.[22]

Similarly, Lucretius famously compares his own poetry to honey smeared on a cup of bitter medicine—the sweetness of the verse masks the bitterness of Epicurean doctrine, which, despite its initial unpleasantness, will ultimately cure the soul. In Prudentius's inversion of these motifs, the fortunate man is protected from the assault of worldly pleasures by his discovery that beneath the sweet appearance of this world's beauties lies not medicine, but rather deadly poison. Where Lucretius asserts that a true understanding of nature will dispel the darkness of the disturbed mind, Prudentius suggests that the appearance of nature itself, as far as we can perceive it through our flawed senses, is actually poison deceptively disguised as beauty. This marks a significant change from the opening of the poem, where the analogy of the sun was used to argue that contemplation of nature could lead to apprehension of divine unity.

The *Hamartigenia*'s deep distrust of the senses, and the anxiety Prudentius expresses about performance in particular, may help explain his choice of didactic rather than heroic epic as the vehicle for his study of sin—a choice that his marked allusion to Lucretius at this point in the text underlines.[23] The "feigned orality" of the *Hamartigenia*, which frames the exploration of the topic of sin as a dialogue between poet and interlocutor, offers the poet the opportunity to stage an interior performance in the mind's eye of the reader, thus using all the weapons available in the arsenal of rhetoric—enargeia, ekphrasis, apostrophe, etc.,—and at the same time lessens the chances of the audience being seduced by the dangers that attend actual performances. In a sense, though, this only displaces the problem from the performance space to the mind of the reader.

The bleak appraisal that beneath the beauty of the world of appearances lies poison marks a shift in the argument. The apprehension that the beauties our senses perceive mask poison leads to a standard Manichaean critique: that if there is evil in the world, God must be responsible for it, for he created all things. Prudentius immediately moves to fend off this line of attack:

> sed fuit id quondam nobis sanctumque bonumque
> principio rerum, Christus cum conderet orbem.
> vidit enim Deus esse bonum velut ipse Moyses
> historicus mundi nascentis testificatus,
> "vidit," ait, "Deus esse bonum quodcumque creavit."
> hoc sequar, hoc stabili conceptum mente tenebo,
> inspirante Deo quod sanctus vaticinator
> prodidit antiquae recolens primordia lucis,
> esse bonum quidquid Deus et Sapientia fecit.
>   (*H.* 337–45)

> Once it was holy and good for us, when God,
> in the beginning, created the universe.
> God saw that it was good indeed, as Moses,
> our historian, bore witness—Moses,
> who wrote the story of the infant world
> and said, "The Lord saw that everything
> He made was good." And I will follow this,
> and steadily hold within my mind the concept
> uttered by the holy seer, inspired
> by God, as he went over in his mind
> the origins of ancient light: "Whatever
> God and Wisdom have created is good."
>   (*H.* 442–53)

In response to the anxiety induced by contemplation of man's inability to distinguish between appearance and reality and the corruption of the cosmos, Prudentius turns to the lawgiver Moses, whom he calls *historicus*. As author of the Pentateuch, Moses is, in a sense, the author of the Creation story, and stands in a privileged relation to divine truth.[24] Conybeare (2007, 231) argues that "Moses bridges the gap between inspired song and historical truth, between, we might say, *fides* and *ratio* (in this case manifest as *historia*): he seems to be cast as a mediator between the two testaments." When Lucretian *ratio* would seem to lead directly to the conclusion that God created a flawed universe, scripture is invoked to bring us back to correct doctrine. To recapitulate, Prudentius moves from pointing out the dangers posed to the Christian soul by the senses and by the deceptive nature of appearances to asserting the necessity of faith—a faith based on scripture, which is to say, on the act of reading. But even as the text turns to the authority of Moses, the act of citation begins to reveal the distance between

Prudentius's words and those of Moses. The assertive "Moses himself" (*ipse Moyses*) breaks down into the historian (*historicus*) and the seer (*vaticinator*); what is presented as a direct quotation is (necessarily, because of the meter) a paraphrase of whatever Latin version of the Old Testament Prudentius read, which was translated from the Greek, which was, in turn, translated from the Hebrew. The speech attributed to "Moses himself" is many steps removed from Moses' original words. Even the poet's confident recapitulation of Moses' words introduces difference: "'*vidit*,' ait, '*Deus esse bonum quodcumque creavit*'" is not the same as "*esse bonum quidquid Deus et Sapientia fecit*." The poet's restatement of Moses' words introduces Sapientia to the scene of creation, and Sapientia takes on different attributes in different places in Prudentius's poetry—most notably a few lines later, at H. 529–30 (Lat. 402), where she appears holding the club of Hercules and representing pagan philosophy or sophistry.[25]

On Moses' authority, Prudentius emphatically reasserts the goodness of God's creation and the unity of the divine:

> conditor ergo boni Pater est et cum Patre Christus
> nam Deus, atque Deus Pater est et Filius unum;
> quippe unum natura facit, quae constat utrique
> una voluntatis, iuris, virtutis, amoris.
> non tamen idcirco duo numina nec duo rerum
> artifices, quoniam generis dissensio nulla est,
> atque ideo nulla est operis distantia, nulla
> ingenii, peperit bona omnia conditor unus.
> nil luteum de fonte fluit nec turbidus umor
> nascitur aut primae violatur origine venae,
> sed dum liventes liquor incorruptus harenas
> praelambit, putrefacta inter contagia sordet.
>   (H. 346–57)

> The Father, then, created what is good,
> and with the Father, Christ, for he is God,
> and God the Father and the Son are one.
> For nature makes them one: one nature
> of will, of law, of strength, of love exists
> in both. It doesn't mean, therefore, that there
> are *two* divinities or *two* creators
> of things, since there is no discrepancy
> in kind, no separation of powers, none
> of intellect: everything that's good
> was born from one creator. From this spring
> no mud can flow, no murky waters rise;

its source, still pure, remains intact. But as
its crystal waters, uncorrupted, lap
against the dirty sands, the sad decay
surrounding it infects its purity.
   (H. 454–69)

Prudentius moves from asserting the goodness of all creation to a metaphor comparing creation to a *fons*, a pure spring that is contaminated by the dirty sands around it, and then pivots to put the blame for nature's fall where it belongs, on man's misuse of nature (470–95; Lat. 358–74). He begins with the rhetorical figure of *enumeratio*, listing specific examples of the perversion of nature's goods: horses, iron, bulls, lions, ropes, and olive trees. All of these were created good, but man has perverted their use. Horses are misused for racing; iron is misused to kill; olive oil is misused by wrestlers; ropes are misused by tightrope walkers in acrobatic performances; lions and bulls are misused in beast shows in the arena. While murder is mentioned, the emphasis in this list is on spectacle and performance—horse racing, wrestling, rope dancing, the beast show, the death of criminals in the arena. The particular misuse of nature that Prudentius stresses over and over—in his diatribe against women's makeup, men's clothing, pantomime dancers, theaters, racing, wrestling, and amphitheatrical displays—is man's tendency to misdirect his gaze. Instead of looking to the heavens, he gazes at the earth, his head down (*pronus*) like a beast (H. 496–506; Lat. 378–84).[26]

Distracted by the spectacle offered to the senses by the world, men are left vulnerable to the devil, who returns to the text once more as a *praedo*, a robber, who stealthily infiltrates men's souls. Men's hearts drink in the devil's agents as if they were a silent poison, and he sows evils deep in the marrow (*medullitus*) of the human frame (marrow is an image with highly erotic connotations in the Greek and Latin poetic tradition):[27]

his aegras animas morborum pestibus urget
praedo potens, tacitis quem viribus interfusum
corda bibunt hominum; serit ille *medullitus* omnes
   nequitias spargitque suos per membra ministros.
   (H. 389–92)

The highwayman attacks our weakened souls
with these diseases and plagues; with hidden force
he penetrates the thirsty hearts of men.
He sows the seeds of every wickedness
deep within, and scatters his agents through
all the body's parts.
   (H. 512–17)

126] AN INTERPRETIVE ESSAY

This is the second appearance of Satan in the guise of a robber in the poem. As we saw earlier, he was thus described in the first simile of the poem, the wording of which suggests that his theft included the appropriation of language. As was the case with the first appearance of the robber, the image of the devil ushers in a figural innovation in the text, in this case the introduction of a series of personifications who act as the devil's *ministri*, or agents:

> Ira, Superstitio, Maeror, Discordia, Luctus,
> Sanguinis atra Sitis, Vini Sitis, et Sitis Auri,
> Livor, Adulterium, Dolus, Obtrectatio, Furtum.
> informes horrent facies habituque minaces.
> Ambitio ventosa tumet, Doctrina superbit,
> personat Eloquium, nodos Fraus abdita nectit,
> inde canina foro latrat Facundia toto.
> hinc gerit Herculeam vilis Sapientia clavam,
> ostentatque suos vicatim gymnosophistas,
> incerat lapides fumosos Idololatrix
> Religio et surdis pallens advolvitur aris.
>   (H. 395–405)

>   Anger, Superstition,
> Grief, Despair, Discord, and Thirst for Blood,
> Thirst for Wine and Thirst for Gold, and Spite,
> Cunning, Slander, Theft, Adultery,
> and Malice. Hideous, with deformed faces,
> their every gesture threatens. Swelled Ambition
> swaggers, Learning boasts, and Oratory
> thunders, while Deceit, in hiding, weaves her snares.
> On this side, bitchy Eloquence fills the forum
> with barking, and on that, cut-rate Philosophy [Sapientia],
> her staff the size of Hercules' club,
> draws a crowd with her troupe of naked sages.
> Idolatrous Religion prays before
> the smoky statues, and pale with fear, she bows
> down low before unhearing altars.
>   (H. 520–34)

A host of fourteen personified abstractions takes the field to fight against the soul, several of them recognizable as Vices from the *Psychomachia*: Ira, Discordia, Sitis Auri (= Avaritia in the *Psychomachia*), and Idololatrix Religio (= Veterum Cultura Deorum). They mingle with seven nations (Canaanites, Amorites,

Girgashites, Hittites, Perizzites, and Hivites) whom Joshua and the Israelites defeated after they arrived in Israel, just as the Virtues and Vices share the field with figures from the scriptures.[28] Origen had interpreted these nations allegorically, as types of sin, as Morton Bloomfield has noted.[29] The resemblance of this passage to the *Psychomachia* is striking enough to suggest that it contains in miniature the ideas Prudentius was later to develop in the form of a full-fledged personification allegory.

The enemy in this passage operates by deception. The weak minds of men believe, because of their *simplicitas* (now a negative quality, radically different from the *generatio simplex* that earlier characterized God's generative power), that the Vices are allies; they think they are operating under a treaty; and they are led astray by their love for peace. This episode rehearses, in brief, the final battle of the *Psychomachia*: the Virtues, believing that peace has been declared, fail to recognize the Vice Discordia in her disguise as an ally and fall prey to her attack. In other words, as the figure of Satan returns in his robber guise, Prudentius deploys personification allegory, the trope that he will later deconstruct in the *Psychomachia*. He signals his concern with the linguistic aspect of the Devil's attack by including a host of personified figures associated with language: Doctrina, Eloquium, Fraus, Facundia, and Sapientia.[30] Especially noteworthy here is the allegiance of Sapientia: as the pejorative adjective *vilis* and her association with the gymnosophists indicate, Sapientia here represents pagan Philosophy, with its dangerous arsenal of deceptive argumentation. In contrast, the *Psychomachia* concludes triumphantly with the construction of a temple to a different Sapientia, the incarnation of divine Wisdom.[31] That two opposing forces can share the same name exemplifies the failure of human language to convey a single stable meaning and the dangers that beset the soul as it engages in the difficult process of interpretation.[32]

Indeed, Prudentius's deployment of scripture itself in this passage exhibits the radical instability of the interpretive process. In Exodus and Joshua, the expulsion of the Palestinian tribes is a sign of God helping his people to gain the promised land. The tribes are listed in a speech given by Joshua, reminding the Israelites of the Lord's goodness (the passage begins with Joshua quoting the Lord):

> "'Then you went over the Jordan and came to Jericho. And the men of Jericho fought against you—also the Amorites, the Perizzites, the Canaanites, the Hittites, the Girgashites, the Hivites, and the Jebusites. But I delivered them into your hand. I sent the hornet before you which drove them out from before you, also the two kings of the Amorites, *but* not with your sword or with your bow. I have given you a land for which you did not labor, and cities which you did not build, and you dwell in them; you eat of the vineyards and olive groves which you did not plant.'"

> "Now therefore, fear the LORD, serve Him in sincerity and in truth, and put away the gods which your fathers served on the other side of the River and in Egypt. Serve the LORD! And if it seems evil to you to serve the LORD, choose for yourselves this day whom you will serve, whether the gods which your fathers served that *were* on the other side of the River, or the gods of the Amorites, in whose land you dwell. But as for me and my house, we will serve the LORD." (JOSHUA 24:11–15)

After Joshua's reminder of the Lord's faithfulness to his people, the Israelites renew the covenant made by Moses. But here Prudentius uses these tribes to suggest the victory of the forces of evil. As Taddei notes, Prudentius's deployment of the scriptural passage is remarkable "inasmuch as it transforms a commonly accepted sign of the Lord's fidelity to the covenant and of the deliverence of His people into *a representation of the universal and continuing power of the external forces of evil.*" (Taddei 1981, 178, my emphasis). Unsettlingly, Scripture itself proves as difficult to interpret and as flexible as the deceptively adorned face of the made-up woman or the fluid body of the pantomime dancer.

6. GENERATION OF VIPERS

> *... with sorrow infinite*
> *To me, for when they list into the womb*
> *That bred them they return, and howle and gnaw*
> *My Bowels, thir repast; then bursting forth*
> *A fresh with conscious terrours vex me round ...*
>
>   MILTON, *Paradise Lost*

THE ALLEGORICAL FIGURES emerging from the poison Satan sows (*serit*, line 391) in our veins in the mini-*Psychomachia* of H. 517–34 (Lat. 390–405) gesture, as it were, to the devil's appropriation of figural speech. His seminal role in creating them also associates Satan with the phenomenon of reproduction, a theme the poet takes up at length in lines 733–833 (Lat. 562–636). He begins his excursion on the generation of sin with the assertion that we give birth to sin from our own bodies. To illustrate this, he relates the story of David, whose son Absalom rebelled against his father:

> For we give birth to all our sins
> from our own bodies, just as David did,
> who was the best of fathers otherwise,
> though he produced as offspring Absalom,
> his only crime. The father of many righteous
> children, David also fathered one
> parricide, an evil son who dared
> to draw his sword against the author of
> his being, who came to battle with his standard
> set against his father and opposed
> his army, fighting his own flesh and blood.
> Alas for loyalty! In just the same
> way our hearts give birth to dreadful children,
> a painful generation, whose habit is
> to turn their teeth against us from the start
> and live by the pain of those that gave them life,
> for they destroy their parents' all-too-fertile
> flesh and feed on the family's dying stock.
> But that royal David, king of kings,

God's prophet and a forefather of Mary,
the virgin mother, had begot a mixed
breed of children, the good and loyal with
the bad.
   (H. 733–55; Lat. 562–76)

The underlying metaphor in Prudentius's account of the creation and propagation of sin is that of childbirth, and this brings us back to a linkage made early in the poem between sin and reproduction. In his opening attack on Marcion's teachings, Prudentius compares sinful dualism to the stable, unified paternity that is for him the mark of the transcendent deity:

And since there is no other God and Father,
and Christ cannot be second to the Father,
the One who has a single Son exists
before all number, God, and rightly God,
for He is first and One: first in power
and first in whom He sired. But how does pure
generation make a difference? Both
begetter and the One begot from One
before the darkness of primeval chaos,
free of number and time, will always be
One.
   (H. 53–63; Lat. 37–44)

Here Prudentius frames the argument against dualism by emphasizing not the Trinitarian nature but rather the unity of God. *Simplex generatio* allows for the perfect relationship, a Father who is one with his Son, without a difference. As Nugent (2000, 16) has noted, "Presumably the nature of the opponent [Marcionism] dictates the form of Prudentius's argument, since he chooses to elaborate on the unity of the godhead in terms which repeatedly emphasize *not* the trinity, but the transcendence of binary form." While man is hopelessly divided from himself, God is unfathomably, mysteriously one. *Simplicitas* is impossible for us to attain; as Prudentius says in the *Psychomachia*, "And human nature, not single, rages with discordant weapons" [*fremit et discordibus armis / non simplex natura hominis*] (903–4). In the human and natural world, generation is never *simplex*: reproduction without difference is impossible. Our condition is defined by change and flux.[1]

In the *Hamartigenia*, Prudentius offers several different models of reproduction, all depressingly unable to achieve the imagined stable paternity of the divinity. The first, as we have seen, is the unit in the preface consisting of mother

Eve and sons Cain and Abel, with Adam conspicuously absent. (Sinful) mother gives birth to twin offspring. The fact that there are two sons necessarily means that neither is perfectly sufficient or powerful, and the two are different in character as well.[2] Prudentius provides a different reproductive model in David, a father with multiple offspring. In this scenario, the mother is ignored, and the results are somewhat better, though hardly perfect: the vast majority of the children are good and only Absalom reveals a fatal difference from his father. This preponderance of good offspring is due to David's extraordinary status as Mary's forefather; the rest of us, with a less illustrious lineage, are more likely to breed evil offspring. And in fact, as he constructs his model of how the soul generates vice, Prudentius specifically states that the good model of generation represented by David's fathering of the good son Solomon does not apply to us: "No Solomon / exists in us; we're Absalom—corrupt, / we turn our knives against our family's flesh (*H.* 758–60; Lat. 579–80).

The image of the son turning his sword against his father leads to a new and even worse reproductive model, the viper, a model antithetical in every way to God's perfect conception of Christ, the son who is not different from his father. Prudentius has already told us that the robber Satan (who is also, of course, a serpent) sows vices into our marrow; now through an exemplum drawn either from natural history or from pagan writings (Prudentius goes out of his way in 761–62 (Lat. 581) to draw attention to his unnamed sources—*ethicis* and *physicis*), we learn exactly how the process of reptilian reproduction works:[3]

> No, when she's in heat, inflamed by female
> lust, the obscene creature opens wide
> her gaping jaws, thirsting for her mate
> who's soon to die. Into his spouse's jaws
> he thrusts his three-tongued head; aflame with passion,
> he enters her mouth, injecting poisoned semen
> through oral sex. Amid the sweet accords
> and covenants of love, the bride, wounded
> by such violent delight, draws down
> her lover's head into her mouth and snaps
> his neck between her teeth, drinking in
> the last ejaculation from her dying
> lover's lips. These pleasures kill the father;
> the offspring in the womb destroy their mother:
> for when the seed matures, the little tiny
> bodies begin to crawl in their warm den,
> and lashing about they strike her shaken womb.
>   (*H.* 768–84; Lat. 586–96)

Prudentius draws from numerous sources in his description of the vipers, but the closest seems to be the *Physiologus*, a compilation of materials that explain the Christian symbolism of elements drawn from nature writings, fables, fairy tales, and scripture. In it, the description of the vipers is linked to John the Baptist's rebuke of the Pharisees:

> Of the adder (or viper, *echidna*). Well spoke John the Baptist to the Pharisees: "You vipers' brood! Who warned you to escape from the coming retribution?" [Matthew 3:7, Luke 3:7]. The "Physiologus" says of the adder that the male has the appearance of a man, the female the appearance of a woman. Down to the navel they have human form, but then the tail of a crocodile. In the groin the female animal does not have an entrance, but only the eye of a needle. And so when the male animal wants to impregnate the female, he drops the seed into her mouth. And as the female wants to swallow the seed, it bites off the male's genitals, and the male dies. Now, as the young grow, they eat their mother's belly and come out in that way; thus she also dies and only the young remain. (*Physiologus* 10)[4]

Similarly, in the *Hamartigenia* the female viper conceives by taking the head of her partner into her mouth (*moriturum obscena maritum/ore sitit patulo*, 586–87), biting it off in the heat of her passion (*frangit amatoris blanda inter foedera guttur*), and drinking in his saliva as he dies (*infusasque bibit caro pereunte salivas*, 591). The male thus suffers a combination of decapitation and castration, since his head is the sexual organ by which he sows his seed in the female. She, however, benefits little from her oral transgression, for the offspring of this deadly union, enclosed in her *alvus* (belly or womb) and unable to find a birth passage, gnaw their way through her loins *(viam lacerata per ilia pandit*, 602) and kill her as they emerge. The ungrateful little viper cubs (Prudentius calls them *catuli*) even creep around licking the recumbent body of their mother after they emerge, an unpleasant reversal of the standard image of a mother bear licking her cubs into shape after birth.[5]

This passage has obvious similarities to the description of the fall of Satan earlier in the poem. Like the male viper, Satan has a triple tongue *(trisulco)*. The male viper is either beheaded or strangled when his head, which takes the place of his sexual organ, is snapped by his mate's jaws, an action that combines decapitation and castration. Satan too undergoes a symbolic loss of phallic rigor or vigor when he exchanges his original erect state for limp coils. Like the male viper, whose head *(caput)* injects *genitale venenum*, "fertile poison," into the female's gaping maw, Satan too is a head/source that produces offspring: as the text puts it, once his tongue has split he becomes the *natale caput vitiorum*. But Satan resembles the female viper in some respects as well. Like her, he is swollen and possesses an *alvus*, a womb or belly. Like her, he is destroyed from within, for it is by his own bitter marrow (*deque acidis vim traxit acerba medullis*) that he is poisoned and turns away from God. He even shares grammatical gender with the female viper: he is repeatedly called *bestia* and modified with feminine adjectives in the lines that describe his metamorphosis into a serpent (*bestia . . . acerba, bestia . . . recta*, 196–97).⁶ Like the deviant crowd of *semiviri*, Satan incorporates a monstrous femininity closely allied to his ability to deceive and to reproduce, whether he is reproducing offspring or deceptive imitations (if there is a difference). The female viper's generative act has obvious similarities to the crime of Eve, the act so systematically repressed in the *Hamartigenia*. Like the viper, Eve commits a specifically oral transgression, inappropriately devouring the forbidden fruit and then persuading her husband to do the same. Through this improper act of eating, she condemns Adam to death, just as the viper bites off the head (or breaks the neck) of her amorous spouse. Inappropriate consumption of food, sexual transgression, and persuasive speech are all associated with the mouth, the orifice through which language is produced.⁷

Milton struggled with the issues of reproduction, division, and difference as well. His personified Sin, with her serpent shape and her offspring all too active in her womb, shares important characteristics with Prudentius's viper (female gender, serpent form, multiple offspring):⁸

> The one seem'd Woman to the waste, and fair,
> But ended foul in many a scaly fould
> Voluminous and vast, a Serpent arm'd
> With mortal sting: about her middle round
> A cry of Hell Hounds never ceasing bark'd
> With wide *Cerberian* mouths full loud, and rung
> A hideous Peal: yet, when they list, would creep,
> If aught disturb'd thir noyse, into her woomb,
> And kennel there, yet there still bark'd and howl'd
> Within unseen.
>   (*PL* 2.650–59)

Like Prudentius's exemplary viper, Milton's Sin is associated with a deviant form of reproduction. In a parody of the birth of Athena from the head of Zeus, and of the creation of Eve from the rib of Adam, Milton's Satan generates a daughter, Sin, from his own head. In *PL* 2, Sin, who has been hideously changed after Satan's rebellion, confronts her father, who no longer recognizes her, and reminds him of the circumstances of her birth:

> Hast thou forgot me then, and do I seem
> Now in thine eye so foul, once deemd so fair
> In Heav'n, when at th' Assembly, and in sight

> Of all the Seraphim with thee combin'd
> In bold conspiracy against Heav'n's King,
> All on a sudden miserable pain
> Surpris'd thee, dim thine eyes, and dizzie swumm
> In darkness, while thy head flames thick and fast
> Threw forth, till on the left side op'ning wide,
> Likest to thee in shape and count'nance bright,
> Then shining Heav'nly fair, a Goddess arm'd
> Out of thy head I sprung: amazement seis'd
> All th' Host of Heav'n; back they recoil'd affraid
> At first, and called me *Sin*, and for a Sign
> Portentous held me....
>   (*PL* 2.747–61)

The narcissistic Satan, captivated by his own likeness, conceives Death in an incestuous union with his daughter. Her monstrous child then rapes his mother, generating the vicious brood. Like the viper's brood in the *Hamartigenia*, Sin's offspring are born by gnawing their way through their mother's womb:

> I fled, but he pursu'd (though more, it seems,
> Inflam'd with lust than rage) and swifter far
> Mee overtook his mother all dismaid,
> And in embraces forcible and foule
> Ingend'ring with me, of that rape begot
> These yelling Monsters that with ceaseless cry
> Surround me, as thou sawst, hourly conceiv'd
> And hourly born, with sorrow infinite
> To me, for when they list into the womb
> That bred them they return, and howle and gnaw
> My Bowels, thir repast; then bursting forth
> Afresh with conscious terrours vex me round,
> That rest or intermission none I find.
>   (*PL* 2.790–802)

Like Prudentius in the *Hamartigenia*, Milton in *Paradise Lost* lays out various models of creativity. God the Father creates a Son who is a reflection of his father; the Son creates the world and man, made in his own image; Adam and Eve reflect praise back to God, as does the poet, whose poem reflects God's creation. As Maggie Kilgour puts it:

> The creativity of divine narcissism comes full circle.... In its linking of the natural, human, and divine realms, creativity appears as a unifying

energy that works against the forces of division and dissonance that emerge in the Fall. As critics have noticed, however, Milton's creation also involves separation and divorce; when Christ sets out to make the world, he begins by dividing chaos. The chain of divine creativity in fact requires a balance of individuation and identification: it begins with God's self-division, which makes one into two who then further multiply God's image. However, the ultimate goal of creative division is the restoration of unity.[9]

But with differentiation, division, and replication comes the possibility of perversion, and God's creative multiplication is parodied by Satan's generation of his "perfect image" Sin (whom Milton punningly links with "sign"), with whom he incestuously mates to produce Death, and by his intention to remake Adam and Eve in his own image. Sin exemplifies the negative aspects of perverted creativity: she is a copy not only of her father but of numerous literary predecessors, especially Spenser's Errour and Ovid's Scylla—including, perhaps, Prudentius's mother viper. Colin Burrow calls her "the most wearisomely derivative figure in *Paradise Lost*."[10] Kilgour shows how Milton is beset with anxiety about his own poetic creativity, particularly in his invocation to the Muse Urania in book 7, at the beginning of the second half of his poem, as he prepares to relate the creation of the world:

> Upled by thee
> Into the Heav'n of Heav'ns I have presumed,
> An Earthlie Guest, and drawn Empyreal Aire,
> Thy tempring; with like safetie guided down
> Return me to my Native Element:
> Lest from this flying Steed unrein'd, (as once
> Bellerophon, though from a lower Clime),
> Dismounted, on th' *Aleian* field I fall,
> Erroneus, there to wander and forlorne.
> . . . .
> . . . though fall'n on evil dayes,
> On evil dayes though fall'n, and evil tongues;
> In darkness, and with dangers compast round,
> And solitude . . .
> (PL 7.12–28)

At the moment when he is about to rival God's Creation in his retelling of the Creation from Genesis, Milton invites us in his invocation to the Muse to compare him to Satan's daughter, Sin. Kilgour notes that Milton's anxiety here is focused on his creative powers:

The unusual foregrounding of the poet's voice has its own narcissistic edge to it, and the speaker, who describes himself as "fall'n on evil dayes.... In darkness, and with dangers compast round," (7.25, 27) sounds strikingly like his infernal creatures. While "fall'n" links the narrator with Satan, the language echoes Sin's earlier description of her own situation, "With terrors and with clamors compasst round" (2.862).... The parallel between her situation and that of the narrator suggests his fears lest his own creations, born of a narcissistic energy that originates not in God but his own ego, turn upon him.[11]

Prudentius, too, expresses his anxieties about the creative process, and his own work, in terms of reproduction. In particular, we can link the anxieties about reproduction expressed in the exemplum of the mother viper with an anxiety about the process of reading, for serpents in late antiquity were associated with a particular technology of reproduction: *reading*. Catherine Conybeare (2007) cites a number of passages where this association is explicitly made, including a vision in which a serpent binds Caesarius of Arles to the book he is reading and gnaws at his arm and shoulder (he is reading a book of "worldly wisdom," *sapientia mundi*), and a passage from Martianus Capella's *De nuptiis* where Dialectica appears holding a snake in her hand (unambiguously interpreted centuries later by Eriugena: *per serpentem sophisticas subtilitates intellige*, "by the snake, understand the logic chopping of the sophists").[12] Like the viper's brood, interpretations can be produced and reproduced, and turn murderous against the mind that conceived them. As Conybeare (2007, 238) says, "Sometimes the result is not the generation of sin as such, but the *generation of sinful meanings*; the mind, 'pregnant with lethal offspring, bears the conceptions of a malign disposition from the seed of the tortuous snake.' And such interpretations kill the mind, or soul, that generates them." Hence it is not surprising to find that after the lurid exemplum of the vipers, the narrator steps in to ensure that the reader will interpret the figure correctly. But the apostrophe to the reader itself raises interpretive issues even as it makes a rare, explicit appeal to biblical authority:

> Hence that just rebuke of Christ when He
> accused, "Is your father not a demon, sinners?
> Were you not begotten when he joined
> with flesh that thirsted for his evil seed?"
> Reader, go through the holy book: you'll see
> that as I said, the Lord brought true indictments
> against iniquitous men: "Holiness
> itself, or works of holiness, would prove
> that you were truly offspring of my Father."
>   (*H.* 815–23; Lat. 621–28)

Conybeare notes several peculiar features in this passage, including the confusion among the various participants in the reading process, and remarks that "the passage is subtly manipulative. Who, for example, is the 'you' at different stages? Who are the *peccatores,* and does every instance of 'you' refer to them? What about the address to the reader in the middle? Who is that?" (Conybeare 2007, 233). Up to this point in the poem, all other singular imperatives have been addressed to Prudentius's imagined interlocutor, Marcion; the reader may well be shocked to find himself thus suddenly accused. Further, as written, without the punctuation introduced by later editors, it is not at all clear who is speaking: Is it Prudentius or Christ who apostrophizes the reader? "Prudentius is conflating his own voice with that of Christ, blurring the boundaries between their two speaking/writing voices.... Prudentius is, in fact, manipulating the reading of the *sanctum volumen* and blurring the boundaries between his own literary production and the Scriptures.... There is a remarkable displacement of authority going on here" (Conybeare 2007, 233–34).

What Prudentius presents here as the actual words of Christ are not an exact quotation but rather an allusion to Jesus' dispute with the Pharisees and the Jews over the meaning of their descent from Abraham in the Gospel of John: "You are of your father the devil, and the desires of your father you want to do" (John 8:44). As Conybeare points out, Prudentius has entirely elided the context of the allusion, so that the *peccatores* Christ upbraids in his text seem to exist in the realm of metaphor and represent the soul or mind.[13] This passage, then, whose purpose seems to be to provide an unambiguous interpretation of the fable of the vipers, actually exemplifies the hermeneutic crisis that the vipers represent: it confuses internal and external audience, alters scripture, and conflates the voices of Prudentius and Christ through the device of scriptural paraphrase. Indeed, the biblical citation itself raises the issue of interpretation and misunderstanding: the reader who turns to the biblical passage Prudentius alludes to will find that at John 8:43, the verse immediately before the one Prudentius "quotes," Jesus says: "Why do you not understand my speech? Because you are not able to listen to my word."

The chain of associations we have traced in the viper passage is certainly not unprecedented in the discourse of his Christian contemporaries. Virginia Burrus has examined the construction of paternity in several patristic authors, and finds in them a number of the themes that are prominent in the *Hamartigenia*. Athanasius, for example, in his attack on Arianism, links together the heretic Arius, the serpent Satan, femininity, illegitimate reproduction, and effeminacy.[14] Ambrose similarly associates Arianism with a serpentine and monstrous femininity:

> Ambrose compares heresy to "some hydra of fable," the two-headed serpent that ever survives its own decapitation; for heresy—as Ambrose explains—"hath waxed great from its wounds and, being ofttimes lopped

short, hath grown afresh, being appointed to find meet destruction in flames of fire." Heterodoxy is also likened to "some dread and monstrous Scylla," whose many-headed form seems to suggest to Ambrose the multiplicity, as well as the fanged threat, of heresy's deceptive guise; her lower body is "girded with beastly monsters," and her cavern, "thick laid with hidden lairs" and resounding with the howling of her black dogs, is a place of danger that can only barely be avoided by the prudent pilot who sails, with stopped ears, close along "the coasts of the scriptures." There is a subtle blurring of genders in these hideous figures, in which femininity embraces the serpentine, a monstrosity gathering all disavowed carnality into itself.[15]

Ambrose, however, does not restrict his depiction of the feminine to the monstrously carnal. He also deploys language that associates femininity with asceticism and the transcendent. As Burrus argues, "What is striking is the flexibility of the gendering of Ambrose's discourse, represented as both transcendently masculine in relation to a monstrously carnal femininity and ascetically feminized in relation to a grotesquely carnal masculinity."[16] In the *Hamartigenia*, by contrast, the gender blurring in the fallen world leads to contamination rather than transcendence, and the feminine is consistently linked not only with the carnal but also with human language and its inherently deceptive nature.

Augustine too, in the thirteenth book of the *Confessions*, provides an interesting contrast to Prudentius's association of language with the devil and the monstrous in his exegesis of the divine command to be fruitful and multiply. He also describes language in terms of the reproductive processes of animals (both land and sea creatures), but although he employs similar imagery of animal mating and spectacular fertility to describe signification, the multiplicity of signs is for him an indication of the bounteous excess of truth:

> But it is only in the case of signs outwardly given that we find increase and multiplication in the sense that a single truth can be expressed by several different means; and it is only in the case of concepts apprehended by the mind that we can find increase and multiplication in the sense that a single expression can be interpreted in several different ways. I therefore understand the reproduction and multiplication of marine creatures to refer to physical signs and manifestations, of which we have need because the flesh which envelops us is like a deep sea; and I take the reproduction of human kind to refer to the thoughts which our minds conceive, because reason is fertile and productive.... This explains how the fish and the whales *fill the waters of the sea* [Gen. 1:22], because mankind, which is represented by the sea, is impressed only by signs of various kinds; and it explains how the offspring of men *fill the earth* [Gen. 1:28], because the

dry land appears when men are eager to learn and reason prevails. (*Confessions* 13.25, trans. PINE-COFFIN)

In Augustine's metaphysics of language, the word is as fertile as Prudentius's vipers, but as Geoffrey Harpham has argued, "The metaphysical Logos both grounds language in transcendence and anchors transcendence in the world," and a truly converted Christian practice of reading brings bounty and fertility.[17] In the *Hamartigenia*, the focus is not on the divine Logos, but rather on the problems that are generated by our limited abilities to read and interpret properly. The reproductive process, whether sexual or linguistic, is associated not with the transcendent divine Logos, but with the fallibilities of human language, epitomized by Satan and his split tongue, and by the viper and her endless brood of vicious offspring. Even holy scripture is at risk of misinterpretation.

7. SIGNS OF WOE

> *So saying, her rash hand in evil hour*
> *Forth reaching to the Fruit, she pluck'd, she eat:*
> *Earth felt the wound, and Nature from her seat*
> *Sighing through all her Works gave signs of woe,*
> *That all was lost.*
>
> MILTON, *Paradise Lost*

PERHAPS THE MOST PECULIAR feature of the *Hamartigenia* to readers brought up on the Genesis account of the Creation and Fall of mankind and influenced by a literary tradition that has been fascinated by the figure of Eve is the way in which she is minimized, almost eliminated, from the narrative of the origin of sin. In this, Prudentius's account of original sin differs greatly from the biblical account. In Genesis, the woman's temptation is highlighted; she takes center stage:

> Now the serpent was more cunning than any beast of the field which the LORD God had made. And he said to the woman, "Has God indeed said, 'You shall not eat of every tree of the garden'?" And the woman said to the serpent, "We may eat the fruit of the trees of the garden, but of the fruit of the tree which is in the midst of the garden, God has said, "You shall not eat it, nor shall you touch it, lest you die." Then the serpent said to the woman, "You will not surely die. For God knows that in the day you eat of it, then your eyes will be opened, and you will be as gods, knowing good and evil. So when the woman saw that the tree was good for food, and that it was pleasant to the eyes, and a tree desirable to make one wise, she took of its fruit, and ate. She also gave to her husband with her; and he ate. Then the eyes of both of them were opened, and they knew that they were naked; and they sewed fig leaves together, and made themselves coverings. (GENESIS 3:1–7)

In the *Hamartigenia*, on the other hand, Eve's action takes place offstage. She appears (unnamed) in the preface, identified only as the mother of Cain and Abel. She gets less than three lines in the text of the poem itself. We never see her talking with Satan, or plucking and eating the fruit, or offering the fruit to Adam; instead, her actions are almost a footnote to Adam's decision. Instead of Eve conversing with the serpent, Prudentius has God speak directly to Adam, and it is Adam who appears to be persuaded by the serpent:

> transit propositum fas et letalia prudens
> eligit, atque volens, magis utile dum sibi credit
> quod prohibente deo persuasit callidus anguis.
> persuasit certe hortatu, non inpulit acri
> imperio. hoc mulier rea criminis exprobranti
> respondit domino: suadellis se male fabris
> inlectam suasisse viro. vir et ipse libenter
> consensit.
> (H. 709–16)

> [Adam] goes against the law laid down for him,
> and with knowledge and free will he chooses
> the things of death, believing all the while
> that what the clever serpent urged, against
> the will of God, would be more useful to him.
> He, indeed, persuaded by rhetoric
> and not by harsh command. The woman, when
> indicted for the crime, made this reply
> to the charges of the Lord: herself seduced
> by crafty arguments, she had persuaded
> her husband; freely then did man himself
> consent.
> (H. 937–48)

Eve is unnamed. Prudentius's silence here may reflect a significant difficulty: determining Eve's "real" name. Her God-given name, according to Genesis 5:2, is *adam*: "He created them male and female; and blessed them; and called their name *Adam* (Human)." "But the names Adam gives to his helpmate, one before and one after the Fall, play on similitude and difference, registering a shift first from unity to multiplicity—mirroring God's own act of Creation—and then, dismayingly, from integral connection to alienation" (Fyler 2007, 12). At Genesis 2:23, Adam names his wife *isha*, "woman," because she was made woman (*isha*) from man (*ish*), an etymological play that Jerome captures in the Vulgate by translating *isha* with *virago* (mirroring the relationship between the Hebrew *ish* (man) and *isha* in the Latin *vir*, "man," and "virago"). The woman's first name, *adam*, is identical with Adam's; her second, though marked by gender difference, reveals their basic prelapsarian similarity. But her final name, Eve, marks her *dis*similarity and is troublingly polysemous: "The name Eve implicitly plays on such dissimilitude within itself, in effect a kind of punning, which mirrors the dissimilitude the Fall brings to Adam and Eve separately, in their division from God, and together, in their division from each other" (Fyler 2007, 15). According to Jerome, the name Eva means "*aut calamitas aut vae vel vita*," Calamity, Woe, or Life.

The unnamed woman in Prudentius's account of the Fall has a drastically reduced role in the narrative that corresponds to her loss of name. In his treatment of Eve Prudentius departs not only from Genesis but from his own narration of the Fall in *Cathemerinon* 3, where she takes an active role: the woman is the object of the serpent's persuasion, and it is she who persuades her husband:

> hic draco perfidus indocile
> virginis inlicit ingenium,
> ut socium malesuada virum
> mandere cogeret ex vetitis,
> ipsa pari peritura modo.
>   (*Cathemerinon* 3.111–15)

> Now the treacherous serpent
> tempts the virgin's untrained mind
> so that she, now dangerously persuasive,
> forces her ally and husband
> to eat of what was forbidden,
> herself to die in the same way.

The *Cathemerinon* account is much more detailed: it includes the details of the first couple's shame at being naked and their sewing fig leaves to cover their nakedness; their discovery of sex and woman's subjugation to man's rule; the punishment of the serpent, who is doomed to have its three-tongued head trodden on by the woman's foot; and the doom of their descendants, who rush into sin, imitating their ancestors. It would seem, then, that Eve's reduced role in the *Hamartigenia* does not reflect an idiosyncratic belief on Prudentius's part that she was not central to the story of the Fall, but rather is part of a poetic strategy. As I will argue below, Eve's near absence is the logical result of her association in the poem with the process of signification.

The language Prudentius uses in the *Hamartigenia* account of Adam and Eve is significant: the unnamed woman (*mulier*, 943) appears as a defendant (*rea*, 944; Lat. 713) and is legally charged (*exprobanti*, 945; Lat. 713). She replies (*respondit*) to the charge in an indirect statement in which she describes herself as having persuaded (*suasisse*) her husband. Her only acts in the poem are speech acts: she responds, is seduced by persuasive arguments (*suasellis*), and then herself persuades (*suasisse*). Her near invisibility and passivity are in contrast to Adam's active, informed decision making. He is described slightly earlier as the judge of his own actions (*arbiter*, 699 and *iudex*, 700), and in this passage he is described as choosing knowingly, willingly, and freely: *prudens, volens*, and *libenter*. The adjective *prudens* is particularly loaded: Adam's foresight proves to be fatally flawed, and at the same time the adjective links him with the poet himself, *Pruden*tius, just at the moment when he succumbs to the woman's and the serpent's rhetoric.

Adam's choice leaves him in a state of radical doubt, caught between the advice of God and the enticements of Satan:

nunc inter vitae dominum mortisque magistrum
constitit medius: vocat hinc deus, inde tyrannus,
ambiguum atque suis se motibus alternantem.
(H. 720–22)

        And now he stands
between the Lord of life and Master of death:
God summons him from one side, from the other
calls the tyrant: impulse drives him one way,
then the other.
(H. 953–57)

Milton marks this moment of decision dramatically in *Paradise Lost*. When his Adam finally eats of the forbidden fruit, the "signs of Woe" that Nature sighed when Eve first tasted the apple become inextricably, cryptically, acrostically embedded in the text:[1]

      Nature gave a second groan,
Skie lowr'd and muttering thunder, som sad drops
Wept at compleating of the mortal Sin
Original; while Adam took no thought,
Eating his fill.
   (*PL* 9.1001–5)

Milton's adaptation, or perhaps "correction," of Prudentius is quite striking—Prudentius's Adam was explicitly *prudens* when he was persuaded by the woman, while Milton's Adam, equally explicitly, "took no thought"—i.e., was *imprudens*. Quite in keeping with Prudentius's earlier description of nature's sympathetic decline once man has provided a negative exemplum, Milton's Nature reverberates in grief when Adam makes his fatal choice, and the skies "som sad drops / Wept." Further, the acrostic embedded in *PL* 9.1003–5 points beyond Adam's completion of the "mortal Sin / Original" to Eve, its instigator, and to Mary, who gives birth to its redeemer, for "WOE" is an English translation of the Latin *VAE*. Milton's acrostic draws at this pivotal moment on a long-established tradition of playing on the anagrammatic possibilities of Eve's name, EVA: she is associated with the woe (*VAE*) she brought to humanity, and with Mary, whose role in the redemption of humanity is signaled by the greeting (*AVE*) she received from the angel at the moment of the annunciation.² Given the obsessive interest of biblical commentators on the name and nature of Eve, Prudentius's refusal to name her within the narrative framework of the Fall, and his diminution of her pivotal role, seems especially significant.³

The Wife of Lot

At this pivotal moment of decision, it is important to examine closely the rhetorical structure of the *Hamartigenia* as it narrates, or, more to the point, *avoids* narrating the moment of original sin. Adam makes his fateful decision, but we never see him take and eat the fatal fruit. Instead, Prudentius freezes him in the present tense at the moment of decision: "Impulse drives him one way, / then the other" (H. 955–56) (*ambiguum atque suis se motibus alternantem*, H. 722). The narrative of Adam ends here as if it were unresolved, with the fate of Adam and all mankind hovering in the balance. For the next one hundred lines, the narrative too is frozen, as it presents a series of figures that illustrate the dilemma of Adam, which itself adumbrates the dilemma of each individual soul: the ekphrasis of Lot and his wife, the biblical tale of Ruth and Orpah, the tale of two brothers at the crossroads, and the simile of the doves.

The text thus simultaneously represses Eve and generates a multiplicity of figures that both illustrate *and stand in for* (since the eating of the fruit is never narrated) the moment of original sin. Prudentius signals his turn to the series of figures by an apostrophe to the reader:

> accipe gestarum monumenta insignia rerum,
> praelusit quibus historia spectabile signum.
>   (H. 723–24)

>   LISTEN and remember
> these famous monuments of deeds long past,
> a prelude staged by History, a sign
> well worth looking at.
>   (H. 957–60)

Prudentius's language here makes it clear that he will be concerned with the process of signification. What he is about to narrate are *monumenta insignia* and a *spectabile signum*, "a sign worth looking at." Both phrases exploit polysemous language—a *monumentum* can be a record or document, a monument, a tomb, a warning, or a statue; *signum* too has a wide semantic range that includes note, mark, sign, trace, and, again, statue. The apostrophe introduces the tale of Lot's wife, a biblical story that Prudentius presents as an ekphrasis of a work of art that is one of his most extended imitations of a classical text—the story of Niobe from Ovid's *Metamorphoses*. This recapitulates the strategy employed earlier in the poem, when the splitting of Satan's tongue (the point in the poem that Prudentius describes as the true origin of sin) introduces the poem's first simile, and parallels that of both Hesiod and Milton, who link the start of the imitative process of signification with Pandora (represented by her embroidered veil and crown decorated with "wonderful things, like living beings with voices") and Eve (nature reacts to her plucking of the fruit by giving "signs of woe"—the process of signification starts with humanity's original loss).[4] Lot "stands for" Adam, and his nameless wife for the nameless, effaced Eve.[5]

The significance of these scriptural types reverberates across time. By the logic of Prudentius's text, Lot and his wife appear to be acting as *monumenta insignia* of Adam and Eve, their predecessors both chronologically and in the narratives of Genesis and the *Hamartigenia*.[6] But like Lot and his wife, this exemplum looks forward (note Prudentius's use of the verb *praelusit* in 724) as well as back. Lot's wife is compared to the weak-minded Eve, who drew her husband into sin ("*traxerat Eva virum dirae ad consortia culpae;/haec peccans sibi sola perit,*" 741–42), but Lot himself, by refusing to look back, corrects the sin of the wavering Adam and obeys God's order to go forward, leaving behind not only his city but also the remnants of his wife.

In Genesis, the transformation of Lot's wife is told in one brief sentence: *Respiciensque uxor eius post se, versa est in statuam salis* ["His wife, looking behind her, was turned into a statue of salt"] (Genesis 19:26).[7] The much more elaborate treatment Prudentius gives this episode (in terms of narrative structure, it is an inversion of the way he compressed the story of Eve into three lines) suggests that it is of considerable importance in the symbolic structure of the *Hamartigenia*. In this passage he embarks on one of his most extended imitations of a classical source, in this case Ovid's description of the metamorphosis of Niobe into a weeping statue:[8]

>   orba resedit
> exanimes inter natos natasque virumque,
> deriguitque malis. nullos movet aura capillos,
> in vultu color est sine sanguine, lumina maestis
> stant inmota genis, nihil est in imagine vivum.
> ipsa quoque interius cum duro lingua palato
> congelat, et venae desistunt posse moveri;
> nec flecti cervix nec bracchia reddere motus
> nec pes ire potest; intra quoque viscera saxum est.

flet tamen. et validi circumdata turbine venti
in patriam rapta est. ibi fixa cacumine montis
liquitur, et lacrimas etiam nunc marmora manant.
   (*Met.* 6.301–12)

Bereft, she collapsed among her lifeless sons and daughters and husband, petrified by her woes. The breeze stirred none of her hair, the color in her face is bloodless; her eyes stand motionless in her sad face; there is no life in her image. Her very tongue and palate harden and congeal inside; her veins lose the ability to move; her neck cannot bend, nor her arms make gestures, nor her foot move: inside her entrails too are turned to stone. Yet she weeps. And swept up by a vortex of powerful wind, she is snatched back to her homeland. There, fixed on a mountain peak, she melts away, and still today the marble drips tears.

In the *Metamorphoses,* Niobe's transformation is described largely in terms of what she loses in the transformation from living woman to marble statue: there is no hair for the breeze to move, no color remains in her face, her eyes no longer move, *nihil est in imagine vivum,* nothing alive remains in the image. She is pure *imago,* bereft of life but still weeping, an eternal sign of loss. Like Niobe, Lot's nameless wife is turned into a statue, but this monument is even more paradoxical than the petrified, weeping Niobe, for she is made of salt, which Prudentius describes as a sort of liquid stone, eternally dissolving but never losing its form.

   . . . solidata metallo
diriguit fragili *saxumque liquabile* fata
stat mulier, sicut steterat prius, omnia servans
caute sigillati longum salis effigiata,
et *decus* et *cultum* frontemque oculosque comamque
et flexam in tergum faciem paulumque relata
menta retro, antiquae *monumenta rigentia* noxae.
   (H. 742–48)

   Growing stiff
and petrified, she turns to fragile ore;
transformed to solvent stone, the woman stands
just as she had stood before, but now
she's formed into a lofty pillar stamped
into the salt, preserving all her features:
her loveliness, her graceful dress, her brow
and eyes and hair, her face turned back
to look behind her, with her chin just barely

lifted over her shoulder—now a stiffening
monument of ancient sin.
(H. 984-94)

Prudentius works with and adapts a number of details from Ovid's description.⁹ Whereas Ovid's Niobe gradually loses all her human features, the description of Lot's wife emphasizes instead what she keeps; *omnia servans*, all her external features are perfectly preserved. Ovid emphasizes above all Niobe's loss of the ability to move: her eyes are fixed, her tongue freezes, her veins no longer pulse, she cannot move her hands or feet, or turn her neck. Lot's wife, on the other hand, is a paradoxical monument to female mobility. Her image, captured forever in salt, an oxymoronic *liquabile saxum* (literally "fluid stone"), endlessly repeats the gesture that damned her: turning her head and looking back over her shoulder. In this, she recalls and reverses Ovid's Niobe once again, down to the gesture of lifting her chin. In one of the most memorable passages of the Niobe story, the narrator intervenes at the moment when the distraught mother begins to take in the loss of all of her sons and her husband Amphion, who dies of grief:

heu quantum haec Niobe Niobe distabat ab illa,
quae modo Latois populum submoverat aris
et mediam tulerat gressus resupina per urbem,
invidiosa suis, at nunc miseranda vel hosti.
(*Met.* 6.273-76)

Alas, how different this Niobe from that Niobe
who recently drove her people away from Latona's altars
and bore herself, chin proudly lifted, through the middle of the city,
hated by her own people, but now pitied even by her foes.

The narrator recalls Niobe's characteristic pride, epitomized in her haughtily lifted chin (*resupina*); in Prudentius, the gesture of the lifted chin remains but emblematizes Lot's wife's inconstancy rather than her pride.¹⁰ The Ovidian narrator's emotive apostrophe draws attention to Niobe as an embodiment of self-alienation and difference: even before her physical transformation takes place, she is undergoing a change that makes her absolutely different from her former self.¹¹ In contrast, the transformation of Lot's wife, Prudentius specifically informs us, has *not* changed her: she is just as she was before: *stat mulier, sicut steterat prius*.

The petrified remains of each woman, one in the desert of Sodom, one on Mount Sipylus, are signs that beg to be interpreted, and in each case the poet obliges.¹² Niobe's story is framed by acts of interpretation. The episode opens as news of the transformation of Arachne into a spider is racing through the cities of Lydia:

> Lydia tota fremit, Phrygiaeque per oppida facti
> rumor it et magnum sermonibus occupat orbem.
> ante suos Niobe thalamos cognoverat illam,
> tum cum Maeoniam virgo Sipylumque colebat;
> nec tamen admonita est poena popularis Arachnes,
> cedere caelitibus verbisque minoribus uti.
> (*Met.* 6.146–51)

All of Lydia is gossiping, and rumor of what happened spreads through the towns of Phrygia, and fills the wide world with talk. Niobe had known her once, before her own wedding, when still a maiden, she lived in Maeonia and Sipylus: but she was not warned by the punishment of her compatriot Arachne to yield to the gods and to use less boastful words.

Arachne's fate is the subject of gossip. Her former acquaintance Niobe hears of it, but signally fails to interpret the meaning of the metamorphosis properly and to respect the power of the gods. Her own, more dreadful fate causes "everyone" to redouble their worship of the furious Latona:

> tum vero cuncti manifestam numinis iram
> femina virque timent cultuque impensius omnes
> magna gemelliparae venerantur numina divae,
> utque fit, a facto propiore priora renarrant.
> (*Met.* 6.313–16)

Then truly everyone, man and woman alike, fears the evident anger of the divinity, and they worship the great power of the goddess who bore the twins with even more extravagant rites, and, as is often the case, the deed becomes the cause of the retelling of old events.

Rumor and *sermo* leave the meaning of Arachne's transformation open to interpretation, and Niobe herself fails to understand the warning it represents.[13] Niobe's statue, however, is read unambiguously by all as manifest evidence of divine wrath.

Like the tale of Niobe, the story of Lot and his wife is bracketed by passages in which the text calls attention to the process of interpretation. As we have noted, the story is the first in a chain of figures introduced as the fate of the soul hangs in the balance, and the poet/narrator intrudes in the text at this crucial moment with an apostrophe to the reader: "*accipe gestarum monumenta insignia rerum / praelusit quibus historia spectabile signum!*" (Lat. H. 723–24; trans. 957–60).[14] Here, as the description of the hesitating Adam gives way to a figural chain, the poet takes up the mantle of *vates*, directly exhorting his audience to pay attention to and interpret the signs in the text (*monumenta insignia, spectabile signum*).[15] Like the Niobe passage, the story concludes with an explanation of the exemplum.[16] This explanation is offered by Prudentius in propria persona, in another apostrophe to the reader and not, as in the Niobe passage, attributed to a nameless audience:

> en tibi signatum libertatis documentum,
> quo uoluit nos scire Deus, quodcumque sequendum est,
> sub nostra dicione situm, passimque remissum
> alterutram calcare uiam. duo cedere iussi
> de Sodomis; alter se proripit, altera mussat,
> ille gradum celerat fugiens, contra illa renutat.
> liber utrique animus, sed dispar utrique uoluntas.
> dividit huc illuc rapiens sua quemque libido.
>   (H. 769–76)

> LOOK! this allegory offers proof
> of freedom for you: through it God desired
> us to know the choice of path to follow
> remains our own; which road to take is always
> up to us. Two were given orders
> to leave from Sodom: one departs in haste,
> the other hesitates; *he* flees with ever-
> increasing speed, while *she* refuses to go.
> Both are free to decide; the will of each
> is different. Every man is split in two:
> desire pulls in opposite directions.
>   (H. 1023–33)

The intrusion of the poet-narrator into the poem points to the need to guide the reader's interpretation of these figures and signs to ensure that he or she does not misinterpret the lesson of the figure of Lot's wife, as Ovid's Niobe had incorrectly interpreted the story of Arachne.[17]

A passage from Plato's *Republic* suggests that the figure of Niobe might be particularly relevant for Prudentius at this key point in his narrative, when it is vital that the reader not misinterpret the text and blame God for sin or injustice. In *Republic* 3, Socrates discusses the role of poetry in the ideal state, famously condemning the effects of tragic performances on the souls of the citizens. In the course of discussion, he offers advice on the proper way for poets to tell stories about the gods: never tell stories about the gods doing harm, escaping punishments, or making war on one another; do not blame the fate of unhappy characters on the gods; and never show the gods to be changeable. Niobe is adduced as an illustration of the second rule:

If a poet writes of the sorrows of Niobe or the calamities of the house of Pelops or of the Trojan war, either he must not speak of them as the work of a god, or, if he does, he must devise some such explanation as we are now requiring: he must say that what the god did was just and good, and the sufferers were the better for being chastised.... *The poet will only be allowed to say that the wicked were miserable because they needed chastisement, and the punishment of heaven did them good.* (Republic 3, 380a, CORNFORD translation; emphasis added)

Prudentius takes a leaf out of Socrates' rule book here, as he pauses after his imitation of Ovid's Niobe passage to provide guidance on how to interpret the scriptural passage. Mastrangelo sums up Prudentius's use of the figure thus:

By confronting the reader with this story, Prudentius associates the reader with a choice between Lot, who did not look back at the cities being destroyed, and his wife, who did. The implied typological choice for the reader is either Lot/reader or Lot's wife/reader. Free will, then, is a function of choice, which in the story of Lot is determined by whether the human being has the right sense of faith. Lot listens to God, and his wife ignores God. Lot makes a good choice because of his faith, whereas his wife makes a bad choice because of her lack of faith.[18]

But even as Prudentius steps in to guide the reader along the correct interpretive path, the text, by introducing the figure of Lot's wife, raises questions about the process of representation itself.[19] The description of Lot's wife is the only extended ekphrasis in the sense of "verbal description of a work of visual art" in the *Hamartigenia*, though as we have seen, many of Prudentius's descriptions are ekphrastic in the broader sense of the word. Prudentius uses the device of describing visual artworks frequently in his other works; indeed, his *Dittochaeon* consists of a series of captions to go with narrative paintings, though whether the cycle described in the collection is real or imaginary is unclear.[20] It is quite possible that Prudentius here is describing an actual work of art—Lot's wife appeared in a narrative cycle of Old Testament paintings in the inner courtyard of Paulinus's shrine to Saint Felix at Nola. Paulinus started construction on the shrine complex in 395 and completed it in 404; Maria Kiely (2004, 448) argues that "extended, chronological series of images entered monumental Christian art only during this time." Paulinus's *Carm.* 27 describes the painting cycle in some detail. Several of the Old Testament passages to which Prudentius alludes in the *Hamartigenia* are also depicted on the walls of Paulinus's courtyard, including Joshua crossing the Jordan, the Israelites crossing the Red Sea, and the parting of Ruth and Orpah (*H.* 777–88). The paintings were accompanied by *tituli*, inscriptions that revealed the content of the picture "so that the text might reveal what the hand has drawn," *ut littera monstret/quod manus explicuit* (*Carm.* 27.584–85). This adds another layer of complexity to the depiction of Lot's wife: it is a verbal description of a work of visual art (a painting) based on a verbal depiction (a biblical story) of a woman who is transformed into a both a work of visual art (a *monumentum*) and a natural feature (the pillar of salt); and it is at the same time a verbal reproduction (in didactic verse) of Ovid's verbal reproduction (in epic verse) of the story of Niobe, another woman transformed into a work of visual art that is also a natural feature (a crag on Mount Sipylus).

In antiquity the term "ekphrasis" was generally used to mean "descriptive language that brings the thing demonstrated clearly into sight," something very close to enargeia.[21] Philip Hardie (2002, 174) argues that there is an inherent similarity between ekphrasis and Ovidian metamorphosis, in that both stimulate the reader to "see" an image as if with his or her own eyes:

> Ovid's quasi-ecphrastic narratives both require of the reader what might be called an "ecphrastic assent" to the reality of the incredible process of metamorphosis unfolding before our mental vision, and also result in permanent products, the new bodies which fill the landscape with a gallery of "real" images, natural works of art that typically embody some essential quality.... Every picture tells a story; in this respect also metamorphosis is faithful to an essential feature of the rhetorical tradition of ecphrasis, which makes of an image the occasion for narrative.

Lot's wife is, like the petrified Niobe, a "natural work of art," a "permanent product" forever on display decorating the landscape; we know that both rock formations were well-known to ancient travelers. But in their respective poems, these statues are unnaturally real in their uncanny collapse of the difference between art and reality. The distinction between what is real and what is represented is blurred because the signified has become a signifier, as woman hardens into sculpture. In an interesting discussion of ekphrasis in the late Hellenistic novel *Aethiopica*, Tim Whitmarsh makes the point that the device of ekphrasis raises important ontological and interpretative issues:

> Ekphrastic description raises issues that are not just formalist and narratological, but also ontological. Ekphrastic mimesis is a form of deceptive illusionism, involving a fake, surrogate reality. In the case of artworks, this is well-known, both from Socrates' ontological critique of art in Book 10 of the Republic, and from less censorious sources such as Philostratus the Younger, who points to the "sweet deception" (ἡδεῖα ... ἀπάτη) in confronting "things that do not exist as though they did exist ..." (*Imagines* pr. 4). But the broader definition of ekphrasis raises the possibility of a broader contagion for this ontological anxiety and play, which may

infect all description.... Descriptions of artworks bring to a head ... the ontological anxiety and illusionistic play that all description provokes.[22]

The figure of Lot's wife, a permanent monument to flux, embodies such illusionistic play and the ontological anxiety it can generate. There are too many "originals" for this figure: the woman who existed before she was converted into a sign; the rock formation still visible to travelers in Prudentius's day; the scriptural passage to which Prudentius refers; the painting depicting the statue on the wall of the courtyard at Cimitile; and the Niobe passage from the *Metamorphoses* that Prudentius imitates so extravagantly.

As a figure who calls attention to the hopelessly unstable relationship between sign and referent, Lot's wife has much in common with the "made-up woman" Prudentius castigated earlier, who, not content with the outer appearance God had given her, adorns her face and hair with deceitful ornaments. The woman in that passage is described in terms that stress her weakness and fluidity: "Within the narrow confines of her breast/a tide of sins batters her fragile mind" (*H*. 366–67, Lat. 277–78). The "made-up" woman of Prudentius's diatribe uses deceptive adornment to produce an artificial exterior that makes her a sign needing to be deciphered. The description of Lot's wife and her metamorphosis into a statue reprises this familiar set of feminine qualities: she is *levis, fragilis*, and noted for her *mobilitas animi*. She too is associated with the process of figuration and with linguistic ornament. Like the "made-up" woman, Lot's wife is characterized by her external appearance: her *decus, cultus, facies,* hair, eyes, and forehead all remain, but now exist only as figural signs (*spectabile signum, monumenta rigentia*), making her an appropriate monument to represent original sin, the act that forever sundered human language from meaning. The ekphrasis of the painting of the statue of Lot's wife, who represents Eve, who herself represents all women, as well as the sinful soul, thus embodies representation itself. She is frozen in flux forever, the ultimate sign of humanity's lack of "origin"-ality. In that sense, she *is* the absent Eve.

The Family of Lot

The tale of Lot and his wife fleeing Sodom is highly allusive and complex, and the figure of Lot's wife exemplifies a number of issues having to do with various forms of reproduction. It is helpful to consider what Prudentius has included in his text, and what he has excluded from it. In the biblical account, Lot is advised by two angels to take his wife and daughters and escape the destruction of the city; he tries to save his daughters' fiancés as well, but they refuse to listen to him and perish with the rest of the inhabitants. Lot's wife looks back at the burning city and is transformed into a pillar of salt; Lot and his daughters flee to the mountains near Zoar:

> Then Lot went up out of Zoar and dwelt in the mountains, and his two daughters were with him; for he was afraid to dwell in Zoar. And he and his two daughters dwelt in a cave. Now the firstborn said to the younger, "Our father is old, and there is no man on the earth to come in to us as is the custom of all the earth. Come, let us make our father drink wine, and we will lie with him, that we may preserve the lineage of our father." So they made their father drink wine that night. And the firstborn went in and lay with her father, and he did not know when she lay down or when she arose. It happened on the next day that the firstborn said to the younger, "Indeed I lay with my father last night; let us make him drink wine tonight also, and you go in and lie with him, that we may preserve the lineage of our father." Then they made their father drink wine that night also. And the younger arose and lay with him, and he did not know when she lay down or when she arose. Thus both the daughters of Lot were with child by their father. The firstborn bore a son and called his name Moab; he is the father of the Moabites to this day. (Genesis 19:31–37)

With Lot's wife gone and his prospective sons-in-law dead, the remaining family configuration of a father without a wife and daughters without husbands or children constitutes a reproductive crisis. In their zeal to ensure that their father's lineage continue, Lot's daughters trick him into sleeping with them; the offspring they produce become the founders of tribes that would be hostile to Israel, the Moabites and the Ammonites. But while this story is detailed at length in Genesis, Prudentius does not mention it. Instead, he introduces the story of Ruth and Orpah into the narrative immediately after the metamorphosis of Lot's wife, the point at which the story of Lot and his daughters occurs in the biblical account.

Prudentius draws attention to the interconnectedness of the various biblical exempla he cites in his introduction to the story of Ruth, where he says, "*talem multa sacris speciem notat orbita libris*" (H. 777), "the cycle of tales in holy scripture / offers many such examples" (1034–35). Catherine Conybeare notes the implications of this phrase, in particular the word *orbita*, which she associates with Prudentius's use of snaky imagery to describe the dangers of heretical interpretation:

> Prudentius pauses after his exposition of the "spectabile signum" of Lot to observe, "talem multa sacris speciem notat orbita libris" (777). Though the Thesaurus Linguae Latinae glosses this use of *orbita* as "of a way well-worn by one's ancestors," its primary meaning is of a wheel, or tracks left by a wheel. The sense of the passage seems to be "many a revolution [as of a wheel] marks out such an appearance in the sacred books," for Prudentius goes on to examine how the figural narrative revolves back on itself to treat of Ruth and Orpah, descendents of Lot. The crucial image seems to

be of cyclical repetition. . . . Prudentius tells us of the *obliqua diuortia* that sow themselves in *textis orbitis*—those, it seems, that contain *uiperina . . . dogmata*. The involutions of serpents are once again connected with worldly—in this case, heretical—wisdom, and these sorts of cyclical links are made possible by the typological imaginary, which in its turn depends on the imaginative construction of readers. (CONYBEARE 2007, 238)

The reproductive crisis caused by the disappearance of Lot's wife and sons-in-law triggers an act—incest—that, while it might be justified by the strict logic of patriarchy, is certainly open to misinterpretation and may be better *not* left to the imaginary construction of readers. So just as the problematic Eve is left almost unmentioned in the account of original sin (but is replaced by the ekphrasis of the painting of the statue of Lot's wife), and the problematic Bathsheba is left out of the story of David and his sons, the troublesome daughters of Lot do not appear in the poem, but in their narrative place Ruth and Orpah appear instead:

> The cycle of tales in holy scripture
> offers many such examples. Look
> at Ruth the Moabite and Orpah. Ruth
> lovingly attends her mother-in-law,
> Naomi; Orpah leaves her. Both had been
> released from marriage and the law of wedlock,
> bound no longer by the Hebrew rites,
> and both enjoyed the liberty of their own
> free will. Her old religion's rites and shrines
> persuaded Orpah to prefer the foreskins
> of savages and bear and raise a monstrous
> hybrid son, Goliath. Ruth, meanwhile,
> sweltered through the stubble in the heat
> of summer and earned the marriage bed of Boaz;
> admitted to his chaste embrace, she soon
> conceived and bore the family of Christ,
> the royal line of David, and mingled
> human offspring with divine.
>   (H. 1034–51)

In the biblical account, the Moabites Ruth and Orpah are married to the sons of Naomi, an Israelite who lives in Moab. Naomi loses first her husband, then her two sons, and decides to return to Israel. Orpah remains in Moab and marries again; Ruth refuses to be parted from her mother-in-law and returns with her to Israel, where, following the advice of Naomi, she ends up wedded to Boaz, a kinsman of Naomi's. Ruth and Orpah, both Moabites, are the products of Lot's incestuous union with his daughters (and thus also are descended from Lot's wife). In the *Hamartigenia,* the two are, like Cain and Abel and Absalom and Solomon, evidence of the flawed nature of human reproduction, which produces such mixed results. In particular, Prudentius exaggerates the faults of Orpah, who is presented as a sinful counterpart to the steadfast Ruth. In the biblical account, Orpah parts on good terms with her mother-in-law, who urges her to stay in Moab where she has a chance to remarry. The text says nothing about whether she in fact marries, mentions no offspring, and nowhere condemns her decision. Prudentius, on the other hand, in strikingly vivid language, characterizes her decision to stay as desertion (*deserit,* line 780) based on her preference for the "foreskins of savages" (*praeputia barbara,* line 783), and identifies her as the mother of the Philistine giant Goliath: the mother's lust is revealed by her monstrous (*semiferi*) son.[23]

The biblical Ruth is not an unproblematic figure to choose as a reproductive model; her story is full of odd doublings and riddles, as Wendy Doniger has argued:

> The text of the story of Ruth, and its explicit parallelism with the stories of Leah and Tamar, present us with a series of riddles. There are two fathers and two mothers, for Obed is supposed to be the son of Ruth's dead husband (Mahlon) but is said to be born to Boaz, and although he is born to Ruth he is called Naomi's baby. Two tricky women (Leah and Tamar) are invoked as role models. The law of the levirate is mentioned several times, in a negative form, but the child is not regarded as the descendant of the dead husband. (DONIGER 2000, 259)

Indeed, the story mirrors the tale of Lot and his daughters in a number of ways. Both Lot and Naomi are exiles; both have lost their spouses. Naomi loses her two sons and is left with her two daughters-in-law, while Lot loses his sons-in-law and is left with his two daughters. In both cases, the chances for continuing the family line are slim. Lot's daughters solve the problem by sleeping with their father. Naomi, resigned to the fact that her line will not continue, tries to persuade her daughters-in-law to remain in Moab, where they have a chance to remarry and raise families of their own, while she returns to Israel. Orpah tearfully agrees, but Ruth insists on accompanying Naomi. Together they solve the problem of perpetuating the family line by a sort of trick; they persuade Naomi's relative Boaz, who may have a legal obligation to marry Naomi,[24] to marry Ruth by arranging for her to spend the night with him when he is drunk.

The structural similarities between these stories about reproduction reveal the logic of Prudentius's preference for the story of Ruth over that of Lot's daughters. It allows him to offer a model in which reproduction is the province of the female, and the female is split into two, the weak-minded Orpah with her monstrous offspring, and the virtuous Ruth, who displays faithful love (*fido amore*) for Naomi and whose union with Boaz is described as chaste (*casto cubili*, line 786). Her descendants bear witness to her purity and piety: she is the grandmother of David and ancestress of Christ.

Throughout the poem, Prudentius offers variations on the theme of reproduction, with mother and father playing different roles. The birth of Cain and Abel, two sons whose difference will cause trouble, is assigned to Eve only; Adam is not mentioned. Mary's role in the birth of Christ is omitted in Prudentius's early description of the generation of Christ, so that he can emphasize the unity of essence of father and son. The model of David, who generates an evil son, is immediately corrected or supplanted by the exemplum of the vipers, which rewrites the model of reproduction that David provided by restoring the vicious female to a central role in the reproductive process. The exemplum of the vipers allows Prudentius to recast the paradigm of the generation of sinful offspring (this, of course, is linked to the central problem of the *Hamartigenia*, for it is another way of asking how God could create a world with evil in it), replacing the troubling model of the good father who somehow generates evil offspring with that of a perverted mother whose bestial sexual voracity generates vicious offspring who are accurate replicas of their parents, and fitting agents of their mother's destruction. The story of Lot and his daughters, another tale in which the father plays a role in generating sinful offspring, is left untold. The tale that replaces it, the story of Ruth and Orpah, recasts the paradigm of David and his mixed offspring by presenting two mothers, each of whom produces an offspring like herself—the bestial Goliath and the good David. In the *Hamartigenia*, the evils of reproduction are ascribed, over and over again, to the mother. True *generatio simplex* is the province of the Father alone.

Generatio simplex

Different reproductive models abound in the *Hamartigenia*, which is obsessed with the issue. In the first model of reproduction to appear in the poem, the family is described as consisting of Eve, Cain, and Abel—Adam is left unmentioned in the preface. The one woman produces two offspring; the differences between the brothers result in fratricide. Eve has not succeeded in producing a single son identical to the parent; instead she produces two who are different in age, different in occupation (one a farmer, one a shepherd), different in their sacrificial rituals, and different in God's esteem. The problem of difference occurs throughout the poem in various ways, but there is a consistency in the text's obsessive return to the issues of reproduction, imitation, division, and signification. Prudentius approaches this set of issues early in the poem, when he discusses the unity of the Godhead. He vehemently argues against the notion that Jesus could be in any way different from his father:

ille Deus, meritoque Deus, quia primus et unus,
in virtute sua primus, tum primus in illo
quem genuit. *quid enim differt generatio simplex?*
unum semper erit gignens atque *unus* ab *uno*
ante chaos genitus numeroque et tempore liber. quis
dixisse duos rem maiestate sub una
regnantem propriamque sibi retroque perennem
ausit et unius naturae excindere vires?
numquid adoptivum genitor sibi sumpsit, ut alter
externi gentis numerum praestare duorum
debeat et geminum distans inducere numen?
forma Patris veri verus stat Filius ac se
unum rite probat dum formam servat eandem.
  (H. 40-52)

[He is] God, and rightly God,
for He is first and one: first in power
and first in whom He sired. Now how does pure
generation make a difference? Both
begetter and the One begot from One
before the darkness of primeval chaos,
free of number and time, will always be
One. What man has dared to say the power
that governs in one majesty, belongs
to itself alone, and was eternal
before the world began, is two? Who dares
to rip apart a single nature's strength?
Did the Father adopt a second son
of foreign origin, to make the number
two—a separate being to introduce
a second godly power? God's true Son
is in the form of his true Father and keeps
the same form, duly proving He is One.
  (H. 56-73)

In a sentence that reads like a particularly annoying mathematical word problem, Prudentius asserts that the one begetting, *gignens,* and the one begotten from that one, *unus ab uno . . . genitus,* will always be one, *unum,* free of time and of number. One times One is One. The true son properly (*rite*) proves his unity by keeping the same form as the true father (*se unum probat dum formam servat eandem*). *Generatio simplex,* the creation of an offspring identical to its creator, is the only model of reproduction endorsed in the poem. But humanity is singularly unable to follow this mode of reproduction without difference, and this failure occurs at the level of language (even Prudentius's attempt to assert the unity of God through repeated uses of the word *unus* necessarily reveals difference because difference in case is always marked in Latin) as well as at the level of society, in this poem represented by the family (God and his Son, Adam and Eve, Cain and Abel, the family of Lot, Ruth and Orpah, David and Absalom).

In his exploration of the concept of reproduction, which entails the question of succession in human society, Prudentius stands well within the norms of Roman epic poetry. As Philip Hardie has shown, the question of succession is integral to the Roman epic tradition:

> The epic is an ideal vehicle for the representation of this conception of the relation between individual and family, because of the genre's hospitality to repetition, impersonation, and possession.... Glancing forward to the end of the tradition, in *Paradise Lost* the motif of living up to family expectations is transposed on to a theological plane in the construction of a chain of individuals who may or may not fulfil the requirement laid on them of recognizing and faithfully imitating their progenitor (The Father-The Son/Satan-Adam-Eve-... Milton-the reader). (HARDIE 1993, 89)

In the *Hamartigenia* the question of faithful imitation of the progenitor is the central issue. Reproduction is figured as both problematic and emblematic of deviance and degeneration. Prudentius takes up the issue once again in the *Psychomachia*. As Georgia Nugent has pointed out, the structuring concept of that battle is introduced in the preface as the soul's attempt to bear offspring:

> nec ante prolem coniugalem iungere
> Deo placentem, matre Virtute editam,
> quam strage multa bellicosus spiritus
> portenta cordis servientis vicerit.
>   *Ps. praef.* 11–14

> We beget no child of wedlock pleasing to God, with Virtue as mother,
> before the battling spirit has overcome with great slaughter the monsters
> in the enslaved heart.

Thus, as Nugent (2000, 14) says, "The entire narrative of the battle which comprises the *Psychomachia* serves the purpose of enabling (in an unspecified way) the birth of offspring which will be pleasing to God." The mention of offspring is followed by allusions to Melchizedek (whose origin is a mystery known to God alone) and to Sara, whose conception of Isaac through divine intervention long after menopause is another alternative to normal human reproduction. Like the *Hamar-*

tigenia, the preface to the *Psychomachia* combines a rejection of sexuality—especially female sexuality—with the desire for a perfectly secure male line of descent. As Nugent says, "The imagery of childbearing as a way of discussing the spiritual life is both extremely strong and also very clearly focused on the goal of providing an heir to the male [God-the-father]" (Nugent 2000, 15).

Two Roads Diverged . . .

At *Works and Days* 274–92, Hesiod addresses his errant brother Perses on the subject of justice and truthful speaking:

> But you, Perses, lay up these things within your heart and listen now to right (*dikê*), ceasing altogether to think of violence. For the son of Cronos has ordained this law for men, that fishes and beasts and winged fowls should devour one another, for right (*dikê*) is not in them, but to mankind he gave right (*dikê*) which proves far the best. For whoever knows the right (*dikê*) and is ready to speak it, far-seeing Zeus gives him prosperity, but whoever deliberately lies in his witness and forswears himself, and so hurts justice (*dikê*) and sins beyond repair, that man's generation is left obscure thereafter. But the generation of the man who swears truly is better thenceforward. (trans. H.G. EVELYN-WHITE)

Hesiod sets in opposition to one another true speech on the one hand and false speech on the other, and links them to reproduction and succession. The man who knows and speaks what is right will be prosperous and have a better generation (*geneê ameinôn*); the man who speaks falsely will leave an obscure generation behind him (*amauroterê geneê*). Justice, truthful speech, and successful generation are closely linked together here, as are their opposites. Hesiod follows this admonition with an exemplum, a metaphor of just and unjust behavior:

> To you, foolish Perses, I will speak good sense. Badness can be got easily and in shoals: the road to her is smooth, and she lives very near us. But between us and Goodness (*aretê*) the gods have placed the sweat of our brows: long and steep is the path that leads to her, and it is rough at the first: but when a man has reached the top, then is she easy to reach, though before that she was hard. (*Works and Days* 286–91; trans. EVELYN-WHITE)

Though this is its first appearance in classical literature, the topos of the choice between the steep path to virtue and the easy road to vice was widespread from its origin in Hesiod through late antiquity.[25] Pythagoras of Samos was said to have used the letter *Y* to illustrate the division between the path to good and the path to evil: *novimus Pythagoram Samium vitam humanam divisisse in modum*

Y litterae, scilicet quod prima aetas incerta sit, quippe quae adhuc se nec vitiis nec virtutibus dedit: bivium autem Y litterae a iuventute incipere, quo tempore homines aut vitia, id est partem sinistram, aut virtutes, id est dextram partem, sequuntur (Servius, ad *Aen.* 6.136). The choice of roads appears in the *Hamartigenia* as well:

> saepe egomet memini fratres geminos ad hiulcum
> pervenisse simul bivium nutante iuventa
> et dubitasse diu *bifido* sub *tramite*, quodnam
> esset iter melius, cum dextrum spinea silva
> sentibus artaret scopulosaque semita longe
> duceret aerium clivoso margine callem,
> at laevum nemus umbriferum per amoena virecta
>   ditibus ornaret pomis et lene iacentem
> planities daret ampla viam; squalentibus unum
> contentum spinis reptasse per ardua saxa,
> porro alium campo sese indulsisse sinistro;
> illum in sideribus caput inmiscere propinquis
> hunc in caenosas subito cecidisse paludes.
>   (H. 789–801)

>   Often
> I remind myself of how, in a time
> of indecision, a pair of youthful brothers
> arrived together at a crossroads; long
> they hesitated by the branching fork
> and wondered which would prove the better path.
> On the right, the road is choked by thorns
> and brambles and a rocky path ascends
> steeply up a narrow ridge, while on
> the left, through pleasant lawns adorned with shady
>   orchards bearing golden fruit, the broad
> and gently sloping road descends. Content
> with thorns, one brother creeps along the jagged
> ridge; the other, self-indulgent, takes
> the level left-hand path. One raises up
> his head nearly to the stars; the other
> slipped and fell into a muddy swamp.
>   (H. 1051–67)

The version of the story Prudentius gives is somewhat unusual in that instead of portraying an individual at the crossroads, as was the case in the famous example of Hercules' choice in Prodicus's allegory, he instead recollects *two* brothers who arrive at the same time at the crossroads. At least two pairs of brothers converge here at the crossroads: Cain and Abel, so prominent at the poem's beginning, and Hesiod and Perses, the hostile brothers whose strife helps shape the *Works and Days*, where the first example of the crossroads story appears—for though only one man faces the choice of paths in that text, the example is directed at Hesiod's own bad brother, Perses, and throughout the poem, the divergent fates of Hesiod and Perses are contrasted. Hesiod, aligned with truthful speaking, is suffering the pains of poverty in the poem's fictional setting, but expects the law of Zeus to reward him ultimately; Perses, aligned with deceitful speech, enjoys the inheritance now, but will suffer for his squandering in the end if he does not change his ways.

The use of the verbal tag *saepe egomet memini* at the start of the passage, though, points to a third source as well, the satirist Persius, who recollects a scene from his childhood in *Satire* 3, shortly before he deploys the metaphor of the crossroads:

> *saepe oculos, memini,* tangebam parvus olivo,
> grandia si nollem morituri verba Catonis
> discere non sano multum laudanda magistro,
> quae pater adductis sudans audiret amicis.
> (*Sat.* 3.44–47)

> Often, I remember, when I was small I used to smear my eyes with olive oil if I didn't want to learn the grandiose words of the dying Cato, which my crazy teacher would praise lavishly, and my father would listen, sweating in front of the friends he had invited.

Persius's recall here is excellent, but he is not simply recalling his childhood experiences. Persius's father, Flaccus, is said to have died when Persius was about six, surely too early for him to have had to perform frequent public recitals of Cato's dying words. The apparent recollection of a real incident is in fact a literary reenactment of a scene from Persius's model Horace (another Flaccus), recalling Horace's description of his miserable education (*Epist.* 2.1.69–71, including the word *memini*). In *Satire* 1, Persius had already indicated his distrust of fathers and their role in the linguistic education of their children, in another passage that uses the imagery of bleared vision:[26]

> hos pueris monitus patres infundere lippos
> cum videas quaerisne, unde haec sartago loquendi
> venerit in linguas?
> (*Sat.* 3.1.79–81)

> When you see bleary-eyed fathers pouring these admonitions into their children, do you need to ask how this casserole of speech came to their tongues?

The *sartago loquendi,* a mixed casserole of speech, represents the debased state of rhetoric and poetry in Persius's Rome, a recurring theme in the *Satires.* In *Satire* 3, after the pseudomemory of cheating his father out of a rhetorical performance, there is an exchange between the persona of Persius and an interlocutor on the subject of Persius's misspent youth. Persius attacks education in the form of *suasoriae* and the Stoics, whom he caricatures; his interlocutor responds by pointing out Persius's own poor choices, using as a final example the two-roads topos:

> "et tibi quae Samios diduxit littera ramos
> surgentem dextro monstravit limite callem:
> stertis adhuc laxumque caput conpage soluta
> oscitat hesternum dissutis undique malis!"
>   Sat. 3.56–59

> "You too have been shown the Upward Path by the Samian's
> branching Symbol and its right fork: yet still you snore and
> trail unhinged a head whose jaws are all unstitched by yesterday's yawn!"
>   (trans. JENKINSON)

As in the Hesiod passage, the crossroads image in Persius is adduced to illustrate that choices between proper and improper behavior, truthful and deceptive speech, affect a young man's chances for inheriting his patrimony, though in Persius's jaundiced dialogue, both speakers seem to be equally distant from attaining truthful speech, the straight and narrow path, and a smooth transition of rightful inheritance from father to son.

The fable of the two brothers at the crossroads repeats a pattern we have already seen in the *Hamartigenia.* Like Cain and Abel, like Solomon and Absalom, like Ruth and Orpah, the brothers stand in radically different relation to their ultimate progenitor, God. It is significant that these unnamed brothers enact their differences within, literally, the framework of the letter, the Pythagorean Y that begins in unity and ends in division, like the forked tongue of the devil.

The Wings of the Dove

Next and last in the chain of figures unleashed in the text by Adam's sin (Lot's wife, Ruth and Orpah, the two brothers at the crossroads) is a simile that compares human souls to a flock of white doves:

> Just as sometimes doves in a milk-white cloud,
> descending through the bright and lucid sky,
> settle in a wheat field, where a clever
> fowler set his snares and smeared the twigs
> with sticky lime, baiting his traps with peas
> and poisoned grain, and some are tempted by
> the treacherous grain and caught by nets of woven
> cord that choke their greedy throats, or else
> soft glue traps and binds their wings: but others,
> not seduced by love of eating, stroll
> at ease, unharmed, about the barren grass
> and take good care not to turn their eyes
> toward the suspect food. Soon, when it comes
> time to fly back toward the sky, some freely
> seek the starry heaven and clap their wings
> above the clouds, while others, taken captive,
> lie wounded, struggling on the ground, their feathers
> torn, looking up in vain at the passing
> breezes.
>   (*H.* 1071–89; Lat. 804–18)

The simile of the doves, like the stories of Lot and his wife, Ruth and Orpah, and the two brothers, illustrates the responsibility of the soul for its own fate. The doves settle down in rich agricultural land (*arvum ruris frugiferi*), reminding us of the association of Cain with the fruits of the earth at the beginning of the poem. The cunning fowler with his limed sticks, nets, and poisoned bait recalls the earlier portrait of Satan as the hunter Nimrod (Nebroth) setting his nets and snares for unwary prey (*H.* 191–203; Lat. 139–48). Some of the birds are attracted to the tempting food and are caught in the snares: they are strangled by cords or their wings are gripped by the sticky glue of the traps. The birds that refrain from turning their eyes toward the food fly off to the heavens, clapping their wings as they go; those trapped in the snares are captive, helplessly beating their wounded wings as they gaze in vain at the swift breezes. The dove simile is a complex multiple allusion to passages from the *Odyssey,* the *Aeneid,* and the *Metamorphoses.* In *Odyssey* 22, Odysseus and Telemachus punish the disloyal maids who had slept with the suitors and betrayed the trust of the household, by stringing them up in nooses in the rafters of the house:

> With that, taking a cable used on a dark-prowed ship
> he coiled it over the roundhouse, lashed it fast to a tall column,
> hoisting it up so high no toes could touch the ground.
> Then, as doves or thrushes beating their spread wings

> against some snare rigged up in thickets—flying in
> for a cozy nest, but a grisly bed receives them—
> so the women's heads were trapped in a line,
> nooses yanking their heads up one by one
> so all might die a pitiful, ghastly death....
> They kicked up their heels for a little—not for long.
> *Odyssey* 22.491–500 (trans. FAGLES)

The doves in the *Odyssey* simile appear in the context of the punishment of a crime. The guilty maids are compared to thrushes or doves trapped in a snare; like the foolish doves of Prudentius's simile, their throats are choked by nooses (Gk. *brokhos*; Latin *laqueus* means both "noose" and "snare"). The Odyssean punishment of the maids' sexual crime by hanging is an example of what Nugent (2000, 23) has summarized as "the emphasis on the throat as the corollary of the problematically sexual body of the female." In both Greek and Roman culture, women were conceived of as being "caught between two throats" (Loraux 1987, 61); there is a cultural logic to punishing female sex crimes by strangulation or stabbing the throat. The doves in Prudentius's simile represent the sinful soul, who has earlier been described by Prudentius as an adulterous bride who forsakes her true lord and husband for sex with the devil.

Finally, Prudentius's dove simile echoes the language used by Ovid in his description of the transformation of the Thracian women in *Metamorphoses* 11. This metamorphosis concludes the Orpheus cycle that takes up all of *Metamorphoses* 10. As Ovid tells it, Orpheus goes to the underworld and his grief-stricken song persuades Proserpina to let him bring Eurydice back from Hades. She agrees with a condition: he is not to look at her until they have arrived in the upper world. Orpheus is unable to resist looking back at her, and Eurydice is forced to return to Hades. The double loss of his wife turns Orpheus away from the love of women, and most of *Met.* 10 is taken up by his song, which celebrates tales of male pederasty and indicts female passion. Maddened by his misogyny, a band of Thracian bacchantes attack the poet and tear him limb from limb, a spectacular punishment enhanced by a simile comparing his death to the death of beasts in the amphitheater. His head, still singing, and his lyre, still sounding, float down the Hebrus River, and his soul is reunited with Eurydice in the underworld, where they are finally free to walk as they please ("hic modo coniunctis *spatiantur* passibus ambo,/ nunc praecedentem sequitur, nunc praevius anteit,/ Eurydicenque suam iam tuto respicit Orpheus," *Met.* 11.64–66). Bacchus, angered by Orpheus's murder, transforms the women who had seen the crime into trees; as the women are rooted to the spot, they are compared to birds caught by a clever fowler:

> Yet Lyaeus does not allow this crime to go unpunished,
> and grieving the loss of the priest of his sacred rites,

there in the woods at once he bound all the Thracian mothers who had seen the crime (*quae videre nefas*) with twisted roots. For he drew out their toes, and, as far as each root extended, he thrust its tip into the solid earth. And just as a bird, when she has put her leg into a snare (*laqueis*) that the clever fowler (*callidus auceps*) had set, and senses she is caught, mourns, and as she trembles, tightens her bonds by her own movement, so, when each of these women had been rooted to the ground, she tried in terror to escape, but in vain. (*Met.* 11.67–77)

Prudentius's language describing the fowler closely echoes Ovid's (*laqueos* ubi *callidus auceps*, H. 806; *laqueis* quos *callidus* abdidit *auceps*, *Met.* 11.73), and his doves caught fast in the sticky lime and struggling to get off the ground share the fate of Ovid's bird, who struggles to escape but only tightens the noose with every movement. Like the *Odyssey* simile, the bird simile in the *Metamorphoses* occurs in the context of punishment for a crime. The crime of Odysseus's maids is obvious—they have betrayed their master's household and slept with his enemies. The faithful servant Eurykleia is brought in to report which of the maids are guilty, and only the guilty ones are punished. The situation of the Thracian women, however, is not quite so straightforward. Bacchus, angered not so much by the fate of Orpheus as by the fact that he has lost the priest of his own rites, punishes not just the women who committed the crime, but also all the women who *saw* the crime (*omnes quae videre nefas*, *Met.* 11.70). *Seeing* the murder of Orpheus is as criminal an act as actually killing him.

It is unlikely that Ovid's choice of the verb *videre* is a casual one, since vision plays such a central role in the whole Orpheus story. Orpheus loses Eurydice when he is unable to restrain his gaze. Orpheus performs his songs in a theatrical setting, surrounded by an audience of trees, beasts, and (unbeknownst to him) bacchants. Ovid compares the bacchants at the murder of Orpheus to birds flocking to chase away an owl, and, more elaborately, to a beast fight in a matinee show at the amphitheater:

Then they turn on Orpheus with their bloody hands and flock together like birds do, when once they see a bird of night wandering in the light, and like when in an amphitheater (*theatro*) a stag is doomed to fall prey to the dogs in an early morning performance (*matutina ... harena*), they hunt the bard and hurl their thyrsoi, wreathed with green, not made for such games (*munera*). (*Met.* 11.23–28)

Orpheus, who is unable to control his gaze, becomes in death a spectacle (note the repeated use of terms that evoke performance: *theatro, matutina ... harena, munera*) for the gaze of others; those who watch it are themselves subjected to punishment from the offended deity. The simile of the fowler occurs in a context of punishment; significantly, it is a context that links punishment to spectacle. The Thracian women are punished for seeing the spectacle of Orpheus's death, a death that is itself the result of Orpheus's misdirected vision. The birds in the *Hamartigenia* fall for the deceptively alluring food of the fowler and end up being trapped in the fowler's net; their wings are held by the sticky lime, and they gaze in vain at the air from which they came (*pars captiva iacet laceris et saucia plumis/pugnat humi et volucres nequiquam suspicit auras*, 817–18). Prudentius expands the parameters of Ovid's simile, linking the foolish doves' appetite for poisoned food to the misdirected gaze: he describes the downfall of the foolish doves as *amor edendi*, but when he turns to the wise doves, he calls attention not to their refusal to succumb to their appetites, but rather to their refusal *to turn their gaze* toward the dangerous food (*H.* 812–14, quoted above). The birds' refusal to look at the poisonous food reverses the visual errors committed by Lot's wife within the poem, and by the Thracian women and Orpheus from the Ovidian intertext, whose misdirected gazes lead to their doom.

The importance of proper direction of the gaze is not merely metaphorical for Prudentius. It is based on ancient understanding of the physics of vision, which held that the mind of the viewer energizes and projects a ray of light toward an object and is thus connected to that object. Not only is the object touched by the ray, but the object is printed on the soul of the viewer. Augustine posited three different kinds of vision: perception through the eyes, by which the soul perceives objects through the body; perception through imagination, by which the soul sees likenesses of physical things that are not present; and perception through intuition, by which the soul understands noncorporeal realities.[27] As Margaret Miles says, in Augustine's theory of vision, the act of seeing requires the viewer's effort and selectivity; it is initiated by will:

> Vision, then, connects or attaches the viewer to the object. Moreover, the soul of the viewer both initially projects the visual ray, and it also "absorbs into itself" the form or image of the object, which is then permanently retained by the memory. Vision is definitely, for Augustine, a two-way street: the soul forms images of sensible things "out of its own substance" (*substantiae suae*), but the result is that the mind itself is formed by the very images it formulates and carries. The soul is "fitted together" with, or "takes the shape of" (10.5.7–8), the objects of its focused attention. (Miles 1983, 128)

The wise doves have clearly learned the lesson that Ovid's Orpheus and the Thracian women who tore him apart did not. Their exercise of will in controlling their gaze keeps their souls free from the imprint of sin. They stroll at their ease on the sterile grass, like Orpheus's shade, united at last with Eurydice in the underworld (*spatiantur* in *H.* 812 echoes *spatiantur* in *Met.* 11.64):

umbra subit terras, et quae loca viderat ante,
cuncta recognoscit quaerensque per arva piorum
invenit Eurydicen cupidisque amplectitur ulnis,
hic modo coniunctis *spatiantur* passibus ambo,
nunc praecedentem sequitur, nunc praevius anteit
Eurydicenque suam, iam tuto, respicit Orpheus.
   (*Met.* 11.61–66)

His shade goes beneath the earth, and he recognizes all the places he had seen before, and seeking her through the fields of the pious, he finds Eurydice and greedily throws his arms around her, and sometimes as they stroll they walk together, sometimes she leads and he follows, sometimes he leads the way and goes ahead and—now safely—looks back at his Eurydice.

Where the foolish doves suffer different punishments for their weakness, the wise doves avoid the snares of the fowler and fly off to the heavens, clapping their wings joyfully (*H.* 815–16). The applauding birds recall a pair of passages in *Aeneid* 5 describing the funeral games for Anchises. In the ship race, Mnestheus, captain of the *Pistris* (*Sea Monster*) is compared to a dove taking flight after being frightened from her nest:[28]

qualis spelunca subito commota columba,
cui domus et dulces latebroso in pumice nidi,
fertur in arua uolans plausumque exterrita pennis
dat tecto ingentem, mox aere lapsa quieto
radit iter liquidum celeris neque commouet alas:
sic Mnestheus, sic ipsa fuga secat ultima Pristis
aequora, sic illam fert impetus ipse uolantem.
   (*Aen.* 5.213–19)

Think: if you suddenly frighten a dove from her home, from her cosy
Nest in a secret bubble of pumice deep in a cavern,
Out above farmlands, in terror she flies, wings frantically, loudly
Clapping. Yet after awhile, she'll be gliding aloft in the calm air,
Hardly touching her frictionless road, not moving her swift wings.
That's how Mnestheus sails, as the *Pristis* sails, on the final
Stretches of the sea. For her own sheer impetus keeps her in motion.
   (trans. AHL, with slight modifications)

The frightened dove, like Prudentius's good soul, is able to soar through the air, clapping her wings, to her home. In the case of the soul, Prudentius goes on to explain, home is the heavens. Nature has sent all souls to earth innocent (*unicoloras*, literally "unicolored" or "spotless");[29] some will be stained by sin and stuck on earth, while a few will return to their heavenly home. Some of the doves trapped by the fowler are, as we have seen, choked to death by his snares, but others are caught fast in birdlime and helplessly beat their wounded limbs. The fate of Prudentius's trapped birds brings to mind another passage from *Aeneid* 5, where the dove in the ship-race simile materializes as a dove that Aeneas tethers to the mast of a ship to serve as the target in an archery contest. The first contestant hits the mast, causing the terrified bird to flutter its wings in a vain attempt to escape:

intremuit malus micuitque exterrita pennis
ales et ingenti sonuerunt omnia plausu.
  (*Aen.* 5.505–6)

As the mast shivers, the dove is dislodged, wings beating in frenzied
Terror. The whole place erupts in a thunder of cheering and clapping.
  (trans. AHL)

The second contestant is Mnestheus, who had earlier been compared to a terrified dove; he misses the frightened bird and instead shoots the cord that tethers her to the mast and sets her free:

ast ipsam miserandus avem contingere ferro
non valuit: nodos et vincula linea rupit
quis innexa pedem malo pendebat ab alto;
illa Notos atque atra volans in nubila fugit.
  (*Aen.* 5.509–12)

Still the poor man cannot quite hit his target, the bird, with its iron
Point; but he severs the cordage of hemp and the slipknot that tethers
One of her feet to the masthead and dangles her high like a pennant.
Off she now speeds into lowering skies on the wings of the south wind.
  (trans. AHL)

Unfortunately, the tethered dove does not have the same good fortune as the dove in the simile: as she soars joyfully into the sky and claps her wings, the next contestant, Eurytion, pierces her with his arrow and she falls from the sky:

iam vacuo laetam caelo speculatus et alis
plaudentem nigra figit sub nube columbam.

decidit exanimis vitamque relinquit in astris
aetheriis fixamque refert delapsa sagittam.
   (*Aen.* 5.516-19)

[He] sets eyes on the dove, bright white on a backdrop of black cloud,
Flapping and clapping her wings in joy at escape through the empty
Skies. Lifeless, she drops to the earth, soul lost in the billowing stardust,
And as she falls, transfixed, she restores spent arrow to archer.
   (trans. AHL, with slight modifications)

Unlike the Ovidian and Homeric similes of trapped birds, the doves in *Aeneid* 5 with their contrasting fates do not illustrate punishment, whether just or unjust. Instead, each dove plays a role in a visual spectacle: the flight of the terrified mother dove illustrates the movement of Mnestheus's ship, and the dove tethered to the mast of the ship is the target of an archery competition. Vergil draws attention to the spectators and the spectacular setting at various moments in the description of the funeral games. For example, as Mnestheus gains on Cloanthus, the crowd roars (*tum vero ingeminant clamor cunctique sequentem/instigant studiis, resonatque fragoribus aether, Aen.* 5.226-27); the footrace takes place in a landscape shaped like a natural theater (*Aen.* 5.286-88); and the Sicilian and Trojan spectators are stunned by the omen of the fiery arrow that concludes the archery contest (*attonitis haesere animis superosque precati/Trinacrii Teucrique viri, Aen.* 5.529-30). Even the noise produced by the beating of the dove's wings suggests spectatorship: Prudentius repeats Vergil's punning use of the verb *plaudo*, which suggests both the beating of the doves wings and the applause of an audience (a wordplay cleverly brought out in Ahl's translation by his rendering of Vergil's *plaudentem* as "flapping and clapping").

The simile of the doves is the last in the chain of figures that illustrate the soul as it hesitates on the verge of sin. As such, it is the pivotal trope, as the poem moves away from the figural chain to a description of the possible fates awaiting the soul after death: for the sinful soul, the fiery torments of the underworld; for the innocent soul, a return to its heavenly home. Through its multiple allusions, the complex simile of the doves brings together two themes of vital importance to the final section of the poem: punishment and spectacle.

8. *IN AENIGMATE*

> *Poore intricated soule! Riddling, perplexed, labyrinthicall soule!*
>
> JOHN DONNE, sermon 48

THE *HAMARTIGENIA* BEGINS after the beginning, starting with the sacrifice of Cain and Abel (not the story of Adam and Eve with which the story of man begins in Genesis), and it ends both before and after the end—before and after the end of the world, in the vision of the Apocalypse as imagined by John the Evangelist, and before and after the end of Prudentius himself, as he imagines his own death and afterlife in his closing prayer. The *Hamartigenia* displays a preoccupation with eschatology that is typical of the late antique period. Eschatology, the study of "last things," includes both the end of time, which would culminate, Christians believed, in the Apocalypse, and the end of the individual, the "hour of death" that each soul must endure. In examining the eschatological vision laid out in the *Hamartigenia*, it is useful to keep in mind the observation of Caroline Walker Bynum and Paul Freedman in their introduction to a collection of essays on death and the Apocalypse in the Middle Ages. They argue that there is

> a disjunction and incompatibility throughout the medieval texts between an eschatology of resurrection—a sense of last things that focuses significance in the moment at the end of time when the physical body is reconstituted and judged—and an eschatology of immortality—in which the experience of personal death is the moment of judgment, after which the good soul ... either gains glorification and beatific vision at once or moves into the experience of growth through suffering known as purgatory.[1]

They further identify a third "eschatology of apocalypse": a belief that the collective end of humanity is imminent, and that the Last Judgment, which would vindicate the good and punish the bad, was at hand. Carole Straw, in her exploration of eschatology in the early church (ca. 100–313 CE), summarizes the apocalyptic mentality of the church of the martyrs thus:

Revelation and subjective conversion replaced discursive reasoning; violence often succeeded persuasion. The concrete and material prevailed over the abstract and immaterial: heaven and hell, the soul and body of the afterlife were elaborated in terms easily understood by analogy with realities known. People, motivations, and actions tended to be reduced to moralistic types: monster and martyr, cruelty and altruism, tragedy and triumph. So, too, polarities of spirit and flesh were fastidiously antithetical, never approaching harmony and reconciliation. The universe was divided and embittered: the ancient mentality of the vendetta overwhelmed the more subtle ideas of justice and moral reform.[2]

Although the *Hamartigenia* postdates the period Straw analyzes by close to a hundred years, the fierce apocalypticism of the period of the martyrs left an indelible stamp on Christian theology, and its stark polarities are deeply embedded in Prudentius's imagination.

Dramatic Justice

In the final section of the poem (*H.* 1095ff.; Lat. 818ff.), the themes of judgment and vision are closely interwoven, as the poem takes its eschatological turn and addresses the fate of the soul after judgment, which is the culmination of the forensic metaphors and language that permeate the poem. Indeed, Prudentius portrays himself as an active participant in a legal process, though his role shifts as the poem unfolds. In the opening of the poem (*H.* 1–172; Lat. 1–123), Prudentius takes on the persona of a defense lawyer defending the accused (God) against the charges lodged against him by the prosecutor (Marcion, who takes on the Satanic role of accuser or prosecutor).[3] After disproving the charges, he turns the tables and launches a counteraccusation against Marcion (*H.* 173–216; Lat. 124–57). Later, as Prudentius builds up to the pivotal moment of Adam's choice (834–918; Lat. 636–696), he again assumes the role of defense attorney, this time defending God against the charge that he is responsible for sin, and the text stages a trial, with an adversary posing objections that the poet/advocate refutes. He makes extensive use of legal language, such as *litem* (637), *calumina* (638), *convicia* (656), *probat* (659), and *argumentum* (667). The moment of original sin is presented as if it were an account of a law case. The still unnamed Woman (*mulier*) appears as a defendant (*rea*, 713) and is legally charged (*exprobanti*, 713). As Taddei (1981, 232) has pointed out, the simple instructions God gives to Adam in Genesis are recast in the *Hamartigenia* as a detailed exposition of Adam's legal duties, with Adam as the judge of his own actions (*arbiter*, 699 and *iudex*, 700).

All of this legal language and imagery culminate spectacularly in a theodicy in which the souls of the damned are condemned to never-ending torment amid the flames and voracious worms of hell, while the good soul ascends, returning like an exile to her homeland, where she is greeted by her old nurse, Faith (Fides), and reclines on a bed of roses. After an excursus on the clarity of the soul's vision, Prudentius describes how the souls of the damned and the souls of the blessed gaze across the gulf that separates them and eternally contemplate each other's fate. The poem concludes with another trial scene, this time with Prudentius himself now in the role of defendant on the day of judgment, addressing Christ as Judge, admitting his guilt, and pleading that his sentence be mitigated.

The judicial trial was by no means a dead metaphor in the late fourth century, and was something that Prudentius, who twice served as governor of a province, a position whose duties included acting as *iudex*, would have experienced firsthand as a participant in the public spectacle of judgment. He draws attention to his legal training and experience in the preface to his collected works, and trial scenes feature repeatedly in his account of the sufferings and deaths of the martyrs in the *Peristephanon*. Judicial imagery was widespread in late antique writings of all kinds. Jill Harries (1999, 214) has pointed out that the figure of the governor as *iudex* "became the prisoner of highly tendentious rhetoricians, whose various portraits of 'the Judge' are almost invariably conditioned by the wider purpose of their text." Thus we find portraits of the ideal judge (God or Christ) in Christian literature along with portraits of venal officials in imperial legislation and persecuting judges in the polemical acts of the martyrs. Whether a good judge or a bad judge presides, the proceedings are always public spectacles, always intended to impress the spectators as well as to administer justice, and always charged with the drama of the state-supplied apparatus of torture and punishment.

In late antiquity, judicial hearings were held in public, in front of crowds; hearings in private rooms were expressly forbidden because of the possibility of bribery.[4] In an article that explores the reasons for the prevalence of accounts of memories and dreams of judicial punishment in the early Christian period (such as the famous dream of Perpetua, and similar dreams of the martyrs Cyprian of Carthage and Marianus, among many others),[5] Brent Shaw (2003, 535) draws attention to the public, spectacular nature of the judicial punishments staged by the Roman state, which he calls "an ekphrasis of administrative power and of undisguised coercion so riveting that it was further developed in internal pictures of the mind. Hence the significance of judicial dreams and punitive nightmares. They are symptoms of a collective picturing and memory of a specific kind of power." As early as the Neronian era, the philosopher Seneca commented on the powerful psychological effect that the familiar sight of the apparatus of torture evoked in the audience:

> Our judicial procedure is a spectacle that surrounds itself with fiery torches, iron chains, and the claws of wild animals that are unleashed to tear out human innards. Consider what you see in the place of trial: the prison,

crosses for crucifixion, the torture rack, the iron claw, the stake driven so far through the middle of a man that it juts out from his mouth, the limbs of a human body wrenched apart by chariot wheels drawing them in opposite directions, the so-called "fiery shirt" laced with pitch and acid, and other instruments of savagery that I have not yet mentioned. So it isn't surprising, is it, that there is such a great fear of all this process in which there is such wonderful variety and such a terrible apparatus. The torturer does not have to do much more than simply set out the instruments of pain. The defendants are mentally overcome by the mere appearance of those things which they would have resisted with physical endurance. In fact, the instruments with which torturers subjugate and dominate our minds are more efficient to the precise degree that they are simply displayed.[6]

The apparatus Seneca describes appears to have been deployed by the state over centuries; Shaw cites a fourth-century Arian commentary on Matthew that describes the spectacle of punishment in terms strikingly similar to Seneca's:

The judge who will hear the cases of criminals in public, places his tribunal in a high location ... and you will see there the officials arranged in their proper order: in the middle of the judicial hearing chamber are placed the horrible devices of punishment, which are painful not just to suffer, but even to see. There stand close at hand and at the ready the torturers themselves, crueler in their appearance than ghostly apparitions. The whole appearance of the court is clothed in the dress of terror. When the criminals are led into the midst of this scene, even before any interrogation has actually begun by the judge, they are already broken by the terrible sight of the court itself.[7]

Tertullian describes in detail the physical effects—the visual indicators of guilt—that were induced in defendants by the sight of the apparatus of judicial ritual: blushing, sweating, bowing, and weeping.[8] The judicial process, which could produce bodily reactions that (at least apparently) were visual indicators of the state of the defendant's invisible soul, was appropriated by Christian writers and thinkers, who urged the Christian believer to internalize it, as Augustine urged his congregation: "Question your faith, lift your soul onto the defendant's tribunal of your conscience, torture yourself with the fear of judgment, and then answer the questions: In whom do you believe? Why do you believe?"[9] (*Ennarationes in Psalmos* 96.16 [CCL 39:1367–68]).

The spectacle of judgment had a clear didactic intent, but it also depended on a cultural belief that punishment of the body served a corrective function. Early Christian thought on punishment was shaped both by the realities of the Roman judicial system and its public enforcement, and by the authority of the Bible, where in both the Old and the New Testaments, God repeatedly subjects his chosen people to punishment. The soul could be improved by purificatory punishments while one was alive. Writers from the second and third centuries such as Irenaeus and Clement of Alexandria believed that even after death the soul could be educated and improved; Clement thought that "in the afterlife purgation would proceed by two types of fires: the educational fire that corrected the corrigible and the punitive fire that devoured the incorrigible."[10] Clement and Origen represent the deeply rooted classical belief that the self could be perfected through labor, a notion, as Peter Brown puts it, that "always looked back across the centuries to the long, austere labor on the self associated with the moral world of the classical philosopher . . . that search for exacting, personal transformation that was the hallmark of the classical tradition of philosophical ethics."[11]

Well into the sixth century, there were many who thought about the Last Judgment less in terms of purgation and purification of the soul and more in terms of intercession and amnesty—of *clementia*, the mercy that was the prerogative of the emperor. Augustine describes such notions in *Civ. dei* 23, as Brown summarizes:

> [Augustine] was touching the outlines of an imaginative structure endowed with exceptional long-term solidity. What he heard was that, at the Last Judgment, the power of the saints would prevail to obtain forgiveness for all but the worst sinners. For, so the argument went, if the saints had prayed for the persecutors when alive, how much more effective would their prayers be when they stood in the presence of God? . . . The amnesty granted by God in answer to the prayers of the saints on their great day of intercession would be wide. It would certainly cover all baptized Catholics who had partaken of the Eucharist, and perhaps many others. As for hell itself, its eternity might also be disrupted by God's amnesty.[12]

By the early fifth century, however, a gloomier view of the soul's fate was being developed. Augustine raised these optimistic views of widespread intercession and amnesty only to refute them. He argued that the soul can no longer improve itself after death, and physical suffering is not a means of educating the soul to bring about its salvation, but rather the inevitable punishment for original sin, from which only a few would be saved by undeserved grace:

> The more enjoyment man found in God, the greater was his wickedness in abandoning Him; and he who destroyed in himself a good which might have been eternal, became worthy of eternal evil. Hence the whole mass of the human race is condemned; for he who at first gave entrance to sin has been punished with all his posterity who were in him as in a root, so that no one is exempt from this just and due punishment, unless delivered by

mercy and undeserved grace; and the human race is so apportioned that in some is displayed the efficacy of merciful grace, in the rest the efficacy of just retribution.[13]

It is against this backdrop of violent and public judicial spectacle and contesting Christian beliefs about the punishment of the soul in the afterlife that we should read the final scenes of the *Hamartigenia*.

The Fate of the Soul

After the simile of the doves, Prudentius turns to a vivid description of the punishments awaiting the guilty soul:

> And so the Father, knowing all
> in advance, set livid Tartarus on fire
> with molten lead and under grim Avernus
> dug channels filled with pitch and hellish water
> and ordered greedy worms to dwell beneath
> the fiery waves of Phlegethon, eternal
> punishment for sinners. For He knew
> the soul, the living force of His own breath
> shaped by His own mouth, can never die,
> but neither, stained by sin, can she again
> return to heaven but must be plunged
> into the boiling abyss. To worms and flames
> and tortures he gave eternal life, to keep
> her punishment from perishing with age,
> since the soul's immortal; torments foster
> and gnaw on matter given without end,
> and Death herself retreats from the endless groaning
> and forces sobbing souls to keep on living.
>   (*H.* 1095–1112; Lat. 824–38)

Terrifying punishments await the guilty soul, whose immortality leads God to create immortal worms and flames, along with rivers of molten lead and boiling pitch, to ensure her eternal punishment. In Prudentius's cosmic vision, the underworld of classical paganism—in particular, the underworld of the *Aeneid*, complete with the fires of Tartarus and the rivers of the underworld, Avernus and Phlegethon—is the setting for the suffering of the guilty. As Mastrangelo puts it, "Prudentius' poetry visually conceives of the afterlife in Vergilian imagistic terms. Prudentius has responded to the apophatic drama of the afterlife—we just do not know how to conceive of it—by integrating the Vergilian sensual version into

Christian tradition."[14] The souls of the innocent dwell in a paradise vastly distant (*diversa procul*) from the torments of hell:

> at diversa procul regionibus in Paradisi
> praemia constituit maiestas gnara futuri
> spiritibus puris et ob omni labe remotis,
> quique Gomorraeas non respexere ruinas,
> aversis sed rite oculis post terga tenebras
> liquerunt miseri properanda pericula mundi.
> ac primum facili referuntur ad astra volatu,
> unde fluens anima structum vegetaverat Adam.
> nam quia naturam tenuem declivia bitae
> pondera non reprimunt nec tardat ferrea compes,
> concretum celeri relegens secat aera lapsu
> exsuperatque polum fervens scintilla remensum,
> carcereos exosa situs, quibus haeserat exul.
> (*H.* 839–51)

> But far away in realms of paradise,
> God's majesty, endowed with knowledge of
> the future, has allotted very different
> rewards for spirits pure and free of any
> sin, who didn't turn around to look
> upon the ruins of Gomorrah, but
> with eyes averted, as is right, they turned
> their backs upon the dark and looming dangers
> of our wretched world.
> These souls are first
> uplifted to the stars in easy flight,
> from whence the soul that animated Adam
> after God had shaped him. For because
> the weight of life no longer drags her tender
> nature down toward earth, nor impedes it
> with iron fetters, she cuts her path and glides
> swiftly through the heavy atmosphere
> and, like a glowing spark, she rises far
> above the heaven whence she came, despising
> the prison house of clay where she was exiled.
> (*H.* 1113–31)

As he turns to his description of the fate of the just souls, Prudentius once again aligns proper moral action with proper governance of the gaze. Returning to the story of Lot, he explicitly associates the just souls with those who did not turn to gaze at the ruins of Gomorrah, and draws an implicit contrast with the fate of Lot's wife through verbal allusion to Ovid's Niobe: "*celeri . . . secat aera lapsu*" in 849 echoes *Met.* 6.216, "*celerique per aera lapsu.*" In the *Metamorphoses* the phrase describes the swift downward flight of Apollo and Diana from Mount Cynthus, on their way to exact their revenge on Niobe (who, as we have seen, served as a model for Prudentius's depiction of Lot's wife). Prudentius inverts the direction of the journey, using the phrase to characterize the swift ascent of the innocent soul instead of the descent of the vengeful gods. Unlike Niobe and the wife of Lot, whose fickle mobility led to their permanent immobility through the process of petrification, the soul sheds the body that weighs it down and ascends to the realms of paradise. Drawing on themes entrenched in Platonic and Neoplatonic thought about the nature of the soul, Prudentius casts the ascent as a return to its original home from its term of exile on earth and imprisonment in the body.[15]

In another vivid ekphrastic display, Prudentius presents a synesthetic picture of the soul's reception in Paradise:

> tunc postliminio redeuntem suscipit alto
> cana Fides gremio tenerisque oblectat alumnam
> deliciis, multos post divorsoria carnis
> ore renarrantem querulo, quos passa, labores.
> illic purpureo latus exporrecta cubili
> floribus aeternis spirantes libat odores
> ambrosiumque bibit roseo de stramine rorem.
>   (H. 852–58)

> Returning to her rightful home, the soul
> is swept into the arms of Faith, her white-
> haired, darling nurse, who gently soothes her as
> she tells in plaintive tones the sufferings she
> endured since taking up her lodging in
> the body. Resting on a crimson couch,
> she tastes the sweet perfumes exhaled from ever-
> blooming flowers, and from roses strewn
> about her feet she drinks ambrosial dew.
>   (H. 1132–40)

The soul is greeted by the personified Fides (Faith), portrayed as a wet nurse who receives her nursling (*alumnam*) in her bosom (*gremio*).[16] The language of the passage is highly sensual, evoking the senses of smell (*spirantes . . . odores*), touch (*latus exporrecta cubili*), hearing (*ore renarrantem querelo*), and taste (*libat, ambrosiumque bibit*) as well as sight (*cana Fides, purpureo . . . cubili, roseo de stramine*). In addition to appealing to all the senses, the description has strong erotic overtones—the soul is not only a nursling received by a beloved nurse but also a bride at a wedding banquet.[17] In Prudentius's allegorical scheme, the personified soul awaits the arrival of the bridegroom, Christ, thus reversing the choice of the adulterous soul in *H.* 629–36 who rejected Christ and chose illicit sex with the devil.[18]

The vivid picture of the soul's rewards in paradise is abruptly juxtaposed with a description of the insatiable thirst of the souls burning in hell, and the assertion that the innocent and guilty souls can view each other across the gulf that divides them. This leads to a passage that returns to the theme of optics addressed at the opening of the poem, where Prudentius associated heretical thinking with unhealthy vision.[19] In 1153–1230 (Lat. 867–921), he contrasts the clumsy apparatus of the human eye with the lively, fiery eye of the soul, which is able to penetrate the mists and clouds of the atmosphere (the *aer*, ruled by Satan and his ministers) and see through mountains, to the ends of the earth, and even into hell. Prudentius compares the soul's vision after it has shed the burden of its body to the apocalyptic vision of John, whose soul was temporarily freed from his body as he slept on the island of Patmos. His gaze traverses both time and space, allowing him to see the end of the world. The main argument of the poem now takes its final turn. Instead of ending with the marvelous vision of John, Prudentius returns to the fate of the soul, and to the theme of the souls' mutual spectacle. The two passages about the fate of the souls contemplating one another thus frame the excursus on the eye of the soul and John's apocalyptic vision:

SOULS CONTEMPLATING EACH OTHER
Soul's powers of vision
Vision of John
SOULS CONTEMPLATING EACH OTHER

Here are the frame passages side by side:

Across the great divide, smoke rises from the
wealthy denizens of hell: they are
so thirsty! They could drink entire rivers,
as much rain as the heavens could unleash.
They beg her just to wet her finger and lift it
to their mouths to quench the surging flames, but she
says no.
        Don't be surprised to find that both
guilty souls and innocent can clearly
see each other despite the yawning gulf
that separates their homes: the just deserts

of each in turn are noted across the great
abyss the axis of the sky marks off
from middle earth.
    (*H.* 1141–53; Lat. 859–66)

Our faith is certain that the gloomy world
below is lit by blazing furnaces
that burn polluted souls for centuries
in the eternal flame, and that these souls
are seen by the poor whose home is far away
across that great divide, and that, despite
the distance, the golden gifts and shining crowns
belonging to the just are visible
to souls submerged in seas of pain. And this
is why the guilty spirit, sadly wailing
in her desolation, is presented
to the happy soul that dwells in paradise,
healed of her dreadful sores and pains! Each one
sees in turn the fate the other earned.
    (*H.* 1231–44; Lat. 923–30)

The stark juxtaposition of the fates of the saved and condemned souls appears even harsher when contrasted with another description of the afterlife from Prudentius's hymn *Cathemerinon* 5. In it, Christ appears, guiding the souls to the country of the just:

He calls the weary over the world's waves
    parting the stormclouds, guiding his people,
and bids the souls tossed by a thousand troubles
    to ascend to the country of the just.
There all the ground, covered with crimson roses,
    is perfumed; watered with rippling streams
it abounds in rich marigolds, soft violets, slender crocus.
    There balsam flows like beads from a slender
stalk, rare cinnamon sighs its fragrance, and there is
    nard carried downstream from the secret source
of the river by whose banks it grows.
    Through the grassy meadows happy souls
sing their songs together in harmony,
    the melodies of their hymns sweetly sounding,
and they tread with shining feet upon the lilies.
    And there are frequent holidays from punishment

> even for the guilty spirits below the Styx
> > on that night when holy God returned to the upper air
> > from the waters of Acheron. . . .
> . . . .
> Tartarus wilts, its punishments mild,
> > and the nation of the dead, free from the fires,
> > rejoices in its holiday from prison, and the rivers
> > of sulfur boil with less than their usual heat.
> > (*Cathemerinon* 5.109–36)

In this vision of the afterlife, we see once again the separation of the just from the unjust souls. Prudentius portrays Christ bringing his people to the country of the just, which, with its crimson rose petals and fragrances, resembles the synesthetic sensuality of the abode of the just soul in the *Hamartigenia*. But he also imagines that Easter provides a reprieve from punishment for the souls of the guilty. This idea that there might be a periodic respite from hell again reflects the way that the Christian imagination was shaped by the experience of imperial justice: Peter Brown notes that even the harsh emperor Valentinian I celebrated Easter by freeing inmates from prison, and that the pious emperor Honorius would allow prisoners in Ravenna to be released from jail on Sundays to go to the baths (under suitable guard).[20] In the *Cathemerinon*, the reprieve for the damned, though it is mentioned, is only temporary. No such holiday from hell awaits the damned in the grim description of the afterlife in the *Hamartigenia*, which is notable for its detailed account of the flames and worms that await the guilty, and its sadistic insistence on how pleasurable it is to watch the torments of the damned.

The Spectacle of Judgment

The souls' mutual contemplation of each other's fate after death is the last image in the poem before the concluding prayer for the poet's soul. Prudentius not only describes the contrasting fates of the souls but emphasizes that each group of souls is a spectacle for the other: the just are rewarded by the sight of the tortures of the damned, and the damned are tormented further by the sight of the bliss enjoyed by the just. The notion that the spectacle of the damned would provide pleasure for the viewer is present in Christian thought as early as Tertullian, who imagines in graphic detail the pleasures to be offered by the spectacle of Judgment Day at the end of his treatise *On Spectacles* (chapter 30, trans. Glover):

> But what a spectacle is already at hand—the return of the Lord, now no object of doubt, now exalted, now triumphant! What exultation will that be of the angels, what glory that of saints as they rise again! What the

reign of the righteousness thereafter! What a city, the New Jerusalem! Yes, and are still to come other spectacles—that last, that eternal Day of Judgment, that day they laughed at, when this old world and all its generations shall be consumed in one fire. How vast the spectacle that day, and how wide! What sight shall wake my wonder, what laughter, my joy and exultation? As I see those kings, those great kings, welcomed (we are told) in heaven, along with Jove, along with those who told of their ascent, groaning in the depths of darkness! And the magistrates who persecuted the name of Jesus, liquefying in fiercer flames than they kindled in their rage against Christians! Those sages, too, the philosophers blushing before their disciples whom they taught that God was concerned with nothing, that men have no souls at all, or that what souls they have shall never return to their former bodies! And, the poets trembling before the judgement-seat, not of Rhadamanthus, not Minos, but of Christ whom they never looked to see! And, then there will be the tragic actors to be heard, more vocal in their own tragedy; and the players to be seen, lither of limb by far in the fire; and then the charioteers to watch, red all over in the wheel of flame; and next, the athletes to be gazed upon, not in their gymnasiums but hurled in the fire.[21]

The laughter Tertullian anticipates so gloatingly has little to do with what we would associate with a sense of humor. As Robert Levine says, "For the Christian rhetorician, engaged in a battle against the forces of darkness, laughter expresses power, not pleasure, and therefore becomes both a weapon and a sign of victory."[22] Since Tertullian has spent most of the treatise condemning the visual pleasures offered by theatrical and amphitheatrical spectacles, it is easy to take this savage affirmation of the pleasures to be attained from contemplation of the sufferings of the damned as hypocritical—as Simon Goldhill (2001, 183–84) puts it, Tertullian's "visual politics lapses into violent self-contradiction."

In response to Goldhill, Webb points out that Tertullian's spectacle takes place in the imagination, not in the real world, and that, for Tertullian, Chrysostom, and other patristic writers, the dangers to the senses offered by theatrical performances might be countered by an alternative form of spectacle, an internal spectacle always available to the mind for contemplation. Chrysostom suggests the contemplation of the divine creation, of the sufferings of the martyrs, and even of suffering prisoners (he recommends visiting a prison) as antidotes to the vain spectacles of the theater and as a means to improve the soul of the spectator. Tertullian's conjuration of the Last Judgment as the ultimate in Christian entertainment is repugnant, but logical "from the perspective of the committed Christian, for whom the Last Judgment was the ultimate truth, not an invention made up by the human imagination."[23] Such a spectacle had the potential to impress the soul of the Christian viewer while he was still alive and corrigible. Before death, there was some possibility that the soul could change, repent, and perhaps improve its fate through compensatory penance; after death, when the soul was incapable of change, punishment was nearly inevitable. "The debt of pain owed by all Christians at death was the debt of simply being human. Suffering was inevitable for all Christians, so there was no question that sinners whose lifestyle repudiated Christ's suffering must also suffer. Born guilty into a world governed by an angry God, humanity's plea for mercy was its only recourse."[24]

The grim doctrine of the suffering of the soul after death as a spectacle is thus expressed in the *Hamartigenia* in terms that are characteristically late Roman. Justice was a matter of exact requital.[25] Observation of the pain of others was institutionalized and harnessed in amphitheatrical displays and public judicial proceedings in order to reinforce social order and shape the identity of citizens. As Martin Zimmerman (2006, 347) puts it, "The pain of the other, seen on the distorted faces of public and private monuments, or heard in the screams of criminals in the amphitheatre, reassured Romans of their own space in the world." The gleeful prospect of watching the brutal torture of the damned must serve at least in part to affirm the identity of the Christian soul. As is the case with late antique mosaics of amphitheatrical scenes, vivid descriptions like Tertullian's of the spectacle of the tormented served not to create empathy but rather to emphasize the distance between the spectator (the good Christian) and the victim.[26] The spectacle of the torments of the damned reinforces the notion that history is progressing toward a Christian Rome, where Christian citizens become triumphant spectators rather than oppressed victims.

The pleasures of watching the torments of others are complicated—perhaps contaminated—by that other violent spectacle that so gripped the early Christian imagination: martyrdom. Like the spectacle of the Last Judgment, the spectacle of martyrdom was frequently invoked by Christian writers as an alternative to the dangerous spectacles of the theater and amphitheater, and offered the same prurient, erotic appeal.[27] The audience contemplating martyrdom is encouraged to empathize with and imitate the martyr, while deriving pleasure from the bloody spectacle. As David Frankfurter says, "It is a simple matter of impulse projection and fantasy as the audience identifies alternately with the brutalized martyr and the monstrous forces of brutality, cringes at the torture, and relishes the blood."[28] Prudentius explores various aspects of this dynamic in the *Peristephanon*, from a surprisingly analytical perspective. *Peristephanon* 9, for example, which describes the death of Saint Cassian, puts the martyrdom of the saint very self-consciously in the context of viewing (the martyrdom is portrayed as a work of art), a viewer's response to art, and the problematics of writing. It opens with a description of Prudentius standing before the tomb of Cassian, and looking at a painting of the martyrdom of the saint (a schoolmaster stabbed to death by the styluses of his pupils):

> stratus humi tumulo aduoluebar, quem sacer ornat
>   martyr dicato Cassianus corpore.
> dum lacrimans mecum reputo mea uulnera et omnes
>   uitae labores ac dolorum acumina,
> erexi ad caelum faciem, stetit obuia contra
>   fucis colorum picta imago martyris
> plagas mille gerens, totos lacerata per artus,
>   ruptam minutis praeferens punctis cutem.
>   (*Pe.* 9.5–12)

> I am stretched on the ground, prostrate before the tomb, which holy
> Cassian, the martyr, honors with his consecrated body.
> While I reflect, weeping, on my wounds and all the labors
> of my life and the pricks of grief,
> I lifted my face to heaven, and there stood opposite me
> an image of the martyr painted in colored hues,
> bearing a thousand wounds, all limbs mangled,
> reproducing his skin ripped with tiny points.

The position of Prudentius at the opening of *Pe.* 9 is strikingly reminiscent of the position of the guilty soul at the end of *Hamartigenia*. The poet is in tears, wounded, reflecting on his sins. But where the damned soul in the *Hamartigenia* stares across the gulf and sees the souls of the just residing in bliss in paradise, Prudentius gazes at a painting of the saint (who is by definition a just soul) in torment. The result for Prudentius and for the guilty soul is initially the same: contemplation of the image of a just soul produces profound grief and pain. The martyrdom is described in a complex ekphrasis: Prudentius sees the image but needs the help of a guide to understand its meaning; the martyrdom is narrated by the guide. At the end, the poem returns to the frame story of the poet's visit to the tomb. The guide advises him to pray to Cassian, evoking this emotional response from the poet (*Pe.* 9.99–102):

> I obey: I embrace the tomb, I pour tears too,
> The altar is warmed by my lips, the stone by my breast.
> Then I reflect on all the hidden parts of my labor,
> Then I murmur what it was I sought and what I feared.

Prudentius responds to the sight of the painting and the narration of the martyrdom with tears and contemplation of his uncertain future, but as Goldhill has noted, the way the poem is framed complicates how we read the tears of the poet, for in the final two lines, we learn that Prudentius is recalling his visit after his successful return home to Spain: *audior, urbem adeo, dextris successibus utor, / domum reuertor, Cassianum praedico* ("I am heard, I enter the city, I meet with success, / I return home, I proclaim Cassian").

As Goldhill says,

> The question might be phrased like this: in what posture, with what expression, is one to read the story of Prudentius prostrate before the tomb of Cassian? With what joy, what embrace? What tears? If the tearful poet imitates the torn martyr, and yet that scene is recalled from the vantage point of a successful return to Spain (established by the inset and framed narrative), how are the different claims of joy and grief, for poet and martyr, to be experienced?[29]

In the most obvious reading of the narrative of *Pe.* 9, the sight of the painting of the saint produces a therapeutic response in the poet, who is clearly portrayed as a parallel to Cassian. His wounds and "pricks of grief" at the beginning of the poem evoke those of the martyr later in the narrative (*vulnera* [7] and *dolorum acumina* [8] are chiastically echoed by *ferrea acumina* [51] and *vulnera* [58]). In the poem's concluding couplet, Prudentius represents his prayer for a successful return home as having been efficacious. The poem offers a lesson for the reader; contemplation of the martyr's triumph and the poet's contrition will help the reader purge sin from his own soul and position himself as abjectly before God as the poet does before the saint's tomb. Tears here offer poet and reader an Aristotelian catharsis, which, together with the opportunity to learn from the spectacle of the suffering saint, produce a therapeutic feeling of pleasure in the reader, who has been guided to interpret the tortures depicted (in the poem, in the painting, and in the inset narrative of martyrdom) as signs of spiritual triumph.[30] Through his deployment of literary tropes, Prudentius hopes to earn for himself the heavenly rewards Cassian earned through suffering torture. Goldhill cites a similar presentation of the pleasures evoked by the contemplation of the suffering martyr from a sermon of Augustine's on the martyrdom of Cyprian:

> The passion of St. Cyprian has just been read. We heard it with our ears, we watched it in our minds, we saw him struggling, we feared somehow for him in his danger, but we trusted in the help of God. Do you then want to know in brief what the difference is between our spectacles and theatrical spectacles? We, inasmuch as a sane mind flourishes in us, want to imitate the martyrs we watch.

Augustine's reaction to the verbal image of Cyprian's passion is unambivalent: "*Specto, delector, quamtum valeo lacertis mentis amplector: video certatorem, gaudeo victorem*" ["I see him, I delight in him, with all the strength of the arms of my mind I embrace him. I see the competitor. I rejoice in the victor"].[31]

But Prudentius's presentation of the martyrdom of Cassian is far more complex than Augustine's evocation of the triumph of Cyprian, and the extent to which the reader can unambivalently identify with the poet and the saint is not clear. The poem's disturbing wit destabilizes the triumphalist reading—Cassian's suffering affords his torturers a chance to mock him, and, unlike Eulalia and Laurence, other martyrs celebrated in the *Peristephanon* who display a caustic wit, Cassian does not respond to the jibes of his tormentors with any capping joke of his own. As Goldhill says, "The poem offers its cruel wit as a further sadistic twist to the suffering of the martyr. A reader's pleasure in the language of the poem is harder to assimilate simply to the celebration of the martyr's triumph. There remains a difficult interplay between pleasure and tears here" (1999, 117).

Another disturbing element in the poem is the negative portrayal of the saint himself, whose harsh sternness, we are explicitly told, earned the fear and anger of his students; indeed, there is no praise at all for the saint's piety or bravery in the lengthy account of his martyrdom. Rather, the whole emphasis in the torture scene, as the students mutilate their master with pens and make ironic jokes about writing errors, is on what Goldhill aptly terms "textual criticism of the flesh." The master of writing who perishes when his students turn their pens on him exists in an uneasy relationship with the poet who imitates his suffering. (Or is it the other way around? In the narrative of the poem, it is the poet's *vulnera* and *acumina* that precede and give rise to the story of the *vulnera* and *acumina* of his literary creation.)[32]

To rephrase Goldhill's questions about *Pe.* 9, we can ask why, if the text portrays Cassian's suffering as an elaborate joke and the saint as a sadistic schoolmaster, is Prudentius crying? Or why, if the poet's tearful response is the appropriate one, is the portrayal of the martyrdom such a joke? If we are meant to experience pleasure, shouldn't the pleasure be that of viewing the triumph of Christian faith rather than the narration of the Pythonesque farce of the schoolboys' revenge? The narrative as it is constructed, with its complex framing, double ekphrasis, black humor, and Ovidian delight in paradox and wordplay, seems oddly out of line with a triumphalist interpretation along the lines of Augustine's sermon on the passion of Saint Cyprian, a model in which contemplation of the saint's suffering and final victory leads to both a desire to imitate the saint and the experience of pleasure on the part of the audience. And yet we are clearly led to adopt such an interpretation by the instructions of the guide and by the external frame of the poem. Commenting on Prudentius's ambiguous use of language in this poem, Ballengee says, "Conveying the account of the martyrdom to his audience depends on the specific logic of language; yet suggesting the awesome (and, by nature, incommunicable) power of the Christian God at the heart of these martyrdoms depends upon Prudentius's moving beyond literal language, releasing language from its logical limits—from its own law—by means of rhetorical trope" (2009, 93). As is so often the case with Prudentius, his linguistic excess forces us to see the tension between a clear interpretive model and a complex and polysemous text that resists simplification.

The spectacle of the contrasting fates of just and unjust souls as Prudentius presents it in the *Hamartigenia* is, similarly, more complicated than the triumphant assertion of God's justice presented by Tertullian at the end of *On Spectacles*. Though not as detailed and grotesque as Tertullian's evocation of the tortures of the damned, Prudentius's presentation of the eschatological confrontation of the souls across the void of the cosmos and the role that the punishment of the damned plays in the pleasures of the just is, on reflection, confounding, in particular because of the elaborate excursus on the mechanics of the soul's vision after death. The swift ascent of the soul to her heavenly home, and the liberated vision she enjoys after being freed from the body might, one would expect, lead to something like the vision of God that Augustine imagined the soul would enjoy after the resurrection (emphasis added): "And when purged from all contagion of corruption, they are placed in peaceful abodes until they take their bodies again, their own, but now incorruptible, to adorn, not to burden them. For this is the will of the best and most wise Creator, that the spirit of a man, when piously subject to God, should have a body happily subject, and that this happiness should last forever. *There we shall see the truth without any difficulty, and shall enjoy it to the full, most clear and most certain*" (*De trin.* 15.25.44–45, trans. Haddan).[33] Similarly, Milton, who shares Prudentius's interest in the technicalities of optics, offers his fallen Adam a glorious vision—not of God, but of the future of his descendants, a grand unfolding of human history that culminates in the Second Coming. In order for Adam to view it, his eyes must be cleared by the angel Michael:

> but to nobler sights
> *Michael* from *Adams* eyes the Filme remov'd
> Which that false Fruit that promis'd clearer sight
> Had bred: then purg'd with Euphrasie and Rue
> The visual Nerve, for he had much to see
> And from the Well of Life three drops instill'd.
> (*PL* 11.411–16; Milton's italics)

Prudentius's adoption of the Neoplatonic motif of the return of the soul and his evocation of the apocalyptic vision of John the Evangelist gives us reason to think that the poem is leading toward the resolution that is Revelation, when the soul at last sees "face to face." But instead of concluding with the soul's contemplation of God, or a glimpse of salvation history, Prudentius shows us a very different kind of "face to face" viewing when he snaps us back to the torments of the damned and creates a vivid picture of the souls at their opposite ends of the universe, each gazing intently at the spectacle of the other. Following ancient optical theory, we can assume that from the eye of each emanates a visual ray that pierces and leaves its mark on the mind of the other, in a dizzying *mise en abyme* of mutually enforcing agony and joy. We are part of this process as well: Prudentius's ekphrastic language impresses this spectacle on the inner eye of his reader. What delight do we find in it? What effect will it have on us?

Occultum per proxima quaerere verum

Prudentius has, as we have seen, set up pairs of opposites throughout the poem, culminating in the opposing fates of the saved and the damned. Each opposition highlights the importance of choice or free will, without which neither sin nor salvation is possible. The argument of the *Hamartigenia* ends with the mutually locked gazes of the souls, but the poem itself is not over yet. Like *Pe.* 9, it ends with the figure of the poet in prayer. In the *Hamartigenia*'s thirty-six-line concluding prayer, Prudentius completes the chain of legal imagery by assuming the role of guilty prisoner himself, with God as his judge. Admitting his sinfulness, he begs for mercy, and imagines the hour of his own death. His guilty body, seduced by earthly pleasures, must be purged and punished for its sins, much as Cassian suffered bodily torment to earn his soul's salvation. At this crucial moment, the figure of the highwayman returns one last time, as Prudentius prays that his soul not have to confront the devil in the guise of a robber (*aliquem de gente latronum, praedo*):

> omne malum merui, sed tu bonus arbiter aufer
> quod merui; meliora favens largire precanti
> dona animae quandoque meae, cum corporis huius
> liquerit hospitium nervis, cute, sanguine, felle,
> ossibus exstructum, corrupta quod incola luxu
> heu nimium complexa fovet, cum flebilis hora
> clauserit hos orbes, et conclamata iacebit
> materies oculisque suis mens nuda fruetur,
> ne cernat truculentum aliquem de gente latronum
> inmitem, rabidum, vultuque et voce minaci
> terribilem, qui me maculosum aspergine morum
> in praeceps, ut praedo, trahat nigrisque ruentem
> inmergat specubus, cuncta exacturus ad usque
> quadrantem minimum damnosae debita vitae.
> (H. 938–51)

> Although what I deserve is evil, when
> my soul takes leave forever of her host,
> my body, built of nerves and skin and blood
> and gall and bones, whose loving arms, alas!
> seduced by pleasure, she cannot bear to leave—
> when that unhappy hour has closed these eyes
> and wailing mourners lay my corpse to rest,
> when my naked soul at last can see
> with her own eyes—Good Judge, I beg that then
> you grant her greater gifts than I have earned.
> May she never have to know a thief
> as mad and cruel, as terrible in face
> and voice as he who wants to drag me
> stained as I am with sin, and throw me headlong
> into caves of darkness, and there extort
> in full the payment, down to the last penny
> that I owe for such a sinful life.
> (H. 1253–69)

In this final evocation of the highwayman, Prudentius merges the metaphor of the robber with an allusion to the Sermon on the Mount, where Christ gave some legal advice to his followers: "Agree with your adversary quickly, while you are on the way with him, lest your adversary deliver you to the judge, the judge hand you over to the officer, and you be thrown into prison. Assuredly, I say to you, you will by no means get out of there till you have paid the last penny (*quadrantem*)" (Matthew 5:25–26). Prudentius is both the victim of the robber, about to be robbed of his last penny, and a guilty party who owes payment to the last penny (*quadrantem*) for his sinful life. If we read this in light of his first use of the robber simile (H. 283–92; Lat. 208–15), the specific relevance of the image to Prudentius becomes clearer. As argued above, the original simile of the robber metaphorically enacts the failure of fallen human language to express divine truth, and the rich garment stolen from the traveler symbolizes the appropriation and corruption of language by the devil. In the last appearance of the figure of the robber, Prudentius casts himself as the robber's victim. By the logic of the first simile, it will be *his* skill with language, *his* rhetoric, that is at risk of being appropriated by the devil. At the same time, the intertextual reference to the Sermon on the Mount suggests that the *quadrantem* may also be all the poet has to offer in recompense for his sins.

Mastrangelo's argument that Prudentius's theology is ultimately apophatic, that he believes that human language and reason are incapable of expressing or grasping the divine, is amply borne out by the *Hamartigenia*. The interrelated problems of interpretation, deceptive appearance, heresy, human generation, and signification are generated by the problematic nature of human language, inextricably linked to original sin. The repeated references to flawed vision and optical illusions, to the dangers of sensory perception of all sorts, and the metaphors of wandering, being lost, and going astray suggest that the poet is engaged in a search for illumination and a struggle for control of meaning—even of the meaning of his own text. Like Milton, who begins his account of the Creation with a description of himself that verbally links him to his own creations, Satan and Sin, Prudentius is beset with fear that his own creations will metaphorically turn on him, that his creative efforts are not reflections of perfect divine creativity (*simplex generatio*), but are instead products of the destructive, profligate creativity that characterizes Satan and the female viper.[34] Interpretive templates, invocations of scripture, typological allegories, and assertions of faith gesture repeatedly toward authoritative meaning, but these gestures are often undermined, as Prudentius's text forces its readers to experience in the very act of reading the uncertainty and error produced by original sin.[35]

The conclusion of Prudentius's closing prayer reworks the concluding image of the poem's argument, the spectacle of the just and unjust souls after judgment. In the final lines, he offers to his readers the spectacle of the fate of his own soul after judgment:

> esto, cavernoso, quia sic pro labe necesse est
> corporea, tristis me sorbeat ignis Averno:
> saltem mitificos incendia *lenta* vapores
> exhalent, aestuque calor languente tepescat;
> lux inmensa alios et tempora vincta coronis
> glorificent: me *poena levis* clementer adurat.
>   (H. 961–66)

> But if my body's fall requires this fate,
> then let the gloomy flames devour me
> in cavernous Avernus. Yet grant at least
> that the fire be slow and mild, exhaling
> gentle vapors, and that its heat become
> a mellow warmth and lose its fury. Let others
> glory in boundless light and crowns that bind
> their temples; as for me, this is my prayer:
> may my punishment be light and clement.
>   (H. 1282–90)

Prudentius is now the guilty soul whose fate is contrasted with the boundless light enjoyed by "others," whose crowns suggest that they are martyrs. But the distance so dramatically described just a few lines between the just and unjust souls is collapsed here, as the poet imagines not the hideous torments of the damned but a gentler alternative, more in line with his notion of souls on holiday in *Cath.* 5. Although he contrasts the crowns worn by the "others" with his own punishment, the image of the crowns implicitly links the martyrs in paradise with the poet, who frequently uses the image of the crown or garland to characterize his own verse. The final line of the poem, where Prudentius conjures up the odd notion of a "light punishment" burning him "leniently," contains an allusion that also suggests that Prudentius's poetry will play a role in his ultimate fate. The allusion is to *Tristia* 1.1.29–30 and the context is strikingly relevant: in this opening poem of the *Tristia*, Ovid is writing from exile in the hope of persuading the angry Augustus to pardon him and lighten his punishment. The poem is addressed to Ovid's personified book, who is told to go to Rome and find a reader who has not forgotten Ovid, who "silently, to himself, lest any bad person should hear it, wishes that Caesar relent and my punishment be light" (*et tacitus secum, ne quis malus audiat, optet / sit mea lenito Caesare poena levis*).[36]

In the final line of the *Hamartigenia*, then, Prudentius casts himself in the role of Ovid, who was exiled from Rome for offending the emperor through the double crimes of *carmen et error*, his poetry and some kind of mistake. For Ovid, poetry was both the reason for his punishment (though he stoutly defends his earlier work) and his only hope of placating Augustus. The pointed allusion to *Tristia* 1.1 suggests that Prudentius saw his *carmen*, like Ovid's, as double-edged, as likely to bring down the wrath of his ruler as to redeem him. It cannot but be implicated in the duplicities and snares of human language, but at the same time it offers his only hope for salvation. This, perhaps, is why Prudentius lays such emphasis on the offerings of Cain and Abel at the opening of the preface. How can he tell if his poetry, which he imagines as all he can offer to God, is acceptable or not? In a fallen world, where accurate vision, knowledge, and understanding are unavailable and even the word of God is subject to misinterpretation, how can a writer determine whether his words reflect divine truth or are implicated in the snaky coils of error?

The concluding lines of the poem reveal just how significant this question was to Prudentius. I return here to a suggestion I presented elsewhere: that the *Hamartigenia*'s final figure is cunningly concealed within its final words, *poena levis clementer adurat*, "May my punishment be light and clement."[37] This is an anagram of a *sphragis*, or signature phrase, "Aurelio prudente se clamante," "Aurelius the prudent proclaims himself." It was not unusual for classical poets to include a signature or other significant word cryptically embedded in their texts, either as anagrams or acrostics or other patterned forms, and there was considerable interest throughout antiquity in such figured texts.[38]

There are clear pointers in both the context and the structure of Prudentius's text that give reason to read beneath its surface. The possibility of anagrammatic wordplay is signaled several lines earlier by the adjective-noun pair *cavernoso* . . .

Averno. Then there is the presence of Prudentius himself in the first person in the final line—"*me* poena levis clementer adurat"—where the personal pronoun draws attention to the persona of the poet. In the same line there is a pun on Prudentius's name, Clemens, in the word *clementer*—a pun made more obvious to the reader by the presence of *me* in the same line.[39] And there is a further pointer, not present in the text itself but evident in the source text, *Tristia* 1.1. There Ovid hopes that his book will find its ideal reader: one who is "not forgetful of that one [Ovid]," (*non immemor illi*), who will pray for relief of his punishment—but only silently, secretly, to himself (*tacitus secum*). Ovid's ideal reader knows how to dissimulate, to cloak his true intentions in silence. Through the allusion to *Tristia* 1.1, Prudentius's text, with its silent, hidden anagram, evokes a similarly silent, sympathetic reader, inviting him or her to share Prudentius's secret.

In a crucial passage about understanding and interpretation early in the poem, Prudentius recalled Corinthians 13:12, *videmus nunc per speculum in aenigmate tunc autem facie ad faciem.* The point he makes is about how to read the natural world analogously. His phrasing neatly anticipates the process of interpreting the anagram:

> parvorum speculo non intellecta notamus,
> et datur occultum per proxima quaerere verum.
> (H. 83–84)

> ... in a mirror
> we see in smaller things the images
> of what our minds can't comprehend. And He
> has granted us to search for hidden truth
> in the closest things.
> (H. 114–18)

This encapsulates Prudentius's sense of language as ultimately mysterious and unknowable, yet as something that might lead to comprehension of the vast mysteries of the divine. Small things—in the case of the anagram, the letters of the text, *elementa*, which are analogous to the atoms that in Lucretian physics constitute the smallest building blocks of the universe—gesture toward larger meanings.

In the final lines of the *Hamartigenia,* recognition of the anagram requires the reader to reconsider the grammar of the preceding clause: *lux inmensa alios et tempora vincta coronis/glorificent: me poena levis clementer adurat.* With the anagram unresolved, the lines translate, literally, "Let boundless light and temples bound with crowns glorify *others*: may a light punishment burn *me* leniently." But the resolution of the anagram leaves *me* problematically dangling.[40] Resolving the anagram means reconsidering the syntax of *me.* If it is no longer the object of *adurat*, it can only be another object of *glorificent*, thus: *lux inmensa alios et tempora vincta coronis glorificent me*. This would change the meaning of the phrase before the anagram to "Let boundless light glorify *others*, and temples bound with crowns glorify *me*," with the poet staking his claim to future reward through the crowns of the martyrs. This is in line with Prudentius's assertions throughout the *Peristephanon* that his accounts of the tortures and triumphs of the martyrs will, in the end, bring him triumph and salvation.

But to what end? What could be the point of this hypothetical anagram that so artfully reveals and conceals the poet's name, when it seems so uncomfortably in conflict with the surface conclusion of the poem?[41]

Once again, Milton's practice in *Paradise Lost* offers an interesting parallel to Prudentius's poetics in the *Hamartigenia*. Milton, a master of puns and wordplay of all kinds, incorporates cryptic verbal patterns at thematically important points in the poem. In "Satanic Vision and Acrostics in *Paradise Lost*," Jane Partner examines four significant acrostics hidden within the text;[42] she argues that the way these words, which she calls "an acrostic mini-epic" are concealed, and the way the reader is led to discover them, "exemplify both the argument and the medium of the whole poem," and that the acrostics are a means for Milton to expound on the frailty of human vision and thus on the process of human reading.[43] In *Paradise Lost*, Satan is consistently associated with flawed or skewed viewing, an association that arises from Christian beliefs about good government of the eye, the abuse of which includes the failure to learn about God from the sight of the creation, and the error of being seduced by the spectacle of creation from the duty of beholding the creator. Satan is subject to optical illusions in the poem, and in *Paradise Lost* 3, these lead to his disorientation in the cosmos. The first acrostic occurs during the account of Satan's travel through the *primum mobile*. As he journeys through the stars, he mistakes the celestial poles for the terrestrial poles in 3.557–61, and perceives the cone-shaped shadow of the earth as a circle at 3.555–57.[44] It is during this journey, as his soul is "seis'd" by envy at the sight of the world "so faire," that the first acrostic occurs:[45]

> Such wonder seis'd, though after Heaven seen,
> The Spirit maligne, but much more envy seis'd
> At sight of all this World beheld so faire.
> Round he surveys, and well might, where he stood
> So high above the circling Canopie
> Of Night's extended shade.
>   (3.552–57)

As Satan loses his bearings among the stars—morally, he has no star to steer by— the acrostic appears and forces us to change our visual orientation and reading practice: we must read on a vertical not horizontal axis. Partner (2007, 139) argues that the acrostic draws the reader "into an enactment of this loss of spatial and spiritual coordinates, and by this means Milton's verbal patterning forms a microcosmic part of the larger moral allegory of space that structures his symbolic cosmos."

Similarly, at the crucial moment when Satan first approaches Eve in the garden, winding his way with "tract oblique" (9.510), we are told that his serpentine form was even more beautiful than the snake that was seen

> with her who bore
> *Scipio* the highth for *Rome*. With tract oblique
> *A*t first, as one who sought acces, but feard
> *T*o interrupt, side-long he worked his way.
> *A*s when a Ship by skilful Stearsman wrought
> *N*igh Rivers mouth or Foreland, where the Wind
> Veers oft, as oft so steers, and shifts her Saile;
> So varied hee, and of his tortuous Traine
> Curld many a wanton wreath in sight of *Eve*
> To lure her Eye.⁴⁶

Satan uses his winding approach to insinuate himself into Eve's presence so that she sees him out of the corner of her eye; his oblique approach induces her to partake in his characteristically skewed viewing. As in the *Hamartigenia*, here in Milton's Paradise the eye is a vulnerable gateway to the soul through which vice can attack. The acrostic that reveals the name of the dazzlingly beautiful serpent forces the reader to participate in an act of skewed viewing like Eve's and Satan's. "Inducing the reader to join Eve in imitating Satan's thwart perspective at this decisive moment, Milton leads us to lose our way in the text. Thus partaking of Eve's danger, we are obliged to consider the moral vulnerability of our own unruly eyes."⁴⁷

Milton uses the device of the acrostic to dramatize, and force his readers to enact, the skewed vision and concomitant disorientation and misinterpretation experienced by his Satan. Partner links Satan's skewed vision and disoriented course together, citing Milton's use of a simile that could have come straight from Prudentius, as Satan's temptations are described as a "delusive light" that "Misleads th' amaz'd Night-wanderer from his way" (9.639–40). "It is this vocabulary that reveals the ultimate literary reference point for Milton's dual-directional verbal patterning: the text-labyrinth. Within this context . . . the acrostic uses interwoven words to emblemize the degeneracy of a fallen mind and world."⁴⁸ The acrostics that inveigle the reader into the maze of the text-labyrinth reflect Milton's own self-consciousness about his poetic creation and serve as object lessons for us readers, who must remain vigilantly in control of our eyes.

Like Milton's acrostics, Prudentius's encrypted anagram is emblematic of the fallen nature of language. It is the ultimate example of linguistic instability, and it expresses the poet's radically ambivalent attitude toward his own art. As we have seen, the presence of the anagram destabilizes the meaning of the previous words in the sentence. Its meaning is open to question even when "solved," for both *prudens* and *clamante* present significant interpretive problems. *Prudente*, of course, puns on the poet's own name, *Prudentius*, and suggests foresight and understanding: *providentia* is a divine attribute. But Prudentius uses the adjective *prudens* only once in the *Hamartigenia*, in a context that seems strikingly inappropriate: it describes Adam at the moment that he knowingly chooses death: *et letalia prudens/eligit*, 709–10. And while *clamo* can mean "to proclaim," it also means "to lament" or "to announce the name of a dead person at his funeral."[49]

Throughout the *Hamartigenia*, which attempts to refute dualist doctrine, Prudentius falls into binary oppositions even as he argues for divine unity: Cain and Abel, Flesh and Spirit, himself and Marcion, Lot and his wife, Ruth and Orpah, Absalom and David, the wise and foolish doves, the brothers at the crossroads, the just and unjust souls, God and the unnamed Adversary, Satan—these are among the adversarial figures that populate his text. It is not surprising, then, to find that the final words of the poem cannot be interpreted simply: in Prudentius's worldview, there is no *simplex interpretatio*. The concluding anagram is radically ambiguous. Does it reveal a poet who shares divine foreknowledge (*prudente*) and proudly proclaims (*clamante*) himself, claiming his poetic reward and signing his work in a triumphant *sphragis*? Or does it reveal a poet sharing Adam's disastrously knowing (*prudens*) choice to disobey God and bewailing his own death and damnation? Which Prudentius is reflected *in speculo parvorum*, in the letters of the anagram, the final *aenigma* of this enigmatic text?

Envoi: *Praefatio*

The end of the *Hamartigenia* sheds light on the final lines of the preface to Prudentius's collected poems, which summarizes his life and work and is most likely the last poem he wrote. It ends with the following stanza:

haec dum scribo vel *eloquor*
vinclis o utinam corporis *emicem*
liber quo tulerit *lingua* sono mobilis ultimo!

As I write and speak these words,
would that I could flash forth, free of the chains of the body,
to where my fluent tongue will take me with its final sound.
 (*Praefatio* 43–45)

It is common for poets to make allusions to their own work in the opening or closing poems of collections—another version of the poetic signature. Prudentius too, in the final lines of the poem that introduces his collection, alludes to two passages in his own poetry. The first is *Peristephanon* 14, the signature poem of his "On the Crowns of the Martyrs."⁵⁰ At *Pe.* 14.91–93, the young martyr Agnes is killed, decapitated by the sword of her executioner. At the moment the sword strikes, her soul leaps to heaven (imitating the surprising apotheosis of Pompey's ghost in Lucan's *Bellum Civile* 9):

exutus rude spiritus *emicat*
liberque in auras exilit. angeli
saepsere euntem tramite candido.

Her cast-off spirit flashes forth and leaps
free into the air. Angels fence her in
as she goes along the shining path.

In the concluding lines of the preface, Prudentius imagines himself chained, like the Titan Prometheus, and wishing to make, like Agnes, a transcendent leap to freedom.⁵¹ The imagery of the leap from earth to heaven in both poems, and the close conjunction of *emicem liber quo* in *Praef.* 44–45, echoing *emicat liberque* in *Pe.* 14.91–92, make a strong case for the presence of a deliberate allusion. Such an allusion supports the views of critic Jill Ross, who, in her study of the imagery of the martyr's body as living text in the *Peristephanon*, has suggested that Prudentius viewed his poetry as ultimately redemptive: "The salvific potential of the written word explains why Prudentius' poetic vocation was of such importance to him. It not only enabled him to experience fully his Christianity, but it held out the promise of salvation by virtue of his collaboration in the embodiment of God's writing."⁵² Similarly, in his discussion of Prudentius's unconventional use of language, Bardzell concludes that "Prudentius has found a truer language than ordinary language"(2009, 44).

But Prudentius's view of human language, as we have seen in this study of the *Hamartigenia*, was fraught with tension. If he indulged in the hope, as Michael Roberts beautifully puts it, that he could "build a Holy City with words," that hope was tempered by the fear that his own poetry was unavoidably implicated in the endless traps of language.⁵³ The hopeful allusion to the apotheosis of Agnes in the *Praefatio* is counterbalanced by an allusion that is startling indeed in this context: as he voices his wish for freedom, Prudentius recalls the *Hamartigenia*'s pivotal moment—the description of the fissure of the devil's tongue, the *natale caput* for all sin:

simplex lingua prius varia micat arte loquendi
et discissa dolis resonat sermone trisulco.
 (*H.* 201-2)

> His tongue,
> once single, now is treacherously split,
> and flickers with the art of varied speaking,
> its fissured words reechoing.
> (H. 272-75)

Eloquor, emicem, and *lingua* in the *Praefatio* echo *loquendi, micat,* and *lingua* in the *Hamartigenia*. As we have seen, the tongue of the serpent has special significance in the *Hamartigenia*, linked as it is to the monstrous fertility of the viper. Levine argues that it "provides a negative, perverse mirror image for the creative power of the Logos."[54] The flickering, flashing tongue of the serpent, with its deadly art of speaking, lurks beneath the pious conclusion of the *Praefatio*, which expresses the poet's hope of attaining freedom and salvation through his own skill in speaking. It is the poet's *lingua,* that fallen, fissured instrument, that will determine the fate of his soul.

Bound by the chains of the flesh, lost and benighted, afflicted with imperfect vision, the poet cannot know whether his elaborately patterned and figured texts are acceptable offerings that have successfully avoided the snares and traps of human language, or are instead, like the viper's vicious brood, the products of Satanic creativity. *Caveat lector.*

NOTES

INTRODUCTION

1. See Cook 2006, 63.
2. Briefly discussed by Edwards 1995.
3. See Cook 2006, 63. Dawson 2002 is essential reading for the development of Christian figural reading.
4. See Mastrangelo 2008, 160–75.
5. Prudentius's popularity continues to grow; there have been many significant studies published since the late twentieth century. As an entrée into his work, see, for books, Bardzell 2009, Gnilka 2000, Gosserez 2001, Lühken 2002, Malamud 1989, Mastrangelo 2008, Nugent 1985, Palmer 1989, Paxson 1994, Petruccione 1985, Roberts 1989 and 1993. Unfortunately, Dykes 2011 appeared too late for me to take into account in this book. For articles, see Ballengee 2002, Burrus 1995, Conybeare 2007, Goldhill 1999, James 1999, Kaesser 2002, Machosky 2003, Malamud 1990 and 2002, Miller 2000, Nugent 2000, Ross 1995. Important earlier works include Fontaine 1980 and 1981, Gnilka 1963, Haworth 1980, Herzog 1966, Lana 1962, Mahoney 1934, Smith 1976, Taddei 1981, Thraede 1965.
6. Palmer 1989, 22.
7. Cameron 1970, app. B; Charlet 1982; Fontaine 1980 and 1981; Costanza 1983.
8. Other examples of aristocratic *conversi* include Sulpicius Severus, Paulinus of Pella, and the author of the *Carmen ad uxorem*. Griffe 1965, 128–48 discusses the life of such converts. For the life and work of Paulinus, see especially Conybeare 2000 and Trout 1999.
9. Roberts 1993, 3; Fontaine 1981, 145–47.
10. Mastrangelo 2008, 10.

1. WRITING IN CHAINS

1. *Nam et in hoc philosophi et oratores et poetae perniciosi sunt, quod incautos animos facile inretire possunt suauitate sermonis et carminum dulci modulatione currentium.* [*mella sunt haec venena tegentia*] (*Inst.* 5.1.10–11). See Mastrangelo 2009, 317 for a discussion of this passage and the patristic attitude toward pagan poetry.
2. MacCormack 1998, 190; Mastrangelo 2009, 319.
3. Mastrangelo 2009, 327.
4. Argued by Mastrangelo 2008, especially chapter 2 and the epilogue; briefly recapitulated in Mastrangelo 2009, 324–25.
5. Miller 2001, 7. On figural reading, see Dawson 2002 and Fabiny 1992.
6. Chin 2008, 12.
7. Ibid., citing Sidonius Apollinaris 1.6.44.
8. Roberts 1989, chapter 3, especially 85–89.

9. Very similar scenes occur in Prudentius's *Pe.* 11.111–22, the dismemberment of Saint Hippolytus, and *Psy.* 720–25, the death of Discordia. See Malamud 1989, 98–99. Henderson 1983 discusses violence in the *Peristephanon*.

10. Scholarship on violent spectacle in the Roman world includes Grig 2002, Shaw 1996, Futrell 1997, Kyle 1998, Ballengee 2009, Frankfurter 2009. Enders 1999 focuses on the spectacle of violence in medieval theater, and includes a discussion of the classical background; for a collection of articles on violence in late antiquity, see Drake 2006b.

11. Miller 2001, 3.

12. Mitchell 1986, 8, quoted in Miller 2001, 5.

13. Theon, *Progymnasmata*, 118.1.7. I draw extensively on Webb 2009, chapter 3 in the following discussion of ekphrasis and enargeia. See also the excellent introduction to Miller 2009.

14. Cited and discussed by Webb 2009, 95–96.

15. Brilliant 1999, 224; I owe the reference to Miller 2005, 32.

16. Carruthers 1998 and 1990. Yates 1966 remains indispensable on the topic of memory and mnemonics.

17. Miller, 2005, 37–43, discusses Prudentius's spiritual landscapes, though her emphasis is on landscapes in the *Peristephanon*.

18. For a discussion of Prudentius's mnemonic technique, see Gosserez 2001, 189–92; the classical sources on the notion of memory place include Cicero, *De orat.* 2.353–54; Quintilian, *Inst.* 11.2.23; *Ad Herennium* 3.16–24; Martianus Capella, *De nuptiis* 410–30.

19. Discussed by Carruthers 1998, 147 (although she confuses the characters: "when Hope cuts off the head of Luxuria").

20. Fontaine (1981, 188) remarks on "la puissance de l'imagination visuelle, qui est peut-être la faculté poétique majeure de Prudence."

21. Grig 2002, 328.

22. Prudentius's violence has upset many readers: as Levine (1991, 5) remarks, "They find his use of violence excessive, his mixing of genres anti-classical, and his shifts of tone generally troublesome." On violence in the *Psychomachia*, see Paxson 1994, 66–71; Lewis 1958, 69; Mastrangelo 2008, 145–55; Nugent 2000, 20–25.

23. In addition to Enders 1999 and Carruthers 1990 and 1998, excellent scholarly studies of the art of memory include Yates 1966 and Coleman 1992.

24. There are many versions of this well-known anecdote, including Cicero, *De oratore* 2.351–55; Martianus Capella, *De nuptiis* 177g. See Enders 1999, 63–65. Here is Quintilian's version: Simonides "had written an ode of the kind usually composed in honour of victorious athletes, to celebrate the achievement of one who had gained the crown for boxing. Part of the sum for which he had contracted was refused him on the grounds that . . . he had introduced a digression in praise of Castor and Pollux, and he was told that, in view of what he had done, he had best ask for the rest of the sum due from those whose deeds he had extolled. And according to the story they paid their debt. For when a great banquet was given in honour of the boxer's success, Simonides was summoned forth from the feast, to which he had been invited, by a message to the effect that two youths who had ridden to the door urgently desired his presence. He found no trace of them, but what followed proved to him that the gods had shown their gratitude. For he had scarcely crossed the threshold on his way out, when the banqueting hall fell in upon the heads of the guests and wrought such havoc among them that the relatives of the dead who came to seek the bodies for burial were unable to distinguish not merely the faces but even the limbs of the dead. Then it is said, Simonides, who remembered the order in which the guests had been sitting, succeeded in restoring to each man his own dead" (*Inst. orat.* 11.2.11–13, trans. H.H. Butler).

25. Enders 1999, 68–69.

26. Carruthers 1998, 143; Katzenellenbogen 1964.

27. Miller 2001, 3.

28. Origen, *Hom. in Ex.* 1.1 (Heine) quoted in Miller 2001, 5.

29. Prudentius refers specifically to a number of his poems in the preface to his collected works: the *Cathemerinon* (line 37); the *Hamartigenia* and *Apotheosis* (line 39); the Romanus hymn, now printed as *Pe.* 10 but originally a separate poem (line 40); the *Contra Symmachum* (line 41); and the *Peristephanon* (line 42). As Shanzer 1989 argues, the *Psychomachia* is not referred to in the *Praefatio*'s list of Prudentius's poems, and is probably to be dated after 405.

30. Of all his poems, the one that comes closest to focusing on contemporary events is the *Contra Symmachum*, a two-part poem in which Prudentius dramatizes the controversy that arose over the cessation of state payments for priesthoods and the removal of the statue and altar of Victory from the Senate house in Rome. Quintus Aurelius Symmachus had requested the restoration of the statue in 384, but was successfully defeated by the intervention of the influential bishop Ambrose of Milan. Cunningham 1976 discusses the contexts of Prudentius's poems.

31. Pelikan 1993, 40–74 and 200–31, discussed by Mastrangelo 2008, 82–83.

32. Mastrangelo 2008, 83.

33. Ibid., 87.

34. As Bardzell puts it, Prudentius's artificial use of language in the *Psychomachia* "might not be artificial in the privative sense (i.e., an idiosyncratic deviation from normal language . . .), but rather artificial in an experimental sense, an attempt at rearticulating reality in a radically faithful way" (2009, 44).

35. Mastrangelo 2008, 169.

36. Benson 1966, 75, cited by Fyler 2007, 53.

37. *Peristephanon* 10 was probably originally published as a separate poem, and later included with the other poems of the *Peristephanon*. Its length sets it apart from the other poems in the collection. I have discussed Cyprian's tongue and the ambivalent aspects of his rhetoric in *Pe*. 13 in Malamud 1989, 117–21. Miller (2005, 40) has a good discussion of the surreal aspects of Romanus's tongue. See Frankfurter 2009, 229–30 on the erotic and voyeuristic aspects of Cyprian's martyrdom.

38. See James 1999 for an analysis of the *Psychomachia* as a Christianized form of the spectacle of the arena.

39. Loraux 1987; see also Sissa 1990, 53–70, and King 1983.

40. Nugent 2000, 22. See Loraux 1987, 50–55, and Cixous 1981, 41–55 for further discussion of this motif.

41. Roberts 1989, 28–29.

42. James 1999, 79.

43. Levine (1991, 12–30) discusses the relation between Prudentius's excessive violence in the *Peristephanon* and his stylistic excesses.

44. On Prudentius's sense of humor, which is an important aspect of his poetry, see Conybeare 2002, Goldhill 1999, Malamud 1989 (esp. chapter 5), and Levine 2005.

45. De Man 1986, 76, cited by Paxson, 1994, 69.

46. As Paxson says (emphasis mine), "Prudentius' focus upon the imagery of the destruction of the face, therefore, is a literalized reverse of prosopopeia. *It is the symbolic dismantling of the trope by which the text invents the figural characters who inhabit its actantial narrative.* Prosopopeia, or more precisely, lexopeia, is self-reflexively thematized as a central topical ground in the *Psychomachia*. . . . At times, [the Virtues'] main semiotic function (as opposed to their obvious thematic role) is to reflect not the ethically abstract offices of virtuehood, but rather the self-reflexive figural armature of the entire *Psychomachia*. This 'armature' is the self-conscious omnipresence of the text's foundational figural operator, personification" (Paxson 1994, 69–70).

47. Mastrangelo 2008, 154.

48. Ibid., 154–55.

49. Bardzell 2009, 51.

2. FIGURING IT OUT

1. Claudian, Prudentius's younger contemporary, also uses the device of an iambic preface; see Gruzelier 1993 ad loc. It is not clear when the Greek titles were attached to the poems. Palla 1981, 23n49 argues for taking the *Apotheosis* and *Hamartigenia* as separate poems, not as two parts of the same work, based on the differences between the prefaces of the works.

2. Averil Cameron makes a point about Byzantine antiheretical texts that is worth extending to late antiquity in general: "Whether we like it or not as historians, writing heresy, in all its various forms, did occupy a major place in Byzantium—so much so indeed that a full treatment would in its way constitute a new history of Byzantium. This is far from having been written as yet. But meanwhile, at the very least, I suggest that one ought to read these compositions, so

strange to our minds, as part of Byzantine pedagogy and the Byzantine sociology of knowledge, self-perpetuating constructions that helped to formulate thought and underpin social norms" (Cameron 2003, 484).

3. See below, 78–81, for a discussion of why Prudentius associates Cain with dualism.

4. The importance of rhetorical performance in Augustine's career is briefly discussed by Webb 2009, 16. For the development of a Christian rhetoric in the fourth and fifth centuries, see Cameron 1991, Brown 1992.

5. See the essays of Clark, Miles, and Lim on the dialogue form in late antique Christian writing in Goldhill 2009. Goldhill (2009, 6) casts the *Psychomachia* as a type of dialogue in which there is no exchange of views: "Each virtue gets to deliver a speech, like a Homeric warrior on the battlefield, upholding Christian values, before vanquishing the enemy. It is more like an extended model of the martyr's put-down to his enemies than an exchange. There is no uncertainty, the only questions are rhetorical, and the dominant model is the battlefield boast—where good can only defeat evil, not exchange views." I would complicate this argument somewhat: the destabilizing use of language in the *Psychomachia* works against the simplistic framework, as the apparently stark differences between Vices and Virtues are undermined.

6. Lavarenne 1961, xi. See Stam 1940, 8–13; Evans's (1972) introduction to Tertullian's *Adversus Marcionem*, ix–xxvi; Palla 1981, 16–17. Marcion died in 160 and the heresy named after him was dead long before the end of the fourth century. As various scholars have pointed out, the arguments against Marcionism apply equally well to heresies much more prevalent in Prudentius's day: Priscillianism, Arianism, and Manichaeism, which famously claimed the young Augustine as a convert and teacher. One of Marcionism's salient features was its use of the contradictions between the Old and New Testaments as a theoretical tool to undermine orthodox doctrine: pitting the scriptures against one another was a particularly powerful rhetorical ploy.

7. Though Marcion is accused of believing that matter is inherently evil, this is probably an exaggeration of his views. McGowan 2001 provides a balanced assessment of the evidence. Whatever Marcion's own views were, it is likely that Prudentius's understanding of them was influenced by apologists such as Tertullian (*Adv. Marc.* 1.16.1), Clement (*Strom.* 3.3.12), and others, who claimed that Marcion believed matter was evil.

8. Wyrick (2004, 299–301) discusses Marcion's impact on canon formation in the early church and Tertullian's response.

9. Miller 2001, 261. She adds: "Irenaeus understood Scripture and Tradition as an Author; what came to be called canon functioned for him to guarantee, to specify, and to close the contents of meaning. The *Gospel of Truth*, on the other hand, understood what came to be called canon hermeneutically; its concept of authority was rooted not in the past but in the present, and grew out of its understanding of the dynamics of language."

10. Conybeare 2007, 229. My emphasis. While I agree with Conybeare on most points, I would point out that while Prudentius does not mention any nonscriptural texts, he makes obvious and frequent allusions to nonscriptural texts in the poem, even if he does not refer to them by name.

11. The preface to the *Psychomachia* offers the biblical story of Abraham as an interpretive model for reading the *Psychomachia,* a misleading move that has caused considerable confusion, since the typological allegory from scripture used in the preface is quite different from the personification allegory in the rest of the poem. "Prudentius' allegory is calling attention not so much to metaphysics, but rather to meta-narrative. By translating the story of Abraham to the inner battle for the soul, the narrator is modeling an interpretive methodology, in which the reader learns to recognize narrative truths. These truths are understood as facts, or sequences of cause and effect, rather than objects or things" (Bardzell 2009, 42–43). Paxson (1994, 78–95) has an illuminating discussion of Job, the one scriptural figure who takes part on the primary narrative level of the *Psychomachia*. The other biblical figures mentioned exist outside the narrative frame, in what Carruthers 1998 would call the ornaments: similes or embedded narrations, such as the narration by the Virtue Hope (*Spes*) of the tale of David and Goliath in *Psy.* 291–99.

12. Carruthers 1998, 145.

13. Taddei 1981, 2–3; Tertullian, *Adv. Jud.* 5 (Tränkle, Wiesbaden, 1964); Ambrose, *De Cain et Abel* 2.6 (*CSEL* 32 pars. 1, Schenkle, 1893). Augustine, *De civitate dei* 15.7 offers several different interpretations of Cain's error, concluding *in quo autem horum Deo displicuerit Cain, facile non potest inveniri* (CCSL 48, Dombart, 1955). See Herzog 1966, 122ff. for a discussion of patristic interpretations of the Cain and Abel story.

14. Vetus Latina: *Nonne, si recte offeras, recte autem non dividas, peccasti? Quiesce!* Cf. the Vulgate, which does not mention division: *Dixitque Dominus ad eum quare maestus es et cur concidit facies tua? nonne si bene egeris recipies sin autem male statim in foribus peccatum aderit sed sub te erit appetitus eius et tu dominaberis illius.* See Stam 1940, 41–42 and 120–21; Grasso 1972, 124–35; Palla 1981, 122–23.

15. Not until Prudentius has moved from the iambic trimeter preface to the dactylic hexameter body of the poem is there some attempt at explanation. Taddei argues that *H.* 6–7 (*terrarum tibi forma duplex obludit, ut excors/dividuum regnare Deum super aethera credas*) imply that Prudentius's preoccupation is with dualism, and that he wishes to associate the notion of division with sin.

16. Josephus, *Jewish Antiquities* 1.2.2. See Fyler 2007, 29 for a discussion of the tradition of Cain as master of division.

17. According to Fyler 2007, 28, Philo, commenting on Genesis 4:17, where Cain sets up the first city, explains that this is not literally true, but rather means that Cain was setting up a creed of his own, and the buildings were plausible arguments and sophistic devices.

18. Taddei 1981, chapter 1, provides a summary.

19. Nichols 2010, 122, in a review of Fyler 2007.

20. Joshua Levinson, in his anaysis of late antique rabbinic exegetical narrative, frames the problem as one of competing genres, in which narrative undermines exegesis: "The exegetical narrative is composed of a story which simultaneously represents and interprets its biblical counterpart. As a hermeneutical reading of the biblical story presented in narrative form, its defining characteristic lies precisely in this synergy of narrative and exegesis. As exegesis, it creates new meanings from the biblical verses, and as narrative it represents those meanings by means of the biblical world. As exegesis, it is subservient to the biblical narrative, but as a story in its own right, it creates a narrated world which is different from its biblical shadow. *It is obvious that the combination of these two elements creates a certain dissonance. Narrative and exegesis are two very different methods of persuasion, based upon divergent, if not opposing, presuppositions of 'author-ity.' It is specifically this tension between sameness and difference, subservience and creativity, which establishes the genre's identity"* (emphasis added).

21. Gnilka (2000, 674–90) has argued persuasively, though not conclusively, that *H. praef.* 35–47 is an interpolation. He believes that the identification of Marcion with Cain is misleading, for the poem is more an attack on dualistic theologies in general than on Marcion in particular. For my argument, it does not matter whether the text's turn to allegorical exegesis comes immediately after the story of Cain, or whether it includes the identification of Marcion with Cain; in either case the narrator must guide the reader toward proper interpretation.

3. SEEKING HIDDEN TRUTH

1. Augustine systematically explores the complexities of reading and interpretation in *De doctrina*; see Stock 1996, 190ff. for a good summary of *De doctrina*'s argument.

2. Gosserez 2001, 34–52 discusses this passage and the related images of sun, mirror, and eyes. See also van Assendelft 1976, 18ff., and Gnilka 1980, 411–46, on Prudentius's use of allegory.

3. See Taddei 1981, 74ff. for further discussion of this allegory.

4. *Silvas Academi* refers to Plato's school, the Academy.

5. Mastrangelo 2008, 133–36 discusses the importance of Platonist doctrines of the soul, particularly of Plotinus in *Ad Marcellam* for the *praefatio* of the *Psychomachia*, and notes in particular the importance of the allegory of the cave for the notion of the body as a prison from which the soul strives to be released.

6. E.g., Seneca, *NQ* 1.11.1–3; Cicero, *Rep.* 1.11–15; Livy, 28.11.3 and 40.21.12; Pliny, *NH* 2.31.99.

7. There is no conclusive verbal parallel, but the association of double vision with madness is suggestive.

8. See Sextus Empiricus, *Against the Professors* 7.247–52; Webb 2009, 116.

9. Webb 2009, 118–19.

10. Gosserez also cites Philo, *De decalog.* 12, and Plutarch, *Ad principem iner.* 5.

11. Taddei (1981, 75) comments on Romans 1:20 in her discussion of the metaphor of sight. The context of the Pauline passage is relevant to the *Hamartigenia*, which takes as its subject the origin of sin: in it Paul lays out a catalog of the sins of the unrighteous, who fail to see the truth of God. Sin is linked to a failure to see the truth.

12. See Cook 2006, 35–38, for sources and a discussion of Augustine's comments.
13. Cited ibid., 31, from the edition of Holtz (1981, 672).
14. Aristotle, *Rhet.* 3.11.6, Loeb edition, trans. J.H. Freese, cited by Cook 2006, 33.
15. This is indeed, as Augustine says, an obscure allegory. It seems to indicate insatiable need. Augustine is unusual in saying there are three rather than two daughters (*De trin.* 15.9). The Vulgate has *sanguisugae duae sunt filiae dicentes adfer adfer tria sunt insaturabilia et quartum quod numquam dicit suffici.* ("The horseleech has two daughters, saying 'Give, Give!' There are three things that are never satisfied and a fourth that never says 'enough.'") The horseleech (*sanguisuga*) is a form of leech that attaches to the flesh with two suckers; some rabbinical commentators, however, take the word *'alukoh* to be the name of a prophet rather than the word for leech (see Plaut 1961, 305).
16. Cook 2006, 40–41. Augustine stresses the unlikeness of man to God again a little later: "Wherefore, since we have found now in this enigma so great an unlikeness to God and the Word of God, wherein yet there was found before some likeness, this, too, must be admitted, that even when we shall be like Him, when 'we shall see Him as He is' (and certainly he who said this was aware beyond doubt of our present unlikeness), not even then shall we be equal to Him in nature" (*De trin.* 15.16.26, trans. Haddan).

4. FALLING INTO LANGUAGE

1. The phrase is from Juvenal 14.136, describing the insanity of the miser.
2. Goldhill makes clear in his introduction that his assertion that Christianity meant the end of dialogue in antiquity is intended to provoke contemporary scholarly dialogue. See the contributions of Clark, Miles, and Lim in the same volume for quite different analyses of dialogue forms and the social place of dialogue in the early church.
3. Herzog 1966, 94.
4. *Invidia* is etymologically linked with *videre*, "to see." The verbal form *invideo* means literally "to look askance." Skewed vision, as I discuss below, is of great thematic significance to Prudentius, as it is to Milton. Envy's inability to tolerate the sight of the *gaudia iustorum* foreshadows the vision of the souls of the damned and the just at the end of the poem.
5. Palla 1981,168 reviews other uses of the rare adjective *anguiferum*.
6. Palla 1981, 166 provides a number of parallel passages from patristic literature on the snares of the devil. On the association of sophistry with tricky nets, see Detienne and Vernant 1978, 42, and Cook 2006, 244–45.
7. The version of Genesis quoted by Augustine (*De civitate dei* 22.3) uses the term *gigans* to refer to Nimrod (*Chus autem genuit Nebroth, hic coepit esse gigans super terram; hic erat gigans venator ante dominum Deum*), as does the Septuagint; the Vulgate does not: "*ipse coepit esse potens in terra et erat robustus venator coram Domino.*"
8. *Quaestiones in Genesin* 2.81–82, cited by van der Toorn and van der Horst 1990, 17.
9. Philo, *De gigantibus* 65–66, cited by van der Toorn and van der Horst 1990, 18.
10. Justin Martyr, *Cohortatio ad Gentiles* 28; Origen, *De principiis* 1.5. Leonard 1990, 88–90 discusses the tradition of the names Satan and Lucifer. See also Pagels 1995, 39–43. Satan was more of a divine colleague than an evil adversary in Job.
11. Fragment Targum ad Gen. 10:9, cited by van der Toorn and van der Horst 1990, 24.
12. "And so this giant is to be recognized as a 'hunter against the Lord.' And what is meant by the term 'hunter' but deceiver, oppressor, and destroyer of the animals of the earth? He and his people therefore, erected this tower against the Lord, and so gave expression to their impious pride; and justly was their wicked intention punished by God.... So that man, who would not understand God when He issued His commands, should be misunderstood when he himself gave orders. Thus was that conspiracy disbanded, for each man retired from those he could not understand, and associated with those whose speech was intelligible; and the nations were divided according to their languages, and scattered over the earth as seemed good to God" (Augustine, *Civ. Dei.* 16.4, trans. Dods).
13. Fyler 2007, 37, who cites Pseudo-Clement *Recognitions* 1.30 (*PG* 1:1224–24).
14. Leonard 1990, 87.
15. Ibid., 53–56.

16. The name Lucifer does appear once in the *Cathemerinon* (*C.* 12.32), but in a context that suggests it refers to the morning star rather than the devil.
17. His pride and jealousy lead him to insist that he is his own creator in *H.* 170-74.
18. Edwards 1995, 448.
19. For other examples, see Palla 1981, 217; Bartelink 1967; and Fontaine 1964.
20. Ambrose (*Expositio evangelii secundum Lucam* 7.73, ed. Schenkl, CSEL 32.4, 1902, p. 312, 16), and Augustine (*Quaestiones evang.* 2.19 [PL 35, 1340]).
21. *Est vera secta?* I have translated this phrase, which literally means "Is our doctrine true?" as "Are we on the true path?" to preserve the etymological play on *secta, sectabitur, sequor*. There is also a play on different meanings of *recta*: *rectam fidem*, "right faith," line 2; and *rectam tramitem*, line 12, "the right (correct) path," but also "the straight path," as opposed to the twisting paths of sin.
22. There is another play on words here: *hostilis manus* first appears to mean "an enemy hand," but the second *manus*, construed with *latronum*, has to mean "band."
23. *De doctrina* 1.10-11; Camargo 1998, 399n7 has a good bibliography on Augustine's transformation of the Neoplatonic topos of the journey.
24. Bartelink 1967 traces the topos of the devil as a robber or highwayman in patristic literature and provides an extensive list of references.
25. *At non caede viri tanta perterrita Lausus./pars ingens belli, sinit agmina: primus Abantem/oppositum interimit, pugnae nodumque moramque* (*Aen.* 10.426-28). "Lausus, a major force in the war, did not allow carnage/Pallas inflicted to panic his troops. He started by killing/Abas, *a knot to frustrate any blade*, who rose up to oppose him" (trans. Ahl). The phrase is difficult to translate. Literally it means "a knot and delay of battle," and forms part of the sustained imagery of knots and snares throughout the poem. I have resorted to paraphrase ("a slow and difficult struggle") in my translation.
26. Ahl's translation.
27. Mastrangelo (2008, 100) notes that Superbia leaves out Eve and mentions only Adam putting on clothing—an omission magnified in the *Hamartigenia*, as I discuss below. Superbia also fails to note that originally Adam and Eve put on garments made of fig leaves. It is God who provides them with garments of skin.
28. I do not know whether Prudentius could have known this, but it interesting that in the Haggadic tradition sources say that Nimrod either received from his ancestors the garments of skin given to Adam by God or tried to kill Esau in order to attain them (van der Toorn and van der Horst 1990, 26).
29. Defined by Cicero (*Orat.* 79): "*verecundus erit usus oratoriae quasi supellectilis. supellex est enim quodam modo nostra, quae est in ornamentis, alia rerum alia verborum.*" Cf. Quint., *Inst.* 8.28. Seneca uses it, like Prudentius, in a way that combines both its original and transferred meanings: "*an tu existimas reprendendum, qui ... pretiosarum rerum pompam in domo explicat: non putas eum qui occupatus est in supervacua litterarum supellectile?*" (*Epist.* 88.36).
30. Elegantly explored in Conybeare 2002, esp. 184-86.
31. "*Eandem sententiam milliens alio atque alio amictu indutam referunt,*" Fronto, Ant. (*De eloquentia*) (ed. Haines, 2:104) (157N).
32. E.g., Quintilian, *Inst.* 10.1.87 and 5.14.30; Fronto, *Aur.* (ed. Haines, 1:36) (46N); Cicero, *Fin.* 1.10 and 5.13; *De orat.* 1.80 and 3.185.
33. On the imagery of cosmic dissolution in *H.* 315-34 (Lat. 236-50), see Lapidge 1980, and Malamud 1989, 72-78. On anachronism as an epic technique, see Zissos and Gildenhard 1999.

5. UNDER ASSAULT

1. Tertullian, *De cultu feminarum* 1.1.
2. See especially Richlin 1995, Rimell 2005, Wyke 2002, and Sharrock 1991.
3. Rimell 2005, 194.
4. This double valence is reflected in another word used for makeup, *medicamina*, which carried associations with medicines, drugs, and poisons. Makeup comes in the form of unpleasant ointments to be smeared on the face, and Ovid describes how sickening these ointments can be in his *Remedy for Love* (*Remedia amoris*): "*Tum quoque, compositis cum collinet ora venenis/ad dominae vultus (nec pudor obstet) eas. / Pyxidas invenies et rerum mille colores, / et fluere in tepidos oesypa*

lapsa sinus./Illa tuas redolent, Phineu, medicamina mensas:/non semel hinc stomacho nausea facta meo est" (351–56). A number of ancient texts associate makeup with prostitutes and adulterers (e.g., Xenophon, *Oeconomicus* 10.2-13, where he chides his wife for appearing in makeup; Seneca, *Controv.* 2.7.3–4; Plutarch, *Coniugalia praecepta* 142a).

5. Tertullian, *De cultu feminarum* 1.2-3.

6. Enterline 2000, 62–65 has an excellent discussion of Ovid's strategic play on the analogy between bodies and rhetorical forms, with particular attention to the rhetorical and corporeal meanings of *figura* and *forma*. *Figura* is frequently used as a rhetorical term (see *OLD*, s.v. 11).

7. Note Cicero's use of the term *supellex*, which Prudentius used to describe the "rich resources" of the fallen world in line 281 (Lat. 207).

8. "Nam ut mulieres esse dicuntur nonnullae inornatae, quas id ipsum deceat, sic haec subtilis oratio etiam incompta delectat; fit enim quiddam in utroque, quo sit venustius, sed non ut appareat. Tum removebitur omnis insignis ornatus quasi margaritarum; ne calamistri quidem adhibebuntur; fucati vero medicamenta candoris et ruboris omnia repellentur; elegantia modo et munditia remanebit.... Verecundus erit usus oratoriae quasi supellectilis. Supellex est enim quodam modo nostra, quae est in ornamentis, alia rerum alia verborum." Cicero, *Orat.* 79-80. Translation slightly modified from Hubbell's Loeb translation.

9. See Sen., *Epist.* 114.16 for discussion of unchaste *sententiae*, 114.21 for a description of Maecenas. Richlin 1997 is an excellent analysis of the interconnections between rhetoric and gender in Roman oratory, with many more examples from primary sources. On rhetoric and masculinity, see Gunderson 2000, and the influential Gleason 1995/2008.

10. A theme explored with relish by Juvenal (*Sat.* 2.44–51, 6.286–93, and 11.162–63).

11. As Richlin (1995, 186) notes, the use of makeup marks sexual difference, so its "improper" use within a culture must blur that difference. "A man wearing make-up and long hair, or a woman wearing no make-up and short hair, can in this culture provoke the fascinated question, 'is that a boy or a girl?' Once the signs on top are blurred, the real question comes out: what is the bottom line?" Tertullian shares the same anxiety; in his attack on makeup he includes a passage forbidding men "to cut the beard too sharply; to pluck it out here and there; to shave round about (the mouth); to arrange the hair, and disguise its hoariness by dyes; to remove all the incipient down all over the body; to fix (each particular hair) in its place with (some) womanly pigment; to smooth all the rest of the body by the aid of some rough powder or other: then, further, to take every opportunity for consulting the mirror; to gaze anxiously into it" (*De cultu feminarum* 2.8.2)—in other words, to elide the differences between male and female bodies and to act like females.

12. On *vas* as a term for the male genitalia, see Adams 1982, 42–43, who cites a number of examples including one contemporary with Prudentius (Augustine, *Civ.* 14.23). The phrase *resectam particulam* here may come from Horace, *Carm.* 1.16.13-16: "*Fertur Prometheus addere principi/limo coactus particulam undique/desectam et insani leonis/uim stomacho apposuisse nostro.*" Horace is describing Prometheus's creation of man. Once again, Prudentius melds the Promethean creation story with the biblical account (Gen. 2:21–23), this time using it as a model for the creation of woman from Adam's flesh. See Palla 1981, 196.

13. Chiappiniello 2009, 181 argues that in this passage Prudentius, unlike his predecessors, "does not castigate women for leading men astray but adopts a different approach by satirizing soft (cf. 282 *mollescere*) and effeminate men.... The onus of ensuring moral conduct in life rests entirely on men, who, by God's commandment, are women's guide." Fontaine 1969, 64 also analyzes this passage and Prudentius's insistence on the weakness of female character and the need for men to control women.

14. Tertullian devotes a chapter of *De cultu feminarum* to attacking luxurious textiles (1.8).

15. For a particularly good example, see *Cath.* 3.26–30, where Prudentius speaks of his muse weaving mystic crowns of dactyls, and *Perist.* 3.206–10, in which he offers garlands of (wilted) dactyls to the martyr Eulalia. As I have argued elsewhere, the tension between imagery of binding and imagery of dissolution is a predominant motif of both the *Peristephanon* and the *Psychomachia* (Malamud 1989, especially 75–78 and 172–80).

16. *O fortunatos nimium, sua si bona norint,/agricolas quibus ipsa procul discordibus armis/fundit humo facilem victum iustissima tellus,/si non ingentem foribus domus alta superbis/mane salutantum totis vomit aedibus undam,/nec varios inhiant pulchra testudine postis/inlusasque auro vestis Ephyreiaque aera,/alba neque Assyrio fucatur lana veneno,/nec casia liquidi corrumpitur usus olivi.*

17. See Gunderson 2009, 119, who discusses the language applied to rhetorical ornmament: "Dressing up one's oratory is always liable to charges that it has been overdone: superfluity and effeminacy are the main vectors of criticism. Quintilian argues that the proper rhetorical adornment is always both functional and virile. Thus the well-made argument of the good man is akin to the virile beauty evinced by the muscular bodies of the athletes."

18. Webb 2008, 59.

19. Cassiodorus, *Variae* 4.51, p. 178, ll.61–64 (= Bonaria *Fasti* no. 446), cited by Webb 2008, 64: "*Idem corpus Herculem designat et Venerem, feminam praesentat in mare, regem facit et militem, senem reddit et iuvenem, ut in uno credas esse multos tam varia imitatione discretos.*" Webb 2008, 62 describes the masks and costumes of pantomime dancers.

20. Translation Laistner 1951.

21. See Miller 2005, 30 for a discussion of this passage.

22. Translation Melville 1997.

23. On the tension between didactic and martial epic, see Von Albrecht 1997, 2:1362.

24. "Prudentius associates scripture with the notion of Moses as the chronicler of creation (*Apoth.* 219, 234–35, and 302). Similarly, Augustine at *Conf.* 12.26 argues that Moses wrote words (*signa*) for those who understand the hidden meaning of scripture" (Mastrangelo 2008, 157; see also 42).

25. "Sometimes he juxtaposes *Sapientia* and *Deus*, referring to them now as fellow creators and now as apophatic divine beings with no discernible origins (*H.* 345, 164). In another passage the poet invokes *Sapientia* as an offspring of the Father and therefore an ontological equal of Christ (*Hymn on the Trinity* 2). In all three passages, a Christian context is clear, but their debt to pagan metaphysics is clear from their concern with the ontology of the godhead" (Mastrangelo 2008, 223n32).

26. This is exactly the same condition in which Boethius appears at the opening of *The Consolation of Philosophy*. His soul is sick, and, weighed down by chains around his neck, he gazes at the earth (1m2) and his vision is obscured and needs to be cleansed by Philosophy (1p2.6). On the cleansing of Boethius's eyes, see Goins 2001.

27. Rosenmeyer 1999, 19–47. As Rosenmeyer points out, science writers in antiquity argued that man's semen is made up of marrow, but in erotic contexts the image of marrow as a *locus eroticus* is used almost exclusively of women (and where it is not, it occurs in passages where the male figuratively takes on the woman's role).

28. Paxson 1994, 78–95 discusses the problematic relationship between allegorical levels in the *Psychomachia* and the extent of the interaction between the personifications and the scriptural figures within the narrative, and has a particularly interesting discussion of the figure of Job. See also Barney 1979, 63, and Van Dyke 1985, 34–35 for the semiotic tension generated by the relationship between the biblical or typological dimension of the poem and the personificational one.

29. Bloomfield 1943, 89 cites Origen, homily 12 in *Lib. Jes. Nave.*

30. These personifications do not appear in the *Psychomachia*, where the destabilizing elements of language that they represent are concentrated in the figure of Discordia.

31. Bardzell makes the point that even Sapientia in the *Psychomachia* does not possess intellection, the divine ability to have comprehensive knowledge, but relies instead on reason: "Sapientia, her name notwithstanding, appears to be engaging here in rational inquiry, rather than pure intellection. Thus, the construction of the temple does not indicate that the battles are over and the Vices defeated once and for all" (2009, 51–52).

32. For this point, that the assignment of Sapientia to different sides (Vice in *H.*, Virtue in *Psy.*) reveals the instability characteristic of language, it makes no difference which text was written first. Obsession with linguistic instability is a characteristic of all of Prudentius's work. Shanzer 1989, however, has persuasively argued that the *Psychomachia* should be dated after 405, and thus subsequent to the *Hamartigenia*. She also notes (360n106) that the mustering of the Vices by the devil in the *Hamartigenia* is similar to the *Psychomachia*, and suggests that it "can be seen as a preliminary version of the imagery to be used in the *Psych.*"

6. GENERATION OF VIPERS

1. Athanasius, in his *Orations against the Arians*, makes this point at some length: "For brutes and men, after a Creator has begun them, are begotten by succession; and the son, having been

begotten of a father who was a son, becomes accordingly in his turn a father to a son, in inheriting from his father that by which he himself has come to be. Hence in such instances there is not, properly speaking, either father or son, nor do the father and the son stay in their respective characters, for the son himself becomes a father, being son of his father, but father of his son. But it is not so in the Godhead; for not as man is God: for the father is not from a father; therefore doth He not beget one who shall become a father: nor is the Son from effluence of the Father, nor is He begotten from a father that was begotten; therefore neither is He begotten so as to beget. Thus it belongs to the Godhead alone, that the Father is properly father, and the Son properly son, and in Them, and Them only, does it hold that the Father is ever Father and the Son ever Son" (Athanasius, *Ar.* 1.21).

2. Cf. Prudentius's argument against the possibility of two Gods: "Either God / is one and holds the highest power, or / the two that now exist are both diminished: / both cannot have supremacy. It's clear / that nothing is supreme if it's not one, / omnipotent, since separate things claim power / each for itself, rejecting the other's rule, / and so are not supreme and not almighty. / Dispersed authority is not complete: / one cannot have a thing another has" (*H.* 28–37).

3. As Salvatore 1958, 16–24 has noted, this passage is a tour de force of textual *contaminatio*: Prudentius draws from a number of models from classical poetry and prose, though he acknowledges no specific sources, only the *ethici* and *physici*. His sources include Herodotus 3.109; Pliny, *HN* 10.62.169–70; Petronius poem 32; Lucretius's description of physical love in *De rerum natura* 4; and Horace, *Odes* 1.37.26–28 (on the death of Cleopatra). See Palla 1981, 254–61 for more parallels. There is also a passage in Horace's *Satire* 2.8 (42–44) where diners are presented with a pregnant lamprey to eat; commentators have noted that in antiquity it was believed that lampreys mated with vipers. Miller 1998, 274–75 discusses the satirical implications of the lamprey pregnant with the viper's brood, and compares it to Prudentius's pregnant viper.

4. Cited by Ladner 1995, 127, who uses the Bern *Physiologus*, Cod. 318 of the Burgerbibliothek.

5. Aulus Gellius uses the figure of the mother bear to describe Vergil's painstaking process of composition: "*Ut illa bestia fetum ederet ineffigiatum informemque lambendoque id postea quod ita edidisset conformaret et fingeret, proinde ingenii quoque sui partus recentes rudi esse facie et inperfecta, sed deinceps tractando colendoque reddere iis se oris et vultus lineamenta*" (*Noctes Atticae* 17.10). Cf. *Aeneid* 8.634 and *Georgics* 2.407.

6. Gender confusion is a hallmark of Prudentius's poetry. See Malamud 1990 on Prudentius's violent masculine virgin martyrs, and Nugent 2000, 16 on the transsexual nature of the Virtues and Vices in the *Psychomachia*.

7. Confusion or conflation of the mouth and the vagina is long-standing in ancient medicine. "The view that a female's speech was influenced by and in turn indicative of her sexual experience is enshrined in the linguistic double meaning of the Greek word *stoma*, meaning both oral and genital mouth or lips.... Galen, for example, compared the clitoris to the uvula, for the clitoris protects the uterus from the cold in the same way that the uvula protects the trachea; the logic runs that a female who opens one of her mouths is thought to open the other" (Morales 1999, 50). On the conflation of throat and vagina, see Sissa 1990, 52–67; Hanson and Armstrong 1986. Nugent 2000 insightfully links this conflation to the striking fact that all but one of the Vices in the *Psychomachia* die from wounds to the mouth or throat.

8. Of course, Sin and her offspring in Milton have many forerunners in the literary tradition; see Fowler 1998 ad loc. Spenser's Errour is one of the most exuberant: "Her scattred brood, soone as their Parent deare / They saw so rudely falling to the ground, / Groning full deadly, all with troublous feare, / Gathred themselves about her body round, / Weening their wonted entrance to have found / At her wide mouth: but being there withstood / They flocked all about her bleeding wound, / And sucked up their dying mothers blood, / Making her death their life, and eke her hurt their good" (*FQ* bk. 1, canto 1, st. 25).

9. Kilgour 2005, 308.

10. Ibid., 339, quoting Burrow 1993, 269.

11. Kilgour 2005, 309.

12. Conybeare 2007, 237.

13. Ibid., 234. She argues that John 8:31–32 is relevant here as well.

14. Arius associated with Eve and the serpent (Athanasius, *Ar.* 1.7). As Burrus puts it, "A writhing effeminacy of the word is the shifty mark of the illegitimacy by which he, Arius—motherless like all the sons of this work—is unmasked as the offspring not of God the Father but of Satan the antifather, disseminator of the 'mania' of heresy" (Burrus 2000, 54).

15. Burrus 1996, 467–68.

16. Ibid., 469. It is worth noting that the contamination of the mouth, or more precisely, confusion of the oral and genital areas, is also a figure in Ambrose's rhetoric against Arian, in particular as it applies to language, as Burrus points out (ibid.): "It is a small step from the monstrous to the more graphically grotesque, a step that Ambrose seems to take easily as he recounts the death of the arch-heretic Arius: 'For Arius' bowels gushed out . . . and so he burst asunder in the midst, falling headlong and besmirching those foul lips wherewith he had denied Christ.' Ambrose invites contrast between the grotesque figure of Arius and the sublimated eroticism of the following representation of the evangelist John: 'Whom, then, are we to believe?—St. John, who lay on Christ's bosom, or Arius, wallowing amid the outgush of his very bowels?' he asks. In John, not heresy but the male body of orthodoxy is feminized in an asceticizing rejection of grotesque masculinity." Easterling and Miles (1999, 101) cite an anecdote from Eunapius of Sardis (*Historici graeci minores*, fr. 54, Blockley 1981–83) that contains similar imagery associating language with gushing bowels, about an unnamed *tragoidos* in the time of Nero whose acting powers had an unfortunate effect on a population unfamiliar with tragic performances.

17. Harpham 1986, 249.

7. SIGNS OF WOE

1. Partner 2007, 142: "As the rain comes down like tears, and man falls, Milton gives us a typographical depiction of the fatal cadence."

2. See Fyler 2007, 16–18 for further references.

3. Fyler 2007, 10–17 has a good summary of the tradition of commentary on the problem of Eve's name.

4. Cf. Pucci's (1977, 100) discussion of Pandora, whose creation represents the birth of rhetoric (my emphasis): "The text implies both the human dawn unmarked by imitation and rhetoric and a turning point that initiates the beautifying, imitative, rhetorical process. *In this way, the text reproduces the split between a language identical to reality and a language imitative of reality.*"

5. Butler 2003 discusses the relation drawn between Eve and Pandora by Milton and Tertullian.

6. Lot is the hero of this tale but represents another variant on the model of reproduction without a wife: after the loss of his wife, his two daughters live with him in a cave, get him drunk, and commit incest with him; each bears a son as a result (Genesis 19:30–38). This allows Lot to reproduce without blame (he is unaware of his actions) through his daughters, and thus produce offspring who are more like himself.

7. Patristic commentators on the passage interpret the transformation of Lot's wife as indicating that the convert to Christianity should turn his back on his earlier life, or as symbolizing the weakness of the flesh compared to the strength of the spirit (Augustine, *Civ. dei* 10.8, 16.30; Origen, *In gen. hom.* 5.2). For further discussion, see Palla 1981, 275 and Herzog 1966, 143.

8. See Hollis 1997 for a discussion of ancient sources of the Niobe story.

9. Salvatore 1958, details the verbal similarities between the passages; he sees Prudentius outdoing Ovid at his own game: "Prudenzio si mostra ancor piu *amator ingenii sui*, ancor piu intemperante di Ovidio" (268).

10. Gnilka 2000, 68–90 argues that lines 745 (*caute sigillati longum salis effigiata*), 747–48 (*et flexam in tergum faciem paulumque relata / menta retro, antiquae monumenta regentia noxae*), and 765–68 are later interpolations. I do not find his argument conclusive, but my main point stands even if one accepts his excision.

11. Hardie 2002, 251 discusses how the repetition of the name Niobe in Ovid's text reinforces the theme of self-alienation and absence.

12. Pausanias saw the figure of Niobe on Mount Sipylus: "This Niobe I myself saw when I had gone up to Mount Sipylus. When you are near it is a beetling crag, with not the slightest resemblance to a woman, mourning or otherwise; but if you go further away you will think you see a woman in tears, with head bowed down" (1.21.3, trans. Jones). Josephus similarly claims to have seen the statue of Lot's wife in the desert: "But Lot's wife continually turning back to view the city as she went from it, and being too nicely inquisitive what would become of it, although God had forbidden her so to do, was changed into a pillar of salt; for I have seen it, and it remains at this day" (*Jewish Antiquities* 1.204, trans. Thackeray).

13. As is the case with the metamorphosis of Actaeon, which is the occasion for contesting interpretations from the crowd: *Rumor in ambiguo est; aliis violentior aequo / visa dea est. alii laudant dignamque severa / virginitate vocant: pars invenit utraque causas* (*Met.* 3.253–55).

14. Conybeare 2007, 226.

15. Compare the contest with David and Absalom, where the battle between father and son is conceived as *"signis contraria signa paternis"* (*H.* 567); and *H.* 79–80, where Prudentius expresses his discomfort with comparing God to any sign: *"non conferre deo uelut aequiparabile quidquam / ausim nec domino famulum componere signum"* (Conybeare 2007, 232n16).

16. As Catherine Conybeare (2007, 227) has noted, the *Hamartigenia*, like other Roman epic poems, is a medium of "studied pseudo-orality." Roman epic is a genre that purports to be sung, though in fact it is written. "The text of the *Hamartigenia* is typical," she says, "in that it is dotted with feigned markers of orality, most notably the magnificent prayer with which it closes, but also its references to *fabulae*, its repeated first person interventions, and its direct address to interlocutors outside the text."

17. Kaesser 2002, 158–71 analyzes the layers of exegesis in Prudentius's account of the martyrdom of Saint Cassian. In the poem, the poet describes an encounter in a shrine with a verger who explains the painting of Cassian's martyrdom. Kaesser argues that the point of the exegetical frame is to close the "hermeneutic gap" opened up by the medium of painting and "diminish, if not dissolve entirely, the potential misunderstanding of painting." Like Goldhill (2006), I find it more likely that the point is to increase rather than diminish the complexity of the ekphrasis.

18. Mastrangelo 2008, 163–64.

19. See Salvatore 1958, 266–69 for a discussion of verbal parallels with Ovid's Niobe. Niobe's transformation into a statue is one of several episodes in the *Metamorphoses* involving humans and statues, including the famous story of Pygmalion and his metamorphic statue; the story of Narcissus, who is compared to a marble statue; and Perseus's transformation of his enemies into statues using the severed head of Medusa. Hardie (2002, chapters 3 and 6) provides a comprehensive discussion of Niobe in the context of other metamorphoses into statues.

20. See Goldhill 2000 on Prudentius and his views on art, including (62–63) his defense of Theodosius's decision to preserve classical sculptures (*Contra Sym.* 1.501–5).

21. Whitmarsh 2002, 111–12 quoting Theon, *On Ekphrasis* = p. 2.118 Spengel), and citing the important discussion of ancient ekphrasis in Webb 1997a and 1997b. For enargeia, see section 1 above, pp. 60–61.

22. Whitmarsh 2002, 112.

23. The identification of Orpah as the mother of Goliath also appears in Jewish tradition; she is identified in Sotah 42b of the Babylonian Talmud as the mother of four Philistine giants (including Goliath), but in this tradition her piety toward Naomi is rewarded. See Palla 1981 ad loc.

24. As Doniger (2000, 260) points out, "Boaz is of Naomi's generation, not Ruth's; he is Naomi's brother-in-law, the brother of her husband Elimelech. If Naomi is the sister-in-law whom Boaz *should* marry, then when Naomi sends Ruth to Boaz, she is substituting the desirable younger generation for the appropriate older generation, in *a reversal* of Rachel/Leah and Shelah/Judah, where the appropriate (or, in the case of Judah, necessary) older generation was substituted for the desirable younger generation. I would suggest that Obed is 'Naomi's baby' because he should have been born (physically) to Naomi or (officially) to Naomi's dead son."

25. E.g., Xenophon, *Memor.* 2.1.20ff; Cicero, *Tusc.* 1.30.72; Servius ad *Aen.* 6.136; Philo, *Spec. leg.* 4.108 and 1.12; Lactantius, *Inst.* 6.3–4; Jerome, *Contra Rufinum* 3.39 (*PL* 23, 508c); Ausonius, *Professores* 11.5. A scriptural parallel appears at Matthew 7:13–14. The metaphor of the road is widespread in Greek and Latin. For a thorough list of citations and scholarship on the topos, see Palla 1981, 285–86. Knox 1999 discusses the related image of the narrow road in Lucretius.

26. Bleary vision was something of a topos in Horatian satire. See Gowers 1993, 60, where she cites Horace, *Sat.* 1.5.30, 1.1.120, 1.7.3, and 1.3.25. Prudentius too uses the imagery of blurred vision at *H.* 85ff. as a metaphor for the misunderstanding of a dualist heretic; later, at 865, he offers an extended description of the supernaturally acute vision of the good soul after death.

27. *De gen. ad lit.* 12, esp. 12.6.15. See Miller 2005, 32–33 for a discussion of Augustine's theory of three kinds of vision.

28. Lühken 2002, 76 notes this allusion.

29. In contrast to the devil, who is described as *decolor*, as is Envy at *H.* 186.

8. IN AENIGMATE

1. Bynum and Freedman 2000, 7.
2. Straw 2000, 23.
3. Taddei (1981, 212-20) notes that Prudentius's diction throughout this opening section is juridical in nature, infused with words derived from Roman jurisprudence: *vindicat* (24), *proprium* (23), *ius* (25 and 110), *potestas* (20), *imperio* (24), *dicio* (19 and 108), *testamur* (27), *probat* (52), *adscitus* (53), *signum, adsignare . . . iura* (105), *coheredem* (110), *ratio* (180), and *negat* (180).
4. Codex Theodosianus 1.16.6, of 331 CE, cited by Harries 1999, 214.
5. Passio ss. Perpetuae et Felicitatis, 10.1-13 (SC 417:134-40). Vita Caecilii Cypriani 12 (CSEL 3.3cii-civ); Passio ss. Mariani et Iacobi = P. Franchi de' Cavalieri, La Passio ss. Mariani et Iacobi = Studi e Testi 3 (Rome: Tipografia Vaticana, 1900).
6. Seneca, *Ep.* 14.2.
7. Shaw 2003, 541 citing *Opus imperfectum in Matthaeum, Hom.* 54.31 (PG 56:941). I have quoted Shaw's translation.
8. Tert., *Apol.* 1.1.10-13 (CCL 1:86-87), cited by Shaw, 544n33.
9. Shaw provides extensive evidence that Christians did indeed internalize the judicial process; a particularly striking example is that of Jerome's famous dream in which he is accused of being a Ciceronian, not a Christian: "When suddenly, taken up in the spirit, I was hauled before the judge's tribunal [*ad tribunal iudicis*], where there was so much light and such a great shining from the radiance of those who were standing about that, throwing myself on the ground, I did not dare even to look up. When I was asked my status [*interrogatus conditionem*], I replied that I was a Christian. The one who was presiding as judge intoned: 'You are lying,' he said, 'You are a Ciceronian, not a Christian. *Your treasure is there, where your heart is.*' I remained rooted to the spot, tongue-tied. Amidst the lashes of the whip [*verbera*]—for the judge had ordered that I be beaten—I was tortured more by conscience than by any torturer's firebrands, and I considered that little piece of verse in my mind: *Who will confess you in the fires of hell itself*? I began to cry and shouted out: 'Pity me, my lord, have mercy on me.' Amidst these pleas of mine the lash of the whip resounded. Then the spectators who were standing round about fell on their knees before the tribunal and began to implore the judge that he should have pity on my youth, that he should make allowance and forgive my mistake, and that he should only impose the penalty of crucifixion if I ever again read the books of the gentiles." Jerome, *Ep.* 22.30 (CSEL 54:189-91), Shaw's translation.
10. Moreira 2006, 150, citing Clement, *Stromata* 4.24.
11. Brown 2000, 46.
12. Ibid., 49.
13. Translated by Marcus Dods. From *Nicene and Post-Nicene Fathers*, first series, vol. 2, ed. Philip Schaff (Buffalo: Christian Literature, 1887). Revised and edited for New Advent by Kevin Knight. http://www.newadvent.org/fathers/1201.htm.
14. Mastrangelo 2008, 108.
15. Plato, *Phaedo* 62b and *Cratylus* 400c. See Courcelle 1965 for an analysis of the topos of the body as prison in Platonic and Christian literature.
16. I departed slightly from the literal sense of the Latin in my translation, but tried to keep the nurse-nursling relationship clear. I call Fides a nurse, which Prudentius does not; instead, he identifies the soul as the *alumna* (nursling or foster child) of Fides.
17. The language here is erotic: *cubile*, line 856, refers to the marriage bed; *querulo* is an adjective typical in Latin love elegy.
18. It is typical of Prudentius's highly ambivalent treatment of females that even this passage, which represents the culmination of his allegorical presentation of the soul, associates the feminine soul not only with the mystical brides of the Song of Songs and of Revelation 19, but also, disconcertingly, with an explicitly erotic pagan epigram attributed to Petronius (*Anth. Lat.* 705). See Salvatore 1958, 18n9; Palla 1981, 297. Even the presence of Fides, the faithful nurse, suggests unsettling parallels with classical literature—both Phaedra and Myrrha are assisted by their faithful old nurses in their pursuit of incestuous love. Prudentius, of course, is not alone in deploying highly erotic imagery to describe virgins, and there is much written on this topic. See Burrus 1995, Grig 2005, Averil Cameron 1989, Brown 1988, Clarke 2006, Uden 2009, and Malamud 1989 and 1990.

19. The association of blindness with lack of faith is graphically expressed in the *Psychomachia*, when Fides tramples on the eyeballs of her opponent, Paganism (*Ps.* 32–33), in the first battle scene of the poem. See Bardzell 2009, 44.

20. Brown 2000, 50.

21. See Goldhill 2001, 183–84; Webb 2008, 204–5 for different reactions to Tertullian's views on spectacles.

22. Levine 1991, 21, in the context of his discussion of the long, violent, and grotesque *Peristephanon* 10.

23. Webb 2008, 207.

24. Moreira 2006, 152.

25. Straw 2000, 23.

26. Brown 1992, 208; Van Slyke 2005, 63. The bibliography on violence in the amphitheater is vast. In addition to Brown and Van Slyke, see Drake 2006, Wiedemann 1992, Kyle 1998, Walter 2004, Barton 1989 and 1993, and Coleman 1998 and 1990 for good introductions to this complicated subject.

27. Van Slyke 2005 provides numerous examples, e.g., Augustine, *Sermo 14* (*PL* 46.864–65) invites his congregation to exchange public spectacles for the edifying spectacle of the martyrdom of Saint Cyprian. See also Chrysostom, *In Ioannem Hom.* 60 (*PG* 59.333), who proposes contemplation of the martyrs or of David (Webb 2008, 206).

28. Frankfurter 2009, 231.

29. Goldhill 1999, 82, which presents an excellent analysis of both *Pe.* 9 and *Pe.* 3, the martyrdom of Eulalia. Both martyrdoms involve writing the marks of torture on the body. For writing on the body in the *Peristephanon*, see Ross 1995, Ballengee 2002, and Malamud 1989.

30. Ballengee 2009, 93: "Prudentius creates a certain excess in his writing in his use of literary, rhetorical tropes, by which he hopes to gain for himself as poet the same benefits as the martyr."

31. Augustine, *Sermo Denis* 14.3, as quoted in Goldhill 1999, 81.

32. Prudentius displays a strong dislike of schoolmasters and rhetoricians in the preface to his collected works: *aetas prima crepantibus/flevit sub ferulis. mox docuit toga/infectum vitiis falsa loqui, non sine crimine* (*Praef.* 7–9).

33. Discussed by Miles 1983, 142.

34. Kilgour 2005, 308, cited above.

35. Mastrangelo (2008, 83) sees the narrative allegory of the *Psychomachia* as a response to such a perceived crisis of meaning; it deploys typologies that point beyond the text to biblical texts and Christian teachings that make it "possible for the poet to communicate ideas that are incommunicable through normal object or referent language."

36. In addition to *poena levis*, Prudentius echoes *lenito* in line 963 (*lenta*).

37. Malamud 1989, which prompted an interesting article by Alan Cameron (1995) arguing against the presence of the anagram. Nugent, too, expressed her doubts about the anagram with characteristic wit: "Well, maybe. But if *my* decoder unscrambles the same line as: LETTERS VALUED IN ARCANE POEM, what are we to make of it?" (1991, 326). As Morgan (1993, 143) put it in discussing a related form of wordplay, "Credulity about acrostics is so closely associated with crankdom that legitimate scholars risk contumely and scorn if they are tempted to believe." My response to Nugent's point is that ancient readers, so far as we know, had neither decoder rings nor sophisticated software to unscramble anagrams, and so would have to be guided by textual clues if they were to have any hope of detecting them. See Somerville 2010 for a discussion of the clues to the signature acrostic that Vergil leaves for the reader at *G.* 424–35.

38. Bleisch 1996 reveals an interesting example from Callimachus, with an excellent analysis of its significance and its history. For other examples, see Fowler 1983, Cameron 1995, Courtney 1990, Levitan 1979 and 1985 (the latter on the unquestioned late antique master of figured verse, Optatian), and Morgan 1993.

39. Cameron (1995, 483) objects to the anagram for several reasons, including that the name *Clemens* is absent from it. However, since the name is clearly signaled by the appearance of *clementer* in the surface text, there is no reason for it to reappear in the anagram.

40. As Cameron notes (1995, 482). My original argument was faulty; I argued that the *sphragis* should read *glorificent me: Aurelio prudente se clamante*, ignoring the fact that grammar requires *glorificent* to be construed with the previous line.

41. Cameron 1995, 482–83: "There is a (to me) uncomfortable conflict between the surface conclusion of the poem (in which the poet sees himself as too much of a sinner to hope for paradise; that is for martyrs alone) and the anagrammatic conclusion, in which he boastfully proclaims his name."

42. STARS (3.552–56), SATAN (9.5010–14), WHY (9. 703–6), and WOE (9.1002–5).

43. Partner 2007, 129.

44. Ibid., 137, citing Fowler's notes ad loc.

45. On the SATAN acrostic, see Klemp 1977, 91; Leonard 1990, 136; Fyler 2007, 14–16; and Partner 2007 passim. See also Schnapp 1991, 280, on Dante's use of the acrostic in the *Commedia*.

46. The close visual similarity between the English words "Eve" and "Eye" may well have struck Milton as significant.

47. Partner 2007, 140.

48. Ibid.

49. Compare *H*. 944–45, where the dead body is called *conclamata ... materies*. Like *clamo*, *conclamo* can denote crying out both in approbation and in ritual mourning.

50. On *Pe*. 14 as Prudentius's signature poem in the collection of the *Peristephanon*, see Malamud 1989, chapter 6.

51. I argued in Malamud 1989, 172–80 that Prudentius saw himself as a Promethean figure, and that he interprets his own name, Prudentius, as a translation of the Greek Prometheus. There is also a significant wordplay here on *liber*, "book," and *liber*, "free."

52. Ross 1995, 331.

53. For the image of building the Holy City with words, see Roberts 1993, 186–87.

54. Levine 1991, 24–25; he has a good discussion of the matrix of serpents, sexuality, and procreation in the poem, which he links with similar themes in *Pe*. 10, a poem in which the tongue is excessively important.

REFERENCES

Adams, J.N. *The Latin Sexual Vocabulary*. Baltimore: Johns Hopkins University Press, 1982.
Ahl, Frederick M. *Metaformations: Soundplay and Wordplay in Ovid and Other Classical Poets*. Ithaca, N.Y.: Cornell University Press, 1985.
Ando, Clifford. "The Palladium and the Pentateuch: Towards a Sacred Topography of the Roman Empire." *Phoenix* 55, no. 3/4 (2001): 369–410.
Augustine. *The City of God*. Translated by Marcus Dods. Nicene and Post-Nicene Fathers, first series, vol. 2. Edited by Philip Schaff. Buffalo: Christian Literature, 1887.
———. *On the Trinity*. Translated by Arthur West Haddan. Nicene and Post-Nicene Fathers, first series, vol. 3. Edited by Philip Schaff. Buffalo: Christian Literature, 1887.
———. *Confessions*. Translated by R.S. Pine-Coffin. New York: Penguin, 1961.
Baker, R.J. "Dying for Love: Eulalia in Prudentius *Peristephanon Liber* 3." In *Multarum Artium Scientia: A "Chose" for R. Godfrey Tanner*, edited by K. Lee, C.J. Mackie, and H. Tarrant, 12–25. Auckland: Prudentia, 1993.
Ballengee, Jennifer. "The Wound That Speaks: Prudentius' *Peristephanon Liber* and the Rhetoric of Suffering." *Crossings* 5/6 (2002): 107–43.
———. *The Wound and the Witness: The Rhetoric of Torture*. Albany: State University of New York Press, 2009.
Bardzell, Jeffrey. *Speculative Grammar and Stoic Language Theory in Medieval Allegorical Narrative: From Prudentius to Alan of Lille*. New York: Routledge, 2009.
Barney, Stephen A. *Allegories of History, Allegories of Love*. Hamden, Conn.: Archon Books, 1979.
Bartelink, G.J.M. "Les démons comme brigands." *Vigiliae Christianae* 21 (1967): 12–24.
Barton, Carlin. "The Scandal of the Arena." *Representations* 27 (1989): 1–36.
———. *The Sorrows of the Ancient Romans: The Gladiator and the Monster*. Princeton, N.J.: Princeton University Press, 1993.
Benson, Larry. "The Alliterative *Morte Arthure* and Medieval Tragedy." *Tennessee Studies in Literature* 11 (1966): 75–87.
Bleisch, Pamela. "On Choosing a Spouse: *Aeneid* 7.378–84 and Callimachus' *Epigram* 1." *American Journal of Philology* 117 (1996): 453–72.
Blockley, R.C. *The Fragmentary Classicizing Historians of the Later Roman Empire*. 2 vols. Liverpool: Francis Cairns, 1981, 1983.
Bloomfield, Morton. "A Source of Prudentius' *Psychomachia*." *Speculum* 18, no. 1 (1943): 87–90.
Boyle, A.J., ed. *The Imperial Muse: Ramus Essays on Roman Literature of the Empire; Flavian Epicist to Claudian*. Berwick, Australia: Aureal Publications, 1990.
Brakman, C. "Quae ratio intercedat inter Lucretium et Prudentium." *Mnemosyne* n.s. 48, no. 4 (1920): 34–48.
Brilliant, Richard. "'Let the Trumpets Roar!' The Roman Triumph." In *The Art of Ancient Spectacle*, edited by Bettina Bergmann and Christine Kondoleon, 221–29. Washington, D.C.: National Galleries of Art, 1999.

Bronner, Leila Leah. "A Thematic Approach to Ruth in Rabbinic Literature." In *A Feminist Companion to Ruth*, edited by A. Brenner, 149–66. Sheffield: Sheffield Academic Press, 1993.
Brown, Peter. *The Body and Society: Men, Women, and Sexual Renunciation in the Early Church.* New York: Columbia University Press, 1988.
———. *Power and Persuasion in Late Antiquity: Towards a Christian Empire.* Madison: University of Wisconsin Press, 1992.
———. "The Decline of the Empire of God: Amnesty, Penance and the Afterlife from Late Antiquity to the Middle Ages." In *Last Things: Death and the Apocalypse in the Middle Ages*, edited by Caroline Walker Bynum and Paul H. Freedman, 41–59. Philadelphia: University of Pennsylvania Press, 2000.
Brown, Shelby. "Death as Decoration: Scenes from the Arena on Roman Domestic Mosaics." In *Pornography and Representation in Greece and Rome*, edited by Amy Richlin, 180–211. New York: Oxford University Press, 1992.
Burrow, Colin. *Epic Romance: Homer to Milton.* Oxford: Oxford University Press, 1993.
Burrus, Virginia. "Reading Agnes: The Rhetoric of Gender in Ambrose and Prudentius." *Journal of Early Christian Studies* 3, no. 1 (1995): 25–46.
———. "'Equipped For Victory': Ambrose and the Gendering of Orthodoxy." *Journal of Early Christian Studies* 4 (1996): 461–75.
———. *Begotten, Not Made: Conceiving Manhood in Late Antiquity.* Stanford: Stanford University Press, 2000.
———. *Late Ancient Christianity: A People's History of Christianity.* Minneapolis: Fortress Press, 2005.
Burrus, Virginia, and Catherine Keller. *Toward a Theology of Eros: Transfiguring Passion at the Limits of Discipline.* New York: Fordham University Press, 2006.
Butler, George E. "Tertullian's Pandora and John Milton's *The Doctrine and Discipline of Divorce*." *Christianity and Literature* 52, no. 3 (2003): 325–43.
Bynum, Caroline Walker, and Paul Freedman. *Last Things: Death and Apocalypse in the Middle Ages.* Philadelphia: University of Pennsylvania Press, 2000.
Camargo, Martin. "'Non solum sibi sed aliis etiam': Neoplatonism and Rhetoric in Saint Augustine's *De doctrina christiana*." *Rhetorica* 16, no. 4 (1998): 393–408.
Cameron, Alan. *Claudian: Poetry and Propaganda at the Court of Honorius.* Oxford: Clarendon, 1970.
———. "Ancient Anagrams." *American Journal of Philology* 116 (1995): 477–84.
Cameron, Averil. "Virginity as Metaphor: Women and the Rhetoric of Early Christianity." In *History as Text: The Writing of Ancient History*, edited by Averil Cameron, 184–205. London: Duckworth, 1989.
———. *Christianity and the Rhetoric of Empire: The Development of a Christian Discourse.* Berkeley: University of California Press, 1991.
———. "How to Read Heresiology." *Journal of Medieval and Early Modern Studies* 33, no. 3 (2003): 471–92.
Carruthers, Mary. *The Book of Memory: A Study of Memory in Medieval Culture.* Cambridge Studies in Medieval Literature. Cambridge: Cambridge University Press, 1990.
———. *The Craft of Thought: Meditation, Rhetoric, and the Making of Images, 400–1200.* Cambridge Studies in Medieval Literature. New York: Cambridge University Press, 1998.
Charlet, Jean-Louis. *L'influence d'Ausone sur la poésie de Prudence.* Paris: H. Champion, 1980.
———. *La création poétique dans le Cathemerinon de Prudence.* Paris: Société d'édition "Les belles lettres," 1982.
Chiappiniello, Roberto. "Feminei Furores: Prudentius' *Hamartigenia* and the *Epigramma Paulini*." *Vigiliae Christianae* 63 (2009): 169–88.
Chin, Catherine. "Through the Looking Glass Darkly: Jerome Inside the Book." In *The Early Christian Book*, edited by William E. Klingshirn and Linda Safran, 101–16. Washington, D.C.: Catholic University of America Press, 2007.
———. *Grammar and Christianity in the Late Roman World.* Philadelphia: University of Pennsylvania Press, 2008.
Cicero. *Cicero's "Tusculan Disputations"; also Treatises on "The Nature of the Gods" and on "The Commonwealth."* Translated by C.D. Yonge. New York, 1877.
———. *Orator.* Translated by H.M. Hubbell. Loeb Classical Library. Cambridge: Harvard University Press, 1939.

Cixous, Hélène. "Castration and Decapitation." Translated by A. Kuhn. *Signs* 7, no. 1 (1981): 41–55.
Clark, Gillian. "Desires of the Hangman: Augustine on Legitimized Violence." In Drake, *Violence in Late Antiquity*, 135–44.
Clarke, J. "Bridal Songs: Catullan *Epithalamia* and Prudentius, *Peristephanon* 3." *Antichthon* 40 (2006): 89–103.
Coleman, Janet. *Ancient and Medieval Memories: Studies in the Reconstruction of the Past*. Cambridge: Cambridge University Press, 1992.
Coleman, K.M. "Fatal Charades." *Journal of Roman Studies* 80 (1990): 44–73.
———. "The Contagion of the Throng: Absorbing Violence in the Roman World." *Hermathena* 164 (1998): 65–88.
Conybeare, Catherine. *Paulinus Noster: Self and Symbols in the Letters of Paulinus of Nola*. Oxford Early Christian Studies. Oxford: Oxford University Press, 2000.
———. "The Ambiguous Laughter of Saint Laurence." *Journal of Early Christian Studies* 10, no. 2 (2002): 175–202.
———. "'Sanctum, lector, percense volumen': Snakes, Readers, and the Whole Text in Prudentius' *Hamartigenia*." In *The Early Christian Book*, edited by William E. Klingshirn and Linda Safran, 225–40. Washington, D.C.: Catholic University of America Press, 2007.
Cook, Eleanor. *Enigmas and Riddles in Literature*. Cambridge: Cambridge University Press, 2006.
Costanza, Salvatore. "Rapporti letterari tra Paolino e Prudenzio." In *Atti del convegno 31 cinquantenario della morte di S. Paolino de Nola (431–1981)*, Nola, March 1982. Rome, 1983, 25–65.
Courcelle, Pierre. "Tradition platonicienne et traditions chretiennes du corps-prison (*Phédon* 62b; *Cratyle* 400c)." *Revue des études Latines* 43 (1965): 406–43.
Courtney, E. "Greek and Latin Acrostichs." *Philologus* 134 (1990): 3–13.
Cunningham, M.P. "Contexts of Prudentius' Poems." *Classical Philology* 71, no. 1 (1976): 56–66.
Dawson, John David. *Christian Figural Reading and the Fashioning of Identity*. Berkeley: University of California Press, 2002.
Deferrari, Roy J., and James Marshall Campbell. *A Concordance of Prudentius*. Cambridge, Mass.: Mediaeval Academy of America, 1932.
Delumeau, Jean. *History of Paradise: The Garden of Eden in Myth and Tradition*. Translated by Matthew O'Connell. Champaign-Urbana: University of Illinois Press, 2000.
de Man, Paul. *The Resistance to Theory*. Minneapolis: University of Minnesota Press, 1986.
de Nie, Giselle. "Iconic Alchemy: Imaging Miracles in Late Sixth-Century Gaul." *Studia Patristica* 30 (1997): 158–66.
Detienne, Marcel, and Jean-Pierre Vernant. *Cunning Intelligence in Greek Culture and Society*. Translated by Janet Lloyd. Brighton: Harvester Press, 1978.
Donatus, Aelius. "Ars grammatica: Ars minor, ars maior." In *Donat et la tradition de l'enseignement grammatical*, edited by Louis Holtz, 555–602. Paris: Centre national de la recherche scientifique, 1981.
Doniger, Wendy. *The Bed Trick: Tales of Sex and Masquerade*. Chicago: University of Chicago Press, 2000.
Drake, H.A. "Gauging Violence in Late Antiquity." In Drake, *Violence in Late Antiquity*, 1–12.
———, ed. *Violence in Late Antiquity: Perceptions and Practices*. Aldershot: Ashgate, 2006.
Dykes, Anthony. *Reading Sin in the World: The "Hamartigenia" of Prudentius and the Vocation of the Responsible Reader*. Cambridge: Cambridge University Press, 2011.
Dyson, Julia T. "*Fluctus Irarum, Fluctus Curarum*: Lucretian *Religio* in the *Aeneid*." *American Journal of Philology* 118, no. 3 (1997): 449–57.
Eagan, M. Clement. *The Poems of Prudentius*. 2 vols. The Fathers of the Church. Washington, D.C.: Catholic University of America Press, 1963.
Easterling, Pat, and Richard Miles. "Dramatic Identities: Tragedy in Late Antiquity." In *Constructing Identities in Late Antiquity*, edited by Richard Miles, 95–111. London: Routledge, 1999.
Edwards, M.J. "Chrysostom, Prudentius, and the Fiends of *Paradise Lost*." *Notes and Queries* 42, no. 4 (1995): 448–51.
Enders, Jody. *The Medieval Theater of Cruelty: Rhetoric, Memory, Violence*. Ithaca, N.Y.: Cornell University Press, 1999.
Enterline, Lynn. *The Rhetoric of the Body from Ovid to Shakespeare*. Cambridge: Cambridge University Press, 2000.
Evans, J.M. *"Paradise Lost" and the Genesis Tradition*. Oxford: Oxford University Press, 1968.

Evenepoel, W. "La présence d'Ovide dans l'oeuvre de Prudence." *Caesarodunum* 17 bis (1982): 165–76.
Fabiny, Tibor. *The Lion and the Lamb: Figuralism and Fulfilment in the Bible, Art and Literature.* London: Macmillan, 1992.
Feldherr, Andrew. "Reconciling Niobe." *Hermathena* 177–78 (2004): 125–46.
Fontaine, Jacques. "Démons et sibylles: La peinture des possédés dans la poésie de Prudence." *Collection Latomus* 70 (1964): 196–213.
———. "La femme dans la poésie de Prudence." *Revue des études Latines* 47, no. bis (1969): 55–83.
———. *Études sur la poésie latine tardive d'Ausone à Prudence.* Paris: Les Belles Lettres, 1980.
———. *Naissance de la poésie dans l'occident chrétien: Esquisse d'une histoire de la poésie latine chrétienne du IIIe au VIe siècle.* Paris: Études augustiniennes, 1981.
Fowler, D.P. "An Acrostic in Vergil (*Aeneid* 7.601–04)." *Classical Quarterly* 33 (1983): 298.
Frankfurter, David. "Martyrology and the Prurient Gaze." *Journal of Early Christian Studies* 17, no. 2 (2009): 215–45.
Fronto, Marcus Cornelius. *The Correspondence of Marcus Cornelius Fronto.* Translated by C.R. Haines. Loeb Classical Library. 2 vols. Cambridge, Mass.: Harvard University Press, 1919–20.
Futtrell, Alison. *Blood in the Arena: The Spectacle of Roman Power.* Austin: University of Texas Press, 1997.
Fyler, John M. *Language and the Declining World in Chaucer, Dante, and Jean de Meun.* Cambridge: Cambridge University Press, 2007.
Gale, Monica. "Poetry and the Backward Glance in Virgil's *Georgics* and *Aeneid*." *Transactions of the American Philological Association* 133, no. 2 (2003): 323–52.
Gleason, Maud. *Making Men: Sophists and Self-Presentation in Ancient Rome.* 1995. Reprint, Princeton, N.J.: Princeton University Press, 2008.
Gnilka, Christian. *Studien zur Psychomachie des Prudentius.* Wiesbaden: O. Harrassowitz, 1963.
———. "Die Natursymbolik in den Tagesliedern des Prudentius." In *Pietas: Festschrift Bernhard Kotting*, edited by E. Dassman and K. Suso Frank, 411–46. Jahrbuch für Antike und Christentum Ergänzungsband 8. Munster, 1980.
———. *Prudentiana I, Critica.* Munich: K.G. Saur, 2000.
Goins, Scott. "Boethius' *Consolation of Philosophy* 1.2.6 and Virgil *Aeneid* 2: Removing the Clouds of Mortal Anxieties." *Phoenix* 55, no. 1–2 (2001): 124–36.
Goldhill, Simon. "Literary History without Literature: Reading Practices in the Ancient World." *SubStance* 28, no. 1, issue 88, special issue, *Literary History* (1999): 57–89.
———. "Viewing and the Viewer: Empire and the Culture of Spectacle." In *The Body Aesthetic: From Fine Art to Body Mortification*, edited by Tobin Siebers, 41–74. Ann Arbor: University of Michigan Press, 2000.
———. "The Erotic Eye: Visual Stimulation and Cultural Conflict." In *Being Greek under Rome: Cultural Identity, the Second Sophistic, and the Development of Empire*, edited by S. Goldhill, 154–94. Cambridge: Cambridge University Press, 2001.
———. "On Knowingness." *Critical Enquiry* 32 (2006): 708–23.
———. "Why Don't Christians Do Dialogue?" in Goldhill, *The End of Dialogue in Antiquity*, 1–12.
———, ed. *The End of Dialogue in Antiquity.* Cambridge: Cambridge University Press, 2009.
Goossens, R. "Vilis Sapientia." *Latomus* 6 (1947): 197–205.
Gosserez, Laurence. *Poésie de lumière: Une lecture de Prudence.* Louvain: Peeters, 2001.
Gowers, Emily. *The Loaded Table: Representations of Food in Roman Literature.* Oxford: Clarendon Press, 1993.
Grasso, N.P. "Prudenzio e la Bibbia." *Orpheus* 19 (1972): 79–170.
Green, R.P.H. *Latin Epics of the New Testament: Juvencus, Sedulius, Arator.* Oxford: Oxford University Press, 2006.
Griffe, Elie. *La Gaule chrétienne à l'époque romaine, t. iii: La cité chrétienne.* Paris, Letouzey & Ané, 1965.
Grig, Lucy. "Torture and Truth in Late Antique Martyrology." *Early Medieval Europe* 2, no. 4 (2002): 321–36.
———. "The Paradoxical Body of St. Agnes." In *Roman Bodies: Antiquity to the Eighteenth Century*, edited by A. Hopkins and M. Wyke, 111–22. London: British School at Rome, 2005.
Gruzelier, Claire. *Claudian De Raptu Proserpinae.* Oxford: Clarendon Press, 1993.

Gunderson, Erik. *Staging Masculinity: The Rhetoric of Performance in the Roman World*. Ann Arbor: University of Michigan Press, 2000.
———. "The Rhetoric of Rhetorical Theory." In *The Cambridge Companion to Ancient Rhetoric*, edited by Erik Gunderson, 109–25. Cambridge: Cambridge University Press, 2009.
Hamburger, Jeffrey. "Overkill, or History That Hurts: A Dictatorship of Relativism?" *Common Knowledge* 13, no. 2–3 (2007): 404–28.
Hanson, Ann, and David Armstrong. "The Virgin's Neck: Aeschylus' *Agamemnon* 245 and Other Texts." *British Institute of Classical Studies* 33 (1986): 97–100.
Hardie, Philip. *The Epic Successors of Virgil*. Roman Literature and Its Contexts. Cambridge: Cambridge University Press, 1993.
———. *Ovid's Poetics of Illusion*. Cambridge: Cambridge University Press, 2002.
Harms, Wolfgang. *Homo viator in bivio: Studien zur Bildlichkeit des Weges*. Medium Aevum, Philologische Studien Bd. 21. Munich: Wilhelm Fink, 1970.
Harpham, Geoffrey. "The Fertile Word: Augustine and Hermeneutics." *Criticism* 38, no. 3 (1986): 237–54.
Harries, Jill. "Constructing the Judge: Judicial Accountability and the Culture of Criticism in Late Antiquity." In *Constructing Identities in Late Antiquity*, edited by R. Miles, 214–33. London: Routledge, 1999.
———. "Violence, Victims, and the Legal Tradition in Late Antiquity." In *Violence in Late Antiquity: Perceptions and Practices*, edited by H.A. Drake, 83–100. Aldershot: Ashgate, 2006.
Haworth, Kenneth. *Deified Virtues, Demonic Vices, and Descriptive Allegory in Prudentius' "Psychomachia."* Amsterdam: Adolf M. Hakkert, 1980.
Hayward, Robert. "What Did Cain Do Wrong? Jewish and Christian Exegesis of Genesis 4:3–6." In *The Exegetical Encounter between Jews and Christians in Late Antiquity*, edited by Emmanouela Grypeou and Helen Spurling, 101–24. Leiden: Brill, 2009.
Hedrick, Charles W. *History and Silence: Purge and Rehabilitation of Memory in Late Antiquity*. Austin: University of Texas Press, 2000.
Henderson, W.J. "Violence in Prudentius' *Peristephanon*." *Akroterion* 28 (1983): 84–93.
Henke, Rainer. *Studien zum Romanushymnus des Prudentius*. Vol. 27, Klassische Sprachen und Literaturen. Frankfurt am Main: Peter Lang, 1983.
Henry, R.M. "Review: The *Hamartigenia* of Prudentius." *Classical Review* 54, no. 3 (1940): 154–55.
Hermann, John P. *Allegories of War: Language and Violence in Old English Poetry*. Ann Arbor: University of Michigan Press, 1989.
Herzog, Reinhart. *Die allegorische Dichtkunst des Prudentius*. Vol. 42, Zetemata. Munich: Beck, 1966.
———. *Die Bibelepik der lateinischen Spätantike: Formgeschichte einer erbaulichen Gattung*. Theorie und Geschichte der Literatur und der schönen Künste: Texte und Abhandlungen 37. Munich: Wilhelm Fink, 1975.
Hesiod. *Works and Days*. Translated by H.G. Evelyn-White. Loeb Classical Library. Cambridge, Mass.: Harvard University Press, 1914.
Hollis, A.J. "A New Fragment on Niobe and the Text of Propertius 2.20.8." *Classical Quarterly* n.s. 47, no. 2 (1997): 578–82.
Holtz, L. *Donat et la tradition de l'enseignement grammatical: Étude et édition critique*. Paris: CNRS, 1981.
Homer. *The Odyssey*. Translated by Robert Fagles. London: Penguin Group, 1996.
Ierodiakonou, Katerina. "Stoic Logic." In *A Companion to Ancient Philosophy*, edited by Mary Louise Gill and Pierre Pellegrin, 506–30. Oxford: Wiley-Blackwell, 2006.
James, Paula. "Prudentius' *Psychomachia*: The Christian Arena and the Politics of Display." In *Constructing Identities in Late Antiquity*, edited by Richard Miles, 70–94. London: Routledge, 1999.
Johnson, William. "Towards a Sociology of Reading in Classical Antiquity." *American Journal of Philology* 121 (2000): 593–627.
Josephus. *Jewish Antiquities, Books 1–4*. Translated by H.St.J. Thackeray. Loeb Classical Library. Cambridge, Mass: Harvard University Press, 1930.
Kaesser, Christian. "The Body Is Not Painted On: Ekphrasis and Exegesis in Prudentius *Peristephanon* 9." *Ramus* 31 (2002): 158–74.
Katzenellenbogen, Adolf. *Allegories of the Virtues and Vices in Mediaeval Art from Early Christian Times to the Thirteenth Century*. New York: W.W. Norton, 1964.

Kessler, Herbert L. *Spiritual Seeing: Picturing God's Invisibility in Medieval Art.* Edited by Ruth Mazo Karras. The Middle Ages Series. Philadelphia: University of Pennsylvania Press, 2000.

Kiely, Maria. "The Interior Courtyard: The Heart of Cimitile/Nola." *Journal of Early Christian Studies* 12, no. 4 (2004): 443–479.

Kilgour, Maggie. "'Thy perfect image viewing': Poetic Creation and Ovid's Narcissus in *Paradise Lost.*" *Studies in Philology* 102, no. 3 (2005): 307–39.

King, Helen. "Born to Bleed: Artemis and Greek Women." In *Images of Women in Antiquity*, edited by Averil Cameron and Amélie Kuhrt, 109–27. London: Croom Helm, 1983.

Klemp, P.J. "'Now Hid, Now Seen': An Acrostic in *Paradise Lost.*" *Milton Quarterly* 11 (1977): 91–92.

Knox, Peter. "Lucretius on the Narrow Road." *Harvard Studies in Classical Philology* 99 (1999): 275–87.

Kyle, D. *Spectacles of Death in Ancient Rome.* London: Routledge, 1998.

Ladner, Gerhart B. *God, Cosmos, and Humankind: The World of Early Christian Symbolism.* Berkeley: University of California Press, 1995.

Laistner, M.L.W. *Christianity and Pagan Culture in the Later Roman Empire, Together with an English Translation of John Chrysostom's Address on Vainglory and the Right Way for Parents to Bring Up Their Children.* Ithaca, N.Y.: Cornell University Press, 1951.

Lana, Italo. *Due capitoli prudenziani: La biografia, la cronologia delle opere, la poetica.* Verba seniorum, collana dei testi studi patristici, n.s. 2. Rome: Editrice Studium, 1962.

Lapidge, Michael. "A Stoic Metaphor in Late Latin Poetry: The Binding of the Cosmos." *Latomus* 39 (1980): 817–37.

Lavarenne, M. *Prudence.* 4 vols. Paris: Les Belles Lettres, 1955–63.

Leach, Elizabeth. "'The little pipe sings sweetly while the fowler deceives the bird': Sirens in the Later Middle Ages." *Music & Letters* 87, no. 2 (2006): 187–211.

Leonard, John. *Naming in Paradise: Milton and the Language of Adam and Eve.* Oxford: Clarendon, 1990.

Levine, Robert. "Prudentius' Romanus: The Rhetorician as Hero, Martyr, Satirist, and Saint." *Rhetorica* 9, no. 1 (1991): 5–38.

Levinson, Joshua. "Dialogical Reading in the Rabbinic Exegetical Narrative." *Poetics Today* 25, no. 3 (2004): 497–528.

Levitan, William. "Plexed Artistry." *Glyph* 5 (1979): 55–58.

———. "Dancing at the End of the Rope." *Transactions of the American Philological Association* (1985): 245–69.

Lewis, C.S. *The Allegory of Love.* Oxford: Oxford University Press, 1958.

Loraux, Nicole. *Tragic Ways of Killing a Woman.* Translated by Anthony Forster. Cambridge, Mass.: Harvard University Press, 1987.

Lucretius. *On the Nature of the Universe.* Translated by Sir Ronald Melville. Oxford: Oxford University Press, 1997.

Lühken, Maria. *Christianorum Maro et Flaccus: Zur Vergil- und Horazrezeption des Prudentius.* Gottingen: Vandenhoeck & Ruprecht, 2002.

MacCormack, Sabine. *The Shadows of Poetry: Vergil in the Mind of Augustine.* Berkeley: University of California Press, 1998.

Machosky, Brenda. "The Face That Is Not a Face: The Phenomenology of the Soul in the Allegory of the *Psychomachia.*" *Exemplaria* 15, no. 1 (2003): 1–38.

Mahoney, A. *Vergil in the Works of Prudentius.* Cleveland: J.T. Zubal, 1934.

Malamud, Martha A. *A Poetics of Transformation: Prudentius and Classical Mythology.* Cornell Studies in Classical Philology. Ithaca, N.Y.: Cornell University Press, 1989.

———. "Making a Virtue of Perversity: Prudentius and Classical Poetry." In *The Imperial Muse: Ramus Essays on Roman Literature of the Empire*, edited by A.J. Boyle, 64–88. Victoria: Aureal Publications, 1990.

———. "Writing Original Sin." *Journal of Early Christian Studies* 10 (2002): 329–60.

Markus, R.A. "Fourth-Century Christian Literature: The Social and Historical Setting." In *The Cambridge History of Early Christian Literature*, edited by L. Ayres, F. Young, and A. Louth, 399–413. Cambridge: Cambridge University Press, 2004.

Mastrangelo, Marc. "The Epicurean View of the Soul in Prudentius' *Psychomachia.*" *New England Classical Journal* 26, no. 3 (1999): 11–22.

———. *The Roman Self in Late Antiquity: Prudentius and the Poetics of the Soul.* Baltimore: Johns Hopkins University Press, 2008.

———. "The Decline of Poetry in the Fourth-Century West." *International Journal of the Classical Traditions* 16, no. 3/4 (2009): 311–29.
McGowan, Andrew. "Marcion's Love of Creation." *Journal of Early Christian Studies* 9, no. 3 (2001): 295–311.
Miles, Margaret. "Vision: The Eye of the Body and the Eye of the Mind in Saint Augustine's *De trinitate* and *Confessions*." *Journal of Religion* 63, no. 2 (1983): 125–42.
Miles, Richard. *Constructing Identities in Late Antiquity*. London: Routledge, 1999.
Miller, Patricia Cox. "'Differential Networks': Relics and Other Fragments in Late Antiquity." *Journal of Early Christian Studies* 6 (1998): 113–38.
———. "'The Little Blue Flower Is Red': Relics and the Poetizing of the Body." *Journal of Early Christian Studies* 8, no. 2 (2000): 213–36.
———. *The Poetry of Thought in Late Antiquity: Essays in Imagination and Religion*. London: Ashgate, 2001.
———. "Relics, Rhetoric and Mental Spectacles in Late Ancient Christianity." In *Seeing the Invisible in Late Antiquity and the Middle Ages: Papers from "Verbal and Pictorial Imaging: Representing and Accessing Experience of the Invisible, 400–1000,"* edited by G. de Nie, K.F. Morrison, and M. Mostert, 25–52. Utrecht: Brepols, 2005.
———. *The Corporeal Imagination: Signifying the Holy in Late Ancient Christianity*. Philadelphia: University of Pennsylvania Press, 2009.
Miller, Paul A. "The Bodily Grotesque in Roman Satire: Images of Sterility." *Arethusa* 31, no. 3 (1998): 257–83.
Milton, John. *Paradise Lost: A Poem in Twelve Books*. 2nd ed. London: S. Simmons, 1674.
———. *Paradise Lost*, ed. Alastair Fowler. 2nd ed. New York: Longman, 1998.
Mitchell, W.J.T. *Iconology: Image, Text, Ideology*. Chicago: University of Chicago Press, 1986.
Morales, Helen. "Constructing Genders in Musaeus' *Hero and Leander*." In *Constructing Identities in Late Antiquity*, edited by Richard Miles, 41–69. London: Routledge, 1999.
Moreira, Isabel. "Violence, Purification, and Mercy in the Late Antique Afterlife." In *Violence in Late Antiquity: Perceptions and Practices*, edited by H.A. Drake, 147–56. Aldershot: Ashgate 2006.
Morgan, Gareth. "*Nullam, Vare* . . . Chance or Choice in *Odes* 1.18." *Philologus* 137 (1993): 142–45.
Nichols, Stephen. "Language and the Declining World in Chaucer, Dante, and Jean de Meun (review)." *Comparative Literature Studies* 47, no. 1 (2010): 120–24.
Nightingale, Andrea. *Spectacles of Truth in Classical Greek Philosophy: Theoria in Its Cultural Context*. Cambridge: Cambridge University Press, 2004.
Nugent, S. Georgia. *Allegory and Poetics: The Structure and Imagery of Prudentius' "Psychomachia"*. Frankfurt am Main: P. Lang, 1985.
———. "Review of Martha Malamud, *A Poetics of Transformation: Prudentius and Classical Mythology*." *Classical World* 84, no. 4 (1991): 325–26.
———. "*Virtus* or Virago? The Female Personifications of Prudentius' *Psychomachia*." In *Virtue and Vice: The Personifications in the Index of Christian Art*, edited by Colum Hourihane, 13–28. Princeton, N.J.: Princeton University Press, 2000.
Pagels, Elaine. *The Origin of Satan*. New York: Vintage, 1995.
Palmer, Anne-Marie. *Prudentius on the Martyrs*. Oxford: Oxford University Press, 1989.
Partner, Jane. "Satanic Vision and Acrostics in *Paradise Lost*." *Essays in Criticism* 57, no. 2 (2007): 129–46.
Paxson, James J. *The Poetics of Personification*. Cambridge: Cambridge University Press, 1994.
Pelikan, Jaroslav. *Christianity and Classical Culture: The Metamorphosis of Natural Theology in the Christian Encounter with Hellenism*. New Haven, Conn.: Yale University Press, 1993.
Perkins, Judith. *The Suffering Self: Pain and Narrative Representation in the Early Christian Era*. London: Routledge, 1995.
Petruccione, John. "Prudentius' Use of Martyrological Topoi in *Peristephanon*." PhD diss., University of Michigan, 1985.
Plato. *Republic*. Translated by M.A. Grube. Revised by C.D.C. Reeve. Edited by John M. Cooper and D.S. Hutchinson. Indianapolis: Hackett, 1997.
Plaut, W.G. *Book of Proverbs: A Commentary*. New York: Union of American Hebrew Congregations, 1961.
Potter, D. "Martyrdom as Spectacle." In *Theater and Society in the Classical World*, edited by Ruth Scodel, 53–88. Ann Arbor: University of Michigan Press, 1993.

Prudentius. *Prudentius' "Hamartigenia."* With introduction, translation, and commentary by J. Stam. Amsterdam, 1940.
———. *Prudentius*. Translated by H.J. Thomson. 2 vols. Loeb Classical Library. Cambridge, Mass.: Harvard University Press, 1949-1953.
———. *Prudence*. Edited by M. Lavarenne. 4 vols. 1933. 2nd ed. Paris: Les Belles Lettres, 1955.
———. *Aurelii Prudentii Clementis carmina*. Edited by M.P. Cunningham. Corpus Christianorum, Series Latina 126. Turnhout: Brepols, 1966.
———. *Aurelii Prudentii Clementis carmina*. Edited by Johan Bergman. 1926. New York: Johnson Reprint, 1979.
———. *Hamartigenia: Introduzione, traduzione e commento* a cura di Roberto Palla. Pisa: Giardini Editori e Stampatori, 1981.
Pucci, Pietro. *Hesiod and the Language of Poetry*. Baltimore: Johns Hopkins University Press, 1977.
Quintilian. *Institutio oratoria*. Translated by H.H. Butler. Loeb Classical Library. Cambridge, Mass.: Harvard University Press, 1920-22.
Rapisarda, Emanuele. "Influssi Lucreziani in Prudenzio: Un suo poema Lucreziano e antiepicureo, I." *Vigiliae Christianae* 4, no. 1 (1950): 46-60.
Richlin, Amy. "Making Up a Woman: The Face of Roman Gender." In *Off with Her Head! The Denial of Women's Identity in Myth, Religion, and Culture*, edited by Howard Eilberg-Schwartz and Wendy Doniger, 185-213. Berkeley: University of California Press, 1995.
———. "Rhetoric and Gender." In *Roman Eloquence: Rhetoric in Society and Literature*, edited by William Dominik, 90-110. London: Routledge, 1997.
Rimell, Victoria. "Facing Facts: Ovid's *Medicamina* through the Looking Glass." In *Gendered Dynamics of Roman Love Poetry*, edited by E. Greene and R. Ancona, 177-205. Baltimore: Johns Hopkins University Press, 2005.
Roberts, Michael John. *Biblical Epic and Rhetorical Paraphrase in Late Antiquity*. Liverpool: F. Cairns, 1985.
———. *The Jeweled Style: Poetry and Poetics in Late Antiquity*. Ithaca, N.Y.: Cornell University Press, 1989.
———. *Poetry and the Cult of the Martyrs*. Ann Arbor: University of Michigan Press, 1993.
Rosenmeyer, Patricia. "Tracing *Medulla* as a Locus Eroticus in Greek and Latin Poetry." *Arethusa* 32 (1999): 19-47.
Ross, Jill. "Dynamic Writing and Martyrs' Bodies in Prudentius' *Peristephanon*." *Journal of Early Christian Studies* 3, no. 3 (1995): 325-55.
Salvatore, Antonio. *Studi prudenziani*. Naples: Libreria scientifica editrice, 1958.
Schnapp, Jeffrey T. "Virgin Words: Hildegard of Bingen's *Lingua Ignota* and the Development of Imaginary Languages Ancient to Modern." *Exemplaria* 3 (1991): 267-98.
Shanzer, Danuta. "Allegory and Reality: *Spes, Victoria*, and the Date of Prudentius' *Psychomachia*." *Illinois Classical Studies* 14 (1989): 347-63.
Sharrock, Alison. "Womanufacture." *Journal of Roman Studies* 81 (1991): 36-49.
Shaw, Brent D. "Body/Power/Identity: Passions of the Martyrs." *Journal of Early Christian Studies* 4 (1996): 269-312.
———. "Judicial Nightmares and Christian Memory." *Journal of Early Christian Studies* 11 (2003): 533-63.
Sissa, Giulia. *Greek Virginity*. Cambridge, Mass.: Harvard University Press, 1990.
Smith, Macklin. *Prudentius' "Psychomachia": A Reexamination*. Princeton, N.J.: Princeton University Press, 1976.
Solmsen, Friedrich. "The Powers of Darkness in Prudentius' 'Contra Symmachum': A Study of His Imagination." *Vigiliae Christianae* 19, no. 4 (1965): 237-57.
Somerville, Ted. "Note on a Reversed Acrostic in Vergil *Georgics* 429-33." *Classical Philology* 105, no. 2 (2010): 202-9.
Stock, Brian. *Augustine the Reader: Meditation, Self-Knowledge, and the Ethics of Interpretation*. Cambridge, Mass.: Harvard University Press, 1996.
Straw, Carole. "Settling Scores: Eschatology in the Church of the Martyrs." In *Last Things: Death and the Apocalypse in the Middle Ages*, edited by Caroline Walker Bynum and Paul H. Freedman, 21-40. Philadelphia: University of Pennsylvania Press, 2000.
Taddei, Rosemarie. "A Stylistic and Structural Study of Prudentius' *Hamartigenia*." PhD diss., Bryn Mawr College, 1981.

Tertullian. *Tertullian: Apology, De spectaculis; Minucius Felix, Octavius*. Edited and translated by T.R. Glover. Loeb Classical Library. Cambridge, Mass: Harvard University Press, 1931.
———. *Adversus Marcionem*. Edited and translated by Ernest Evans. Oxford Early Christian Texts. Oxford: Oxford University Press, 1972.
Thomas, Richard F. *Virgil, Georgics*. 2 vols. Cambridge Greek and Latin Classics. Cambridge: Cambridge University Press, 1988.
Thomson, H.J. "Review: The Budé Prudentius." *Classical Review* 60, no. 3 (1946): 116–17.
Thraede, Klaus. *Studien zu Sprache und Stil des Prudentius*. Göttingen: Vandenhoeck u. Ruprecht, 1965.
Trout, Dennis. *Paulinus of Nola: Life, Letters, Poems*. Berkeley: University of California Press, 1999.
Uden, James. "The Elegiac *Puella* as Virgin Martyr." *Transactions of the American Philological Association* 139 (2009): 207–22.
van Assendelft, M.M. *Sol ecce surget igneus: A Commentary on the Morning and Evening Hymns of Prudentius*. Groningen: Bouma's Boekhuis B.V., 1976.
van der Toorn, K., and P.W. van der Horst. "Nimrod before and after the Bible." *Harvard Theological Review* 83, no. 1 (1990): 1–29.
Van Dyke, Carolynn. *The Fiction of Truth: Structures of Meaning in Narrative and Dramatic Allegory*. Ithaca, N.Y.: Cornell University Press, 1985.
Van Slyke, Daniel. "The Devil and His Pomps in Fifth-Century Carthage: Renouncing *Spectacula* with Spectacular Imagery." *Dumbarton Oaks Papers* 59 (2005): 53–72.
Vergil. *Aeneid: A New Translation*. Translated by Frederick M. Ahl. Oxford World Classics. Oxford: Oxford University Press, 2007.
Von Albrecht, Michael. *A History of Roman Literature from Livius Andronicus to Boethius with Special Regard to Its Influence on World Literature*. 2 vols. *Mnemosyne* supplement. Leiden: Brill, 1997.
Walter, U. "'Schoene Wunde, verachteter Tod': Zur Funktion der Gladiatorenkaempfe in der roemischer Kaiserzeit." *Geschichte in Wissenschaft und Unterricht* 55 (2004): 513–20.
Webb, Ruth. "Imagination and the Arousal of the Emotions." In *The Passions in Roman Literature and Thought*, edited by Susanna Braund and Christopher Gill, 112–27. Cambridge: Cambridge University Press, 1997a.
———. "Mémoire et imagination: Les limites de l'enargeia dans la théorie rhétorique grecque." In *Dire l'évidence (Philosophie et rhétorique antiques)*, edited by C. Lévy and L. Pernot, 229–48. Paris: L'Harmattan, 1997b.
———. *Demons and Dancers: Performance in Late Antiquity*. Cambridge, Mass.: Harvard University Press, 2008.
———. *Ekphrasis, Imagination and Persuasion in Ancient Rhetorical Theory and Practice*. Farnham: Ashgate, 2009.
Whitmarsh, Tim. "Written on the Body: Ekphrasis, Perception, and Deception in Heliodorus' *Aethiopica*." In *The Verbal and the Visual: Cultures of Ekphrasis in Antiquity*, edited by Jaś Elsner, 111–25. Bendigo, Australia: Aureal Publications, 2002.
Wiedemann, T. *Emperors and Gladiators*. London: Routledge, 1992.
Wiesen, David. *St. Jerome as a Satirist: A Study in Christian Latin Thought and Letters*. Ithaca, N.Y.: Cornell University Press, 1964.
Witke, Charles. "Recycled Words: Vergil, Prudentius, and Saint Hippolytus." In *Romane Memento: Vergil in the Fourth Century*, edited by Roger Rees, 128–40. London: Duckworth, 2004.
Wyke, Maria. *The Roman Mistress: Ancient and Modern Representations*. Oxford: Oxford University Press, 2002.
Wyrick, Jed. *The Ascension of Authorship*. Cambridge, Mass.: Harvard University Press, 2004.
Yates, Frances. *The Art of Memory*. Chicago: University of Chicago Press, 1966.
Zimmerman, Martin. "Violence in Late Antiquity Reconsidered." In *Violence in Late Antiquity: Perceptions and Practices*, edited by H.A. Drake, 241–56. Aldershot: Ashgate, 2006.
Zissos, Andrew, and Ingo Gildenhard. "Problems of Time in Ovid's *Metamorphoses* 2." In *Ovidian Transformations: Essays on Ovid's "Metamorphoses" and Its Reception*, edited by Alessandro Barchiesi, Philip Hardie, and Stephen Hinds, 31–47. Cambridge: Cambridge University Press, 1999.

INDEX

Abel. *See* Cain and Abel
Abraham story, in preface to *Psychomachia*, 62, 85
Absalom and David, 10n29, 29–30, 77, 129, 131, 155, 156, 158, 162, 194, 208n15
acrostics
    in *Commedia* (Dante), 211n45
    in *Paradise Lost* (Milton), 192–94
Actaeon, metamorphosis of, 208n13
Ad Iovinianum (Jerome), 32n91
Ad Marcellam (Plotinus), 201n5
Ad principem ineruditum or *To an Uneducated Ruler* (Plutarch), 201n10
Adam
    clothing taken up by, 108–9
    judicial process, Christian adaptation of, 172
    Lot as *monumenta insignia* of, 144–45
    Milton's personification of Sin parodying creation of, 133–35
    name of, 3n4
    original sin and fall of, 35–36, 77, 140–45
    traveler motif and, 105, 109
Adversus Judaeos (Tertullian), 200n13
Adversus Marcionem (Tertullian), 14n40, 200n6–7
Aeneid (Vergil)
    Abas, slaying of, 108, 203n25
    Anchises, funeral games of, 167–69
    Aulus Gellius's description of composition process of, 206n5
    Dido in, 11n30, 26n72, 90–91
    Improbe Amor echoed by Prudentius, 13n37
    Servius's *Commentary on the Aeneid of Vergil,* 40n110, 160, 208n25
    translation of, xii
    underworld in, 41n114, 175

Aethiopica, 151
afterlife, fate of the soul in, 41–45, 175–80
Against the Professors (Sextus Empiricus), 201n8
Agnes (saint and martyr), 195
Ahl, Frederick, xii, 169
Ambrose of Milan
    on Arius and Arianism, 137–38, 207n16
    De bono mortis, 46n126
    De Cain et Abel, 200n13
    dynamism of fourth century emerging in works of, 56
    Expositio evangelii secundum Lucam, 203n20
    on Good Samaritan, 105
    on statue and altar of Victory in Roman Senate, 199n30
amictus, 109
Ammianus, 56
amnesty, intercession, and mercy, 47n127, 174–75, 180, 190
"An Ordinary Evening in New Haven" (Stevens), 51
anagram at end of *Hamartigenia,* 190–92, 194, 210n37
analogy, problem of, 85–95
    mirror metaphor, 10, 92–95, 105
    parhelion and problem of human vision, 10–11, 88, 89–92
    riddle or enigma, 93–95
    sun, allegory of, 10, 85–88, 105, 122
Antiquities of the Jews (Josephus), 13n36, 201n16, 207n12
Apocalypse of John, 44n122, 45n123, 170, 178, 186
apocalyptic in *Hamartigenia,* 170–71, 186

apophatic nature of language and meaning
  in poetry in late antique world, 51–52, 53,
    65–67, 68
  in Prudentius, 51–52, 66–67, 83–84, 188–89,
    194, 210n35
apostrophe (as rhetorical device), 16n51, 27n74,
    73, 76–77, 90n32, 97, 122, 136, 144–45,
    147–49
Apotheosis (Prudentius)
  fabula in, 82
  lost travelers and hidden pathways in, 35n96,
    58, 106–7
  Moses as historian in, 205n24
  postlapsarian problem of language and
    meaning in, 66
  preface to collected works referring to,
    198n29
  relationship to *Hamartigenia*, 199n1
  theme/plot of, 65
Arachne, transformation of, 147–48, 149
Arianism, 137, 173, 200n6, 205–6n1, 206n14,
  207n16
Aristotle, 89, 93, 184, 202n14
Ars grammatica (Donatus), 93
"Ars Poetica" (Macleish), 51
art, Prudentius's views on, 208n20
artwork, description of, 150–52, 182–84,
    208n17
Athanasius, 137, 205–6n1, 206n14
Augustine of Hippo
  on Cain, 81, 200n13
  classical poetry, critique of, 57
  Confessiones, 138–39, 205n24
  conversion of, 54
  on Cynic philosophy, 23n63
  De civitate dei or *The City of God*, 23n63, 57,
    81, 174, 200n13, 202n7, 202n12, 207n7
  De doctrina, 107, 201n1, 203n23
  De genesi ad litteram, 208n26
  De trinitate, 88, 93–94, 186, 202n16
  on enigma or riddle, 93–94, 202n15
  Ennarationes in Psalmos, 173
  on justice, judgment, and punishment, 173,
    174–75
  language, metaphysics of, 138–39
  Manichaeism and, 15n46, 200n6
  on martyrdom of Cyprian, 184–85, 210n27
  new forms of Christian literature, develop-
    ment of, 56
  princeps, use of, 16n50
  Quaestiones evangeliorum, 203n20
  Sermons, 15n46, 119, 210n27, 210n31
  traveler motif used by, 105, 107
  vision, theory of, 88–89, 119, 120, 166

Aulus Gellius, 206n5
Aurelius Prudentius Clemens. *See* Prudentius
Ausonius, 40n110, 54, 56, 57, 208n25

Babel, Tower of, 13n36, 100–101
Babylonian Captivity in *Hamartigenia*, 24–25
Babylonian Talmud, 208n23
Ballengee, Jennifer, 60, 69, 185, 210n30
Bardzell, Jeffrey, 74–75, 195, 199n34, 200n11,
  205n31
Bartelink, G. J. M., 203n24
Bathsheba, 154
Bathyllus, 117
The Battle of the Soul (Prudentius). *See*
  Psychomachia
Bellum Civile (Lucan), 195
Bible and biblical stories. *See also specific*
    stories and characters, e.g. Cain and Abel,
    and specific books, e.g. Genesis
  Christian poetry based on, 57
  narrative structure and exegesis, 201n20
  postlapsarian problem of language and
    meaning in, 68
  Psychomachia's use of, 62
  Septuagint, 80, 202n7
  Vulgate, 141, 201n14, 202n7, 202n15
binary oppositions, Prudentius's use of, 187,
  194
Bloomfield, Morton, 127
body as prison house of soul, 42n117–18, 177,
  201n5, 209n15
Boethius, 205n26
brothers at crossroads, 35n96, 40, 159–62
Brown, Peter, 174, 180
Burrus, Virginia, 137–38, 206n14, 207n16
Bynum, Caroline Walker, 170

Caesarius of Arles, 136
Cain and Abel
  brothers at crossroads story and, 161, 162
  in Christian theology, 3n1
  concerns about worthiness of poetic
    offering, reflecting, 190, 196
  Eve as mother of, 130–31, 141, 156
  Flesh and Spirit/Mind, allegorical identifica-
    tion with, 6, 84
  in *Hamartigenia* text, 3–6, 7
  Marcion identified with Cain, 5–6, 7, 76,
    80–81, 201n21
  meaning of Abel's name, 6n21
  meaning of Cain's name, 4n6
  in *Paradise Lost* (Milton), 81
  Prudentius's interpretation of, 3n1, 4n6,
    79–84

INDEX [225

reasons for God's rejection of Cain's sacrifice, 4n6, 4–5n10, 80–81
Roman mythology, warring brothers in, 3n1
Ruth and Orpah compared, 155
Callimachus, 210n38
Cameron, Alan, 210n37, 210n39, 210n41
Cameron, Averil, 199n2
canonicity, concept of, 5n14, 78
Carmen ad uxorem, 197n8
Carmina (Paulinus of Nola), 150
Carmina or *Odes* (Horace), 26n72, 204n12, 206n3
Carroll, Lewis, 71
Carruthers, Mary, 61–63, 64, 79, 198n19, 200n11
Cassian (saint and martyr), 89, 182–85, 187, 208n17
Cassiodorus, 118, 205n19
Cathemerinon (Prudentius), 65, 142, 179–80, 190, 198n29, 203n16, 204n15
Cato, 161
cave, allegory of, 86–88, 91–92, 201n5
Chaucer, Geoffrey, xi, 67, 83
Chiappiniello, Roberto, 204n13
Chin, Catherine, 58–59, 63, 107
Christianity
  eschatology in period of the martyrs, 171–72
  history, *Hamartigenia* reflecting Christian view of, 55–58
  judicial process, adaptation of language of, 171–75
  martyrs and martyrdom, 170–71, 182–86
  traveler motif used to create landscape for, 107
Chronica (Eusebius), 57
Cicero
  De finibus bonorum et malorum, 203n32
  De oratore, 198n18, 198n24, 203n32
  De republica, 89–90, 201n6
  Jerome's dream of being accused of being a Ciceronian rather than a Christian, 209n9
  Orator, 115, 203n29, 204n7–8
  Tusculan Disputations, 40n110, 208n25
The City of God or *De civitate dei* (Augustine), 23n63, 57, 81, 174, 200n13, 202n7, 202n12, 207n7
classical poetry, loss of cultural authority of, 55–58
Claudian, 54, 56, 57, 59–60, 199n1
clemency, desire for, 47n127, 174–75, 180, 190
Clement of Alexandria, 174, 200n7, 209n10
clothing, Adam's adoption of, 108–9
Codex Theodosianus, 209n4
Commedia (Dante), 211n45

Commentary on the Aeneid of Vergil (Servius), 40n110, 160, 208n25
conclamata, 46n126, 211n49
Concordia, in *Psychomachia*, 70, 74–75
Confessiones (Augustine), 138–39, 205n24
Coniugalia praecepta (Plutarch), 204n4
The Consolation of Philosophy (Boethius), 205n26
Constantine I (Roman emperor), 55
Contra Rufinum (Jerome), 40n110, 208n25
Contra Symmachum (Prudentius), 54, 198n29, 199n30
Controversiae (Seneca the Elder), 204n4
conversion to Christianity in late antique period, 54–55, 197n8, 207n7
Conybeare, Catherine, 32n89–90, 77–79, 123, 136–37, 153–54, 208n16
Cook, Eleanor, 93, 94–95
1 Corinthians 13:12, 93, 94, 191
cosmetics and ornament, use of, 18, 112–17, 204n11
Cratylus (Plato), 209n15
creative process, Prudentius's anxieties about, 136–37, 194–96
crossroads, brothers at, 35n96, 40, 159–62
cultural authority of classical poetry, loss of, 55–58
Cynic philosophy, 23n63
Cyprian of Carthage, 68–69, 73, 104, 172, 184–85, 199n37, 210n27

Dante, xi, 83, 211n45
David
  Absalom and, 10n29, 29–30, 77, 129, 131, 155, 156, 158, 162, 194, 208n15
  Bathsheba and, 154
  Goliath and, 27n73, 39n109, 156, 200n11
  in *Psychomachia*, 200n11
  Ruth, as descendent of, 39
Dawson, John, 67
De bono mortis (Ambrose), 46n126
De Cain et Abel (Ambrose), 200n13
De civitate dei or *The City of God* (Augustine), 23n63, 57, 81, 174, 200n13, 202n7, 202n12, 207n7
De cultu feminarum (Tertullian), 112, 113, 203n1, 204n5, 204n11, 204n14
De decalogo (Philo), 201n10
De doctrina (Augustine), 107, 201n1, 203n23
De eloquentia (Fronto), 203n31
De finibus bonorum et malorum (Cicero), 203n32
De genesi ad literam (Augustine), 208n26
De gigantibus (Philo), 202n9

De lingua latina (Varro), 31n87
de Man, Paul, 73
De nuptiis (Martianus Capella), 136, 198n18, 198n24
De oratore (Cicero), 198n18, 198n24, 203n32
De principiis (Origen), 202n9
De republica (Cicero), 89–90, 201n6
De rerum natura (Lucretius), 30n86, 73–74, 121–22, 206n3
De specialibus legibus (Philo), 40n110, 208n25
De trinitate (Augustine), 88, 93–94, 186, 202n16
De viris illustribus (Jerome and Gennadius), 54, 57
the devil, 96–111
   description of, 97–99
   dialectic reasoning of Marcion and, 96–97
   envy, associated with, 98, 102–3
   fall of, 102–4
   forked tongue of, 16, 104–5, 195–96
   in *Hamartigenia* text, 12–16, 29, 36
   as highwayman or robber, 16, 22n61, 35n96, 105–9, 125–26, 187–88
   language and meaning, association with problem of, 99, 100–101, 104–5, 109
   Lucifer, identification with, 14n40, 14n42, 100, 202n10, 203n16
   naming, 100–102
   natural order, corruption of, 109–11
   Nimrod, identification with, 13n36, 99–101, 163
   personifications as agents of, 126–27
   snakes, association with, 98, 104, 131, 132–33
dialectic reasoning, 97
dialogue form, 77, 96–97, 200n5
Dido in *Aeneid* (Vergil), 11n30, 26n72, 90–91
Diocletian (Roman emperor), 55
Discordia in *Psychomachia*, death and dismemberment of, 70–75
Dittochaeon (Prudentius), 65, 150
Divinarum Institutionem (Lactantius), 14n38, 40n110, 208n25
division, as thematic concern of *Hamartigenia*, 80–81
Dog Star, 104
Donatus (Aelius Donatus), 93
Doniger, Wendy, 155, 208n24
Donne, John, 170
double vision of sun (parhelion), problem of, 89–92
doves, simile of, 40–41, 162–69
dualist heresies generally, *Hamartigenia* aimed at, 5n16, 7n22, 15n46, 77–78, 86, 200n6

Easter, reprieve from punishment on, 180
effeminacy of devil, 132–33
effeminate men, 18–19, 115–17
ekphrasis
   artwork, as description of, 150–52, 182–84, 208n17
   Cassian, martyrdom of, 183, 185
   devil, presentation of, 97
   feigned orality of *Hamartigenia* and, 122
   in late antique poetry, 60–61
   Lot and his wife, tale of, 144, 145, 150–52, 154
   spectacle of public justice as, 172
enargeia, 12n34, 17n53, 60–61, 63, 122, 151
Enders, Jody, 63–64, 198n10
enigma or riddle, 93–95
Ennarationes in Psalmos (Augustine), 173
Enterline, Lynn, 204n6
enumeratio, 60, 125
Envy (*Invidia*), 12, 15, 98, 102–3, 192, 202n4
Ephesians
   2:1–2, 28n81
   2:20, 26n70
   6:12, 28n80
Epicurus and Epicureanism, 14n41, 73–74, 122
Epistulae (Horace), 86, 161
Epistulae (Jerome), 209n9
Epistulae (Seneca the Younger), 203n29, 209n6
eschatology of *Hamartagenia*, 170–71, 186
Eteocles and Polyneices, 3n1
etymologies of proper names. *See* names, etymologies of
Eulalia (martyr), 185, 204n15, 210n29
Eunapius of Sardis, 207n16
Eusebius of Caesarea, 57
Eve
   Arius associated with, 206n14
   cosmetics, use of, 112, 113
   judicial process, Christian adaptation of, 46n124, 172
   Lot's wife as *monumenta insignia* of, 37, 144–45, 152
   Milton's account of, 142–44, 145, 193, 211n46
   Milton's personification of Sin as parody of, 133–35
   minimized by Prudentius, 36n98–99, 52, 140–42, 144, 154, 203n27
   name of, 3n4, 36n99, 37, 141–42, 143–44
   oral nature of transgression of, 133
   Pandora and, 145, 207n4–5
   reproduction of Cain and Abel by, 130–31, 141, 156

Exodus
 23:24, 23n64
 expulsion of Palestinian tribes in, 127
Expositio evangelii secundum Lucam
 (Ambrose), 203n20
eyesight. *See* vision
4 Ezra 7:23, 46n126

fabula, 82–83
faces, attacks on, 69–73, 199n46. *See also* throats and mouths
Faerie Queene (Spenser), 135, 206n8
Fasti (Ovid), 4n7
Febris, shrines to, 14n38
feigned orality, 20n58, 77, 96, 122, 208n16
Felix of Nola, 55, 150
Fides (Faith)
 in *Hamartigenia*, 172, 177, 209n16, 209n18
 in *Psychomachia*, 71–72, 210n19
figuration
 cosmetics and ornament, association with use of, 115, 117
 in late antique poetry generally, 65, 67–68, 73
 Prudentius's use of, 10n29, 53, 76, 78, 85
Flesh and Spirit/Mind, Cain and Abel identified with, 6, 84
Fontaine, Jacques, 55, 198n20, 204n13
free will, 35, 77, 102
Freedman, Paul, 170
Fronto (Marcus Aurelius Fronto), 203n31–32
Fyler, John M., 67, 83, 141, 142, 201n16–17

Galen, 206n7
gaze. *See* vision
gender and sexuality, 112–25. *See also* Eve; reproduction and succession; throats and mouths
 Arianism and, 137–38, 206n14, 207n16
 cosmetics and ornament, use of, 18, 112–17, 204n11
 devil, effeminacy of, 132–33
 effeminate men, 18–19, 115–17
 just souls, erotic overtones of description of fate of, 178, 209n18
 Lot's wife in *Hamartigenia* and Ovid's Niobe, 38n105, 144–52
 marrow, erotic connotations of, 125, 205n27
 Odyssey, punishment of Penelope's maids in, 163–64
 pantomime dancers, evocation of, 117–18, 119, 120
 Ruth, Orpah, and Naomi favored over story of Lot's daughters, 77

senses, distrust of, 118–23, 125
sexual difference, markers of, 204n11
transsexuality and gender confusion in Prudentius's work generally, 206n6
generatio simplex, 9n25, 156–59
Genesis
 1:31, 20n59
 2:23, 141
 3:1–7, 140
 3:6, 36n98
 4, 3n1, 4n7
 4:1, 4n6
 4:17, 201n17
 5:2, 141
 6, 99
 10:8–12, 13n36, 99
 11, 100
 19:26, 38n104, 145
 19:30–38, 207n6
 19:31–33, 37n101
 19:31–37, 153
Gennadius, 57
Georgics (Vergil), 31n87, 104, 117, 121, 206n5
giants
 allegorical meaning of, 99
 in Bible, 99
 in classical mythology, 27n73
 Goliath, 27n73, 39, 154, 155, 156, 200n11, 208n23
 Nimrod, 13, 27n73, 76, 99–101, 163, 202n7, 203n28
Gnilka, Christian, 5n14, 38n106, 44n121, 201n21, 207n10
Goldhill, Simon, 97, 181, 183–85, 200n5, 202n2, 208n17, 208n20, 210n21, 210n29
Goliath, 27n73, 39, 154, 155, 156, 200n11, 208n23
Good Samaritan, 105
goodness of God and creation, assertion of, 122–25
The Gospel of Truth, 200n9
Gosserez, Laurence, 86–89, 201n2, 201n10
Grig, Lucy, 63
Gunderson, Erik, 205n17

Hamartigenia or *The Origin of Sin* (Prudentius)
 on analogy, 85–95. *See also* analogy, problem of
 closing prayer of, 45–47, 187–96
 crossroads, story of brothers at, 35n96, 40, 159–62
 devil in, 96–111. *See also* devil
 dialogue form, use of, 77, 96–97, 200n5
 doves, simile of, 40–41, 162–69

Hamartigenia (continued)
  editions of, xii
  as exploration of problem of sin, 51–52
  fall of Adam and Eve, account of, 140–44
  figuration, use of, 53, 76, 78, 85
  gender and sexual issues in, 112–25. *See also* gender and sexuality
  goodness of God and creation, assertion of, 122–25
  humor in, 73
  importance of, xi, 54
  Joshua crossing the Jordan in, 77, 127–28, 150
  justice and judgment in, 170–96. *See also* justice and judgment
  moderation, praise of, 121
  narrative scheme and structure of, 76–79
  Paradise Lost compared, 52–53
  personification allegory in, 73–74, 126–27, 129
  poetry in late antique world and, 56–75. *See also* poetry in late antique world
  preface of, 3–6, 79–84
  reproduction in, 129–39. *See also* reproduction and succession
  Roman world and Christian view of history, reflecting, 55–58
  translation of, xi–xii
Hardie, Philip, 151, 158, 207n11, 208n19
Harpham, Geoffrey, 139
Harries, Jill, 172
Henry, R. M., 12n33
heresy. *See also* Marcion
  Arianism, 137, 173, 200n6, 205–6n1, 206n14, 207n16
  dualist heresies generally, *Hamartigenia* aimed at, 5n16, 7n22, 15n46, 77–78, 86, 200n6
  late antique writing of, 78, 97, 199–200n2
  Manichaeism, 5n16, 15n44, 15n46, 77–78, 82, 122, 200n6
Herodotus, 206n3
Hesiod, 40n110, 41n113, 79, 145, 159, 161–62
highwayman or robber, devil as, 16, 22n61, 35n96, 105–9, 125–26, 187–88
Hindus, 26, 32
Hippolytus (saint and martyr), 198n9
Historici graeci minores (Eunapius of Sardis), 207n16
history
  Moses as historian, 20, 123, 205n24
  typological view of Prudentius, 82–83
Homer and Homeric style, 61, 99, 163–65, 169, 200n5
honey on rim of cup metaphor, 57, 121–22
Honorius (Roman emperor), 180
Horace, xi, 26n72, 86, 161, 204n12, 206n3, 208n26
horseleech and daughters, riddle of, 93, 202n15
Hugo of St. Victor, 64
humor, Prudentius's mastery of, 73, 185
Humpty-Dumpty in *Through the Looking Glass*, 70–71, 72

In genesim homiliae (Origen), 207n7
In Ioannem homiliae (John Chrysostom), 210n27
Indians, 26n72, 32, 32n91
Institutio oratoria (Quintilian), 61, 63, 198n18, 198n24, 203n32
intercession, amnesty, and mercy, 47n127, 174–75, 180, 190
interpretation. *See* language and meaning
Invidia (Envy), 12, 15, 98, 102–3, 192, 202n4
Irenaeus of Lyons, 78, 174, 200n9
Isaiah 14:3–20, 14n40, 100

James, Paula, 72, 199n38
Jean de Meun, 67, 83
Jerome
  Ad Iovinianum, 32n91
  Contra Rufinum, 40n110, 208n25
  De viris illustribus, 54, 57
  dream of being accused of being a Ciceronian rather than a Christian, 209n9
  Epistulae, 209n9
  Eve, on meaning of name of, 142
  new forms of Christian literature, development of, 56
  on promiscuity of Indians/Hindus, 32n91
  traveler motif, use of, 107
  Vulgate, 141, 201n14, 202n7, 202n15
Jerusalem Talmud, 39n109
Jewish Antiquities (Josephus), 13n36, 201n16, 207n12
Job
  1:7, 100
  in *Psychomachia*, 200n11, 205n28
  Satan in, 100, 202n10
John, Gospel of
  1:3, 15n46
  8:31–32, 32n89, 206n13
  8:43, 137
  8:44, 32n89, 137
  14:2, 46n126
John, Revelation of, 44n122, 45n123, 170, 178, 186
John the Baptist, 132

INDEX [229

John Chrysostom, 19n57, 118–20, 181, 210n27
Josephus, 13n36, 81, 201n16, 207n12
Joshua
   24, 23n64
   24:11–15, 127–28
Joshua crossing the Jordan, 77, 127–28, 150
Judith and Holofernes, 62–63
Julian, 56
justice and judgment, 170–96
   afterlife, fate of the soul in, 41–45, 175–80
   body as prison house of soul, 42n117–18, 177, 201n5, 209n15
   Christian adaptation of language of judicial process, 171–75
   in closing prayer of poet, 46n125, 187–94
   eschatology and apocalyptic, 170–71, 186
   intercession, amnesty, and mercy, 47n127, 174–75, 180, 190
   Jerome's dream of being accused of being a Ciceronian rather than a Christian, 209n9
   Prudentius, judicial experience of, 6n18, 24n65, 172
   in Sermon on the Mount, 188
   as spectacle, 172–73, 175, 180–87
Juvenal, xi, 202n1, 204n10

Kaesser, Christian, 208n17
Kiely, Maria, 150
Kilgour, Maggie, 134–36
Knox, Peter, 208n25

Lactantius, 14n38, 40n110, 57, 208n25
Lamentations, 24
lampreys and vipers, 206n3
language and meaning. *See also* analogy, problem of; poetry in late antique world
   apophatic view of Prudentius, 51–52, 66–67, 83–84, 188–89, 194, 210n35
   Augustine on metaphysics of, 138–39
   complexity and ambiguity of, 85
   creative process, Prudentius's anxieties about, 136–37
   devil associated with perils of, 99, 100–101, 104–5, 109
   gushing bowels, association of language with, 207n16
   Hesiod on, 159, 161
   Lot's wife in *Hamartigenia* and Ovid's Niobe, interpretive framing of, 147–50
   martyrdom, portrayals of, 185–86
   Persius on, 161–62
   reading as interpretive act in *Hamartigenia*, 10n29, 78–79
   reading in late antique period, 58–59

Tower of Babel and Nimrod, 13n36, 100–101
wordplay, Prudentius's use of, 6n21, 29n83, 35n95, 67–71, 190–92, 194
Laurence (saint and martyr), 185
Levine, Robert, 181, 196, 198n22, 199n43, 210n22, 211n54
Levinson, Joshua, 201n20
lex talionis, 72
Livy, 201n6
locuples, 109
Loraux, Nicole, 70, 164
Lot and his wife
   Adam and Eve, and *monumenta insignia* of, 144–45
   daughters of, 37n102, 152–56
   fate of just souls and, 42n116, 177
   free will, illustrating concept of, 77
   gaze, significance of, 37n102, 166, 177
   Good Samaritan, links to, 106
   in *Hamartigenia* text, 36–39
   Ovid's Niobe and Lot's wife, 145–52, 177
   in *Psychomachia*, 62
Lucan, 195
Lucifer, devil identified with, 14n40, 14n42, 100, 202n10, 203n16. *See also* devil
Lucretius, xi, 14n41, 30n86, 57, 73–74, 121–22, 123, 206n3, 208n25
Luke
   3:7, 132
   10:30–33, 105
   Marcion's use of, 5n14
luxury, Latin tradition of diatribes against, 116

Macleish, Archibald, 51
Maecenas, 115
Manichaeism, 5n16, 15n44, 15n46, 77–78, 82, 122, 200n6
Marcion, 5n14, 77–78
   as bad reader, 79
   Cain identified with, 5–6, 7, 76, 80–81, 201n21
   canonicity, concept of, 5n14, 78
   Christianized language of judicial process applied to, 171
   the devil and, 96–97, 99, 100
   dialogue with, in *Hamartigenia*, 7–12, 77
   Hamartigenia framed as refutation of, 3n1, 77–78
   in *Hamartigenia* text, 5–6, 7–12, 27
   sin and reproduction, association of, 130
   sun allegory and parhelion problem, 86, 89, 95
   views of, 77–78, 200n6–7
Marcus Aurelius, Fronto's letters to, 203n32

Marianus (martyr), 172
marrow, erotic connotations of, 125, 205n27
Martianus Capella, 136, 198n18, 198n24
martyrs and martyrdom, 170–71, 182–86
Mary, mother of Christ, 30, 130, 131, 143–44, 156
Mastrangelo, Marc
    on Adam's taking up clothing, 109, 203n27
    on afterlife conceived in Vergilian imagistic terms in *Hamartigenia*, 175
    on apophatic nature of Prudentius's theology, 188, 210n35
    on Lot and his wife, 150
    on Moses as historian, 205n24
    on Platonist doctrines of the soul, 42n117, 201n5
    on poetry in late antique period, 56, 66, 69, 73, 74
    on preface of *Hamartigenia*, 82, 83
    on Prudentius's use of *Sapientia*, 205n25
Matthew
    3:7, 132
    5:25–26, 188
    7:13–14, 40n110, 208n25
    16:18, 26n71
    Opus imperfectum in Matthaeum (Arian commentary on Matthew), 209n7
meaning and language. *See* language and meaning
Medicamina faciei feminae (Ovid), 112–13
Medusa, devil associated with, 98
Memmius, 79
Memorabilia (Xenophon), 40n110, 208n25
memory, aesthetics of, 61–65
mercy, amnesty, and intercession, 47n127, 174–75, 180, 190
Metamorphoses (Ovid)
    Actaeon, transformation of, 208n13
    Medusa, description of, 98
    Niobe, Lot's wife based on tale of, 38n104, 145–52, 177, 208n19
    scrobis, use of, 4n5
    Thracian women transformed after murder of Orpheus, 164–67
Metaphysics (Aristotle), 89
Miles, Margaret, 37n102, 88, 166
Miller, Patricia Cox, 58, 64–65, 78, 119, 198n17, 199n37, 200n9, 206n3
Milton, John, Prudentius compared to, xi, 52, 189. *See also Paradise Lost*
Mind/Spirit and Flesh, Abel and Cain identified with, 6, 84
mirror metaphor, 10, 92–95, 105
moderation, praise of, 121

monumenta insignia, 144–45
Morgan, Gareth, 210n37
mosaics and poetry, parallels between, 59
Moses, 20, 25n68, 26n69, 77, 123–24, 128, 205n24
mouths. *See* throats and mouths; tongue

names, etymologies of
    Abel, 6n21
    Cain, 4n6
    Eve, 141–42
    Nimrod, 100
    Satan, 100–101
Narcissus, 208
narrative structure
    exegesis and, 201n20
    of *Hamartigenia*, 76–79
    role in late antique poetry, 62
natural order, corruption of
    cosmetics, women's use of, 112–13
    devil's fall leading to, 109–11
    goodness of God and creation, assertion of, 122–25
    in *Hamartigenia* text, 16–18
    senses, distrust of, 118–23
Naturales quaestiones (Seneca the Younger), 201n6
Naturalis historia (Pliny the Elder), 14n38, 30n86, 201n6, 206n3
Neoplatonism, 42n117–18, 65, 107, 177, 186
nets and snares
    devil associated with, 98–99
    Nimrod associated with, 100, 163
    in simile of the doves, 40, 163
Nightingale, Andrea, 92
Nimrod, 13, 27n73, 76, 99–101, 163, 202n7, 203n28
Niobe in Ovid, Lot's wife based on, 38n104, 145–52, 177
Noricum, plague of, 104
Nugent, Georgia, 69–70, 130, 158–59, 164, 206n6–7, 210n37
Numbers
    13:17–20, 23–25, 25n68
    34:13, 26n69

Odes or *Carmina* (Horace), 26n72, 204n12, 206n3
Odyssey, 99, 163–65
Oeconomicus (Xenophon), 204n4
Oedipus myth, 3n1
On Ekphrasis (Theon), 208n21
On the Nature of the Universe (Lucretius), 14n41

On Spectacles (Tertullian), 180–81, 182, 186, 210n21
On Vainglory and the Education of the Young (John Chrysostom), 19n52, 118
Optatian, 210n38
Opus imperfectum in Matthaeum, 209n7
orality, feigned, 20n58, 77, 96, 122, 208n16
Orations against the Arians (Athanasius), 137, 205–6n1, 206n14
Orator (Cicero), 115, 203n29, 204n7–8
Orestes, disturbed vision of, 91
Origen, 65, 127, 174, 198n28, 202n10, 205n29, 207n7
The Origin of Sin (Prudentius). See *Hamartigenia*
ornament and cosmetics, use of, 18, 112–17, 204n11
ornament, figurative. See figuration
Orpheus, Thracian women transformed after murder of, 164–67
Ovid. See also *Metamorphoses*
  on cosmetics, 112–13, 203–4n4
  exile of, 190, 191
  Fasti, 4n7
  interplay of bodies and rhetorical forms in, 204n6
  irony and skepticism of, 67, 73, 185
  Medicamina faciei feminae, 112–13
  Prudentius influenced by, xi
  Remedia amoris, 203–4n4
  Scylla, Milton's Sin as daughter of Satan mimicking, 135
  Tristia, 190, 191

pagan religion, *Hamartigenia*'s references to, 5n10, 14n38, 41n113, 175–76, 220n60
Palla, Roberto, xii, 6n21, 30n85–86, 199n1, 202n5–6
Pandora and Eve, 145, 207n4–5
pantomime dancers, evocation of, 117–18, 119, 120
Paradise Lost (Milton)
  acrostics in, 192–94
  Cain and Abel story in, 81
  citation of, xii
  on cosmetics, 112
  creative process, Milton's anxieties about, 135–36
  Eve in, 142–44, 145, 193, 211n46
  fall of man in, 143–44, 207n1
  family expectations as theme of, 158
  Hamartigenia compared, 52–53
  Satan in, 98, 101, 103–4
  Second Coming in, 186

Sin personified as Satan's daughter in, 14n39, 133–36
parhelion, problem of, 10–11, 89–92
Parthians, 26, 28
Partner, Jane, 192–93, 207n1
Passio ss. Mariani et Iacobi, 209n5
La Passio ss. Mariani et Iacobi, 209n5
Passio ss. Perpetuae et Felicitatis, 209n5
Paul and Pauline theology, 5n14, 27n77–78, 92–93, 94–95, 107
Paulinus of Nola, 54–55, 107, 150
Paulinus of Pella, 197n8
Pausanias, 207n12
Paxson, James, 69, 73, 74, 199n46, 200n11, 205n28
Peristephanon (Prudentius)
  Agnes, martyrdom of, 195
  binding and dissolution imagery in, 204n15
  Cassian, martyrdom of, 89, 182–85, 187, 208n17
  Eulalia, martyrdom of, 185, 204n15, 210n29
  fabula in, 82–83
  Hippolytus, martyrdom of, 198n9
  humor in, 73, 185
  hymnic style of, 65
  lingua (language, tongue, or speech), wordplay on, 68–69
  preface to collected works referring to, 198n29
  Romanus, martyrdom of, 69, 198n29, 199n37
  trial scenes in, 172
  violence in, 68–69, 198n9, 199n43
Perpetua (martyr), dream of, 172
Perses (brother of Hesiod), 79, 159, 161
Persius (satirist), 161–62
personification allegory
  gender issues and, 126–27
  in *Hamartigenia* text, 4n8, 17n53, 22–23
  in late antique poetry, 73–74
  in *Psychomachia*, 17n53, 126–27, 129, 205n28, 205n30
1 Peter 2:7, 26n70
petra, as reference to Peter, 26n71
Petronius, 206n3, 209n18
Phaedo (Plato), 209n15
phantasia or *visio*, 61
Philistines, 26–27n73
Philo, 40n110, 99–100, 201n10, 201n17, 202n9, 208n25
Physiologus, 30n86, 132, 206n4
Plato and Platonic tradition, 42n117, 86–88, 91–92, 107, 149, 177, 201n5, 209n15
Pliny the Elder, 14n38, 30n86, 201n6, 206n3

Plotinus, 201n5
Plutarch, 201n10, 204n4
poetry in late antique world, 56–75
  apophatic nature of language and meaning in, 51–52, 53, 65–67, 68
  cultural authority of classical poetry, loss of, 55–58
  Epicurean and Stoic language theories, 73–75
  figure and ornament in, 65, 67–68, 73
  memory, aesthetics of, 61–65
  narrative structure, role of, 62
  personification allegory, 73–74
  style and reading of, 58–61
  violence, as literary device, 59–60, 63–64, 68–73
  wordplay, importance of, 67–71
Polyneices and Eteocles, 3n1
polysemy, 65, 67, 71, 74, 141, 144, 186
polyspermy, 39n109
Pompey's ghost, 195
preface to collected works of Prudentius, 54, 198n29, 210n32
Priscillianism, 200n6
Prodicus, 161
Professores (Ausonius), 40n110, 208n25
Progymnasmata (Theon), 198n13
Prometheus, 195, 204n12, 211n51
prosopopoeia, 12n32, 16n51, 73, 77, 95, 97
Prudentius (Aurelius Prudentius Clemens). See also *Apotheosis*; *Hamartigenia*; *Psychomachia*
  Adam in *Hamartigenia* linked to name of, 143
  apophatic nature of language for, 51–52, 66–67, 83–84, 188–89, 194, 210n35
  art, views on, 208n20
  biographical information, 54–55
  Cathemerinon, 65, 142, 179–80, 190, 198n29, 203n16, 204n15
  closing prayer for salvation of, 45–47, 187–96
  Contra Symmachum, 54, 198n29, 199n30
  creative process, apparent anxieties about, 136–37, 194–96
  Dittochaeon, 65, 150
  history, typological view of, 82–83
  importance and influences, xi
  judicial experience of, 6n18, 24n65, 172
  popularity and studies of, 197n5
  preface to collected works of, 54, 198n29, 210n32
Psalms 96:16, 173
Pseudo Clement, 202n13
Pseudo Longinus, 91

Psychomachia or *The Battle of the Soul* (Prudentius)
  on Adam's acquisition of clothing, 108–9
  aesthetics of memory in, 61–63, 64
  apophatic understanding of language and meaning in, 210n35
  binding and dissolution imagery in, 204n15
  black humor of, 73
  blindness associated with lack of faith in, 210n19
  classical poetry, influence of, 57
  complexity and ambiguity of interpretation in, 85
  dating of, 198n29, 205n32
  as dialogue, 200n5
  Discordia, death and dismemberment of, 70–75
  epic style of, 65
  on impossibility of simplicity for humans, 130
  personifications in, 17n53, 126–27, 129, 205n28, 205n30
  postlapsarian problem of language and meaning in, 66–67
  preface of, 79, 200n11, 201n5
  preface to collected works not referring to, 198n29
  reproduction and succession in, 158–59
  theme/plot of, 62, 65
  transsexuality and gender confusion in, 206n6
Pucci, Pietro, 207n4
punishment. See justice and judgment
Pygmalion, 208
Pylades, 117
Pythagoras, 107, 159, 162

Quaestiones evangeliorum (Augustine), 203n20
Quaestiones in Genesin (Philo), 202n8
Quintilian, 61, 63, 87, 198n18, 198n24, 203n32, 205n17

reading
  as interpretive act in *Hamartigenia*, 10n29, 78–79
  in late antique period, 58–59
Recognitions (Pseudo Clement), 202n13
Remedia amoris (Ovid), 203–4n4
reproduction and succession, 129–39
  in Augustine's metaphysics of language, 138–39
  David and Absalom, 129, 131
  Eve, Cain, and Abel, 130–31, 141, 156
  generatio simplex, 9n25, 156–59

literary creativity, Milton's and Prudentius's anxieties about, 135–37
Lot's daughters left out of *Hamartigenia*, 77, 152–56
multiple variations on theme of, 156
polyspermy, 39n109
in Roman epic tradition, 158
Ruth, Orpah, and Naomi, 28n108–9, 77, 152–56
Sin as Satan's daughter, Milton's personification of, 14n39, 133–36
sin, generation of, 129–30
snakes, reproductive process of, 30–32, 131–33
The Republic (Plato), 86–88, 91–92, 149
Revelation of John, 44n122, 45n123, 170, 178, 186
Rhetoric (Aristotle), 202n14
Rhetorica ad Herennium, 64, 198n18
Richlin, Amy, 112, 204n9, 204n11
riddle or enigma, 93–95
Rimell, Victoria, 112–13
robber or highwayman, devil as, 16, 22n61, 35n96, 105–9, 125–26, 187–88
Roberts, Michael, 55, 59–60, 64, 72, 195
Robigo and Robigalia, 14n38
Roman world. *See also* poetry in late antique world
  classical poetry, loss of cultural authority of, 55–58
  Hamartigenia reflecting, 55–58
  pagan religion, *Hamartigenia*'s references to, 5n10, 14n38, 41n113, 175–76, 220n60
Romans
  1:20, 92–93, 201n11
  8:20–22, 27n77
  9:33, 26n70
Romanus (martyr), 69, 198n29, 199n37
Romulus and Remus parallels with Cain and Abel, 3n1, 4n7
Rosenmeyer, Patricia, 205n27
Ross, Jill, 195
Rufinus, death of, 59
Ruth, Orpah, and Naomi, 39, 77, 106, 152–56
Ruth 1, 39n107, 39n109

Salvatore, Antonio, 30n86, 206n3, 207n9, 208n19
1 Samuel 24–26, 39n109
Sant' Apollinare Nuovo, Ravenna, 59
Sapientia, 23n63, 123–24, 126–27, 205n25, 205n31–32
Sappho, 51
sartago loquendi, 162

Satan, 100. *See also* devil
Satires (Horace), 206n3
Satires (Juvenal), 202n1, 204n10
Satires (Persius), 162
scabies, 14n38
Second Sophistic, 56
Seneca the Elder, 204n4
Seneca the Younger, 115, 172–73, 201n6, 203n29, 209n6
senses
  Prudentius on fate of just souls and, 177–78
  Prudentius's distrust of, 19n57, 118–23, 125, 189, 202n4
Septuagint, 80, 202n7
Sermon on the Mount, 188
Sermons (Augustine), 15n46, 119, 210n27, 210n31
Servius, 40n110, 160, 208n25
Sextus Empiricus, 201n8
sexual issues. *See* gender and sexuality
Shanzer, Danuta, 198n29, 205n32
Shaw, Brent, 172, 173, 209n7, 209n9
Sidonius Apollinaris, 59
sight. *See* vision
signification, Prudentius's interest in, 144–45
Simonides, 64, 198n24
snakes
  Arianism linked to, 137–38, 206n14
  Caesarius of Arles bound to book by, 136
  devil associated with, 98, 104, 131, 132–33
  lampreys and vipers, 206n3
  Paradise Lost, oblique approach of snake in, 193
  reproductive process of, 30–32, 131–33
snares. *See* nets and snares
Solomon, 30, 131, 155, 162
spectacle
  in *Aeneid*'s account of funeral games of Anchises, 169
  judgment/judicial process as, 47n120, 172–73, 175, 180–87
  Ovid's account of transformation of Thracian women, 164–67
  Tertullian on, 180–81, 182, 186, 210n21
Spenser, Edmund, xi, 135, 206n8
Spirit/Mind and Flesh, Abel and Cain identified with, 6, 84
Stam, J., 12n33
Statius, xi, 3n1
Stevens, Wallace, 51, 52
Stoicism, 74–75, 91, 162
Straw, Carole, 170–71

Stromata (Clement of Alexandria), 200n7, 209n10
succession. *See* reproduction and succession
Sulpicius Severus, 197n8
sun, allegory of, 10, 85–88, 105, 122
supellex, 109, 204n7
Symmachus (Quintus Aurelius Symmachus), 199n30

Taddei, Rosemarie, 26n70, 80, 89, 128, 171, 201n11, 201n15, 209n3
Targum ad Gen. 10:9, 202n11
Tartarus, 41, 43, 175, 180
Tertullian
 Adversus Judaeos, 200n13
 Adversus Marcionem, 14n40, 200n6–7
 canon formation and, 200n8
 De cultu feminarum, 112, 113, 203n1, 204n5, 204n11, 204n14
 Ennarationes in Psalmos, 173
 Eve and Pandora compared by, 207n5
 on judicial process, 173
 On Spectacles, 180–82, 186, 210n21
textiles and weaving, 19, 116–17
Thebiad (Statius), 3n1
Theodosius I (Roman emperor), 54, 55, 208n20
Theogony (Hesiod), 41n113
Theon, 198n13, 208n21
Thomas, Richard, 104
Thracian women, transformation of, 164–67
throats and mouths. *See also* tongue
 in Athanasius's account of Arius's death, 207n16
 confusion or conflation of mouth and genital area, 206n7, 207n16
 oral nature of Eve's transgression, 133
 Prudentius's focus on attacks on, 69–73, 199n46
 strangulation of women in Greek and Latin literature, 70, 164
Through the Looking Glass (Carroll), 71
Thucydides, 61
To an Uneducated Ruler or *Ad principem ineruditum* (Plutarch), 201n10
tongue. *See also* throats and mouths
 devil, forked tongue of, 16, 104–5, 195–96
 of martyred Cyprian of Carthage, 68–69, 73
 poet's tongue in closing prayer, 194, 195–96
 wordplay involving, 16n49, 68–69
Tower of Babel, 13n36, 100–101
traveler motif
 in *Apotheosis*, 35n96, 58, 106–7
 crossroads, brothers at, 35n96, 159–62
 devil as highwayman and, 16, 22n61, 35n96, 105–9, 125–26, 187–88
 in *Hamartigenia* text, 7, 16, 22, 44
 Prudentius's use of, 35n96, 105–9
Trinity
 Prudentius stressing unity of God over, 130
 sun as allegory of, 85
Tristia (Ovid), 190, 191
Tusculan Disputations (Cicero), 40n110, 208n25
typological scheme in Prudentius's works, 82–83

underworld, Prudentius's use of concept of, 41n113, 175–76
unity of God
 Prudentian argument against dualism framed in terms of, 130
 sun as visible sign of, 85

Valentinian I (Roman emperor), 180
van Assendelft, M. M., 87
Variae (Cassiodorus), 205n19
Varro, 31n87
Vergil. *See also Aeneid*
 afterlife conceived by Prudentius in imagist terms of, 175–76
 Aulus Gellius's description of composition process of, 206n5
 ekphrasis, use of, 61
 Georgics, 31n87, 104, 117, 121, 206n5
 moderation praised by, 121
 Prudentius influenced by, xi, 57
 snake's forked tongue described by, 104
Vetus Latina, 80, 201n14
violence
 apocalyptic and eschatology in *Hamartagenia*, 170–71
 judicial punishment, 172–75
 as literary device, 59–60, 63–64, 68–73
 martyrs and martyrdom, 170–71, 182–86
 spectacle, judgment as, 180–87
vipers. *See* snakes
Virtues and Vices, personifications of, 126–27
visio or *phantasia*, 61
vision. *See also* spectacle
 apophatic theology of Prudentius and, 189
 artwork, description of, 150–52, 182–84, 208n17
 Augustine's theory of, 88–89, 119, 120, 166
 blindness associated with lack of faith, 210n19
 devil's fall associated with, 102–3, 202n4

education and bleared vision in Roman satire, 161–62
in *Hamartigenia* text, 7, 11, 12, 43, 44
Lot's wife, gaze of, 37n102, 166, 177
in Orpheus story, 165–66
Paradise Lost, oblique approach of snake in, 193
parhelion and problem of human vision, 10–11, 88, 89–92
senses, distrust of, 19n57, 118–23, 125, 189, 202n4
soul's eye compared to human eye, 178
Vita Caecilii Cypriani, 209n5
Vulgate, 141, 201n14, 202n7, 202n15

weaving and textiles, 19, 116–17
Webb, Ruth, 64, 91, 117–18, 120, 181, 200n4, 205n19
Whitmarsh, Tim, 151
woe, signs of, 140, 142, 143–44, 145, 146
women. *See* gender and sexuality
wordplay, Prudentius's use of, 6n21, 29n83, 35n95, 67–71, 190–92, 194
Works and Days (Hesiod), 40n110, 159
Wyrick, Jed, 200n8

Xenophon, 40n110, 204n4, 208n25

Zimmerman, Martin, 182

www.ingramcontent.com/pod-product-compliance
Lightning Source LLC
Chambersburg PA
CBHW061346300426
44116CB00011B/2013